THE AGE OF THE VIKINGS

In memory of my Mother and Father

The Age
of the Vikings

Second Edition

P. H. SAWYER

EDWARD ARNOLD

© P. H. SAWYER, 1971

First published 1962
by Edward Arnold (Publishers) Ltd.
41 Maddox Street
London W1R 0AN

Second Edition, 1971

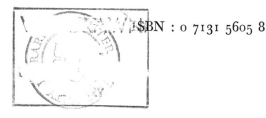

ISBN : 0 7131 5605 8

Printed in Great Britain by
The Camelot Press Ltd., London and Southampton

Preface

THE main argument of this book is that the Scandinavian activity of the Viking period is not so much inexplicable as misunderstood. I have tried to show that the misunderstandings are due partly to mistaken interpretations of the evidence and partly to the uncritical acceptance of some basic assumptions. Some interesting topics such as the settlement of Iceland and the conversion of Scandinavia are neglected, not because they are unimportant or well understood but because they are not relevant here.

As the debts incurred in the preparation of this book are too numerous to mention in detail, I should like to express my gratitude in general to all those who have helped, especially to the staffs of the museums at Copenhagen, Gothenburg, Lund, Oslo, Stockholm, Uppsala and Visby. My particular thanks are due to Holger Arbman, H. A. Cronne, R. H. M. Dolley, R. H. Hilton, Sune Lindqvist, Mårten Stenberger, and Harald Åkerlund as well as to N. L. Rasmusson who has put himself to great inconvenience on my behalf, to Sture Bolin for making available his unpublished work and so generously giving permission to use his material, and to Bertil Almgren for his advice, criticism and encouragement over many years. I should also like to thank the University of Birmingham for making possible a recent visit to Scandinavia. My indebtedness to the published work of others is inadequately expressed in the notes and I should like to take this opportunity of expressing my particular obligation to the fundamental work of Sir Frank Stenton.

Several scholars have given me permission to quote from translations they have made and I should like to thank Professor Dorothy Whitelock, Professor Lee Hollander and Miss Margaret Ashdown's executors as well as the publishers concerned, namely the American-Scandinavian Foundation, Cambridge University Press, Columbia University Press and Eyre and Spottiswoode. I have elsewhere acknowledged my debt to individuals and institutions for permission to reproduce pictures and diagrams.

PREFACE TO THE SECOND EDITION

THE publication of this second edition provides an opportunity to correct some of the mistakes of the first, as well as to take account of recent work. The most important changes are in Chapters 4–7 and 9. The reconstruction of the Gokstad ship and its rigging has been improved and the Skuldelev ships have been taken into account with consequent changes in the discussion of late Viking-period ships. The suggestion that the Hon hoard was assembled in Scandinavia has been abandoned and the interpretation of hoards as evidence of disorder modified. I now accept that the 'Trelleborg' camps can be dated 970–1020 and this has meant important changes in the discussion of the armies that attacked Ethelred's England. Chapter 7 is now limited to the Danish settlements and the hypothetical reconstruction of that colonisation has been greatly improved, thanks to the work of Kenneth Cameron and Gillian Fellows Jensen. The concluding chapter has been extensively rewritten on the basis of a discussion of 'The Two Viking Ages of Britain' published in *Medieval Scandinavia*, 2 (1969). Figures 4, 5, 9, 12a, b, c, and 13 are new or redrawn and Plates VIII, IX, and XIII are new. The notes and the Bibliography have been brought up to date.

In preparing this edition I have been fortunate to have had the advice and criticism of many scholars. I should like to record my particular obligation to Bertil Almgren, Charlotte Blindheim, Kenneth Cameron, Michael Dolley, Gillian Fellows Jensen, Lucien Musset, Olaf Olsen, R. I. Page, Ole Crumlin-Pedersen, N. L. Rasmusson, Kolbjørn Skaare and David Wilson.

CONTENTS

LIST OF FIGURES

LIST OF PLATES

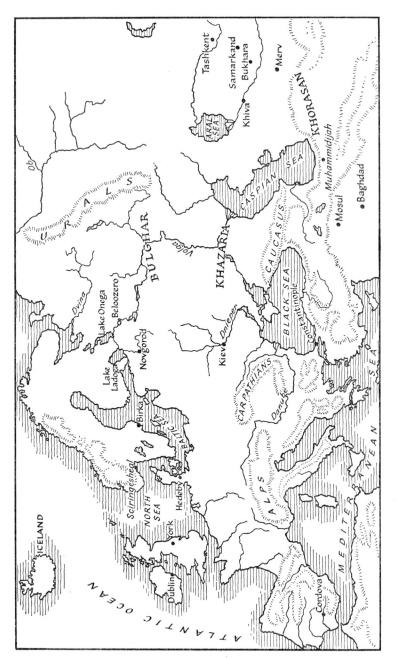

Figure 1 General Map showing areas of Scandinavian activity

1. Introduction

VIKING raiders first began to trouble the coastlands of western Europe at the end of the eighth century and the earliest raid may have been in 793 when the island monastery of Lindisfarne, off the Northumbrian coast, was plundered. The news of this outrage quickly reached Alcuin, a Northumbrian who had for years lived on the Continent, and he wrote several letters expressing his horror, saying in one of them 'it is nearly 350 years that we and our fathers have inhabited this most lovely land, and never before has such a terror appeared in Britain as we have now suffered from a pagan race, nor was it thought that such an inroad from the sea could be made'.[1] At about the same time as this attack on the north-east coast of England, another band of raiders was involved in an incident in the south-west. In a skirmish at Portland the king's reeve Beaduheard was killed and according to the West Saxon Chronicler 'those were the first ships of Danish men which ever came to the land of the English'.[2] It matters less that either Alcuin or the Chronicler must have been misinformed than that they provide independent evidence that the raids that then occurred were unprecedented. They were soon followed by others. In 794 another Northumbrian monastery, probably Jarrow, was looted, and in 795 Iona was attacked. The first raid in Ireland was reported near Dublin in 795, and by 799 raiders reached the coast of Aquitaine. For western Europe the Viking period began in the last decade of the eighth century.[3]

These early attacks were the work of Norwegians, not Danes.

The Anglo-Saxon Chronicle describes the killers of Beaduheard as Northmen, and several versions add that they came from Hörthaland, a district of western Norway. The comment that 'these were the first ships of Danish men to come to England' cannot be taken as evidence of Danish raids in the eighth century for it is obviously a gloss added by the compiler a century later when the Danes had long been the main threat to the English. The raid on Portland, like the contemporary attacks elsewhere in the British Isles was a Norwegian enterprise.[4] The main series of Danish raids only began in 834 with an attack on Dorestad, which was repeated the following year when the first Danish raid on England also occurred and for the rest of the century England and the Carolingian Empire were rarely free of raiding Danes. The English evidence, unfortunately, is unsatisfactory for the middle years of the century but the Frankish annals do something to compensate for this and the Annals of St. Bertin report at least one raid every year but one between 836 and 876.[5]

In the ninth century the areas of Norwegian and Danish activity were generally distinct. The Norwegians raided the Hebrides and Ireland and some of them settled there as well as in Orkney and Shetland. Later generations from Norway and from the original settlements in Britain colonised Iceland and Greenland. The Danes concentrated on lowland England and on those parts of the Carolingian Empire that were accessible by the rivers that flow into the North Sea, the Channel and the Atlantic, although some went further afield, to Ireland, Spain and into the Mediterranean. Their victims may sometimes have confused Danes and Norwegians, or been content to call them indiscriminately pagans, heathen men, pirates or barbarians, but it would be wrong to conclude that they were indistinguishable. In Ireland where Danish and Norwegian zones overlapped, the chronicles sometimes call the Danes 'Black Foreigners' and the Norwegians 'White Foreigners'. Other distinctive names were also used by the Irish, the most interesting being *Lochlannach* for Norwegian. Norway is itself sometimes called *Lochlann*, although that name also seems to have been used for the areas of north-west Britain under the control of Norwegians.[6] Danes and Norwegians were not, of course, invariably hostile to each other: the raids on England in the reign of Ethelred were, indeed, undertaken by armies recruited from all parts of Scandinavia and there are earlier examples of co-operation but in the ninth century the Norwegians and Danes raided and colonised different areas, and at that time Swedes played little part in the west.

Danes or Norwegians, the raiders came, at least in part, for the plunder which they found in the hoarded treasures of the Christian West. Being pagan they had no respect for the undefended holy places and may well have been surprised as well as delighted by the foolishness of their Christian victims, who naturally regarded their assailants with horror. The Christians were, however, rarely able to put up a successful resistance, and often the only alternative to the desecration of their shrines and the indiscriminate looting of their treasures was the payment of tribute with which the raiders might be persuaded, at least for a time, to divert their attention elsewhere. Quite early in the ninth century the raiders were wintering in temporary bases on such islands as Noirmoutier in the mouth of the Loire, or Sheppey in the Thames estuary, and in 859 one band spent the winter in the mouth of the Rhône, on the island of Camargue. From such island bases the raiders were able to continue their work in successive campaigning seasons and before the end of the century the persistent attacks had brought a large part of England, later known as the Danelaw, under the authority of Scandinavians. Across the Channel a similar development led, early in the tenth century, to the formation of Normandy. From these and other permanent settlements the plundering went on but before long the settlers were assimilated into the native populations. In Normandy, for example, by the middle of the tenth century most of the settlers had adopted the religion and speech of 'Frenchmen' and although Normandy always remained distinct, by the second half of the century it was no more of a threat to its neighbours than was the county of Anjou. In England too, the settlers soon accepted Christianity, and there was then very little to distinguish them from the English except, perhaps, their speech.[7] While Normandy remained, until the thirteenth century, a separate duchy, the

Scandinavian areas of England were soon brought under the
authority of the kings of Wessex, and with the final conquest of
the kingdom of York, England was, for the first time, unified.

This process of assimilation was made easier by a lull in
the attacks from Scandinavia.[8] Some raiders may still have
come but most incidents that are reported, and for fifty years
after 930 there were relatively few, involved men who had
already settled in the west or their descendants, not newcomers fresh from Scandinavia. Raiders from Scandinavia do
not seem to have been prominent in western Europe in the
tenth century until its last two decades when the lull abruptly
ended. After 980 England was subjected to fresh, and vigorous,
assaults, led by such men as Olaf Tryggvason, later king of
Norway, Svein, king of Denmark, and his son Cnut. These raids
thoroughly disorganised the English who several times paid
massive tributes to be rid, however briefly, of their tormentors,
and by 1016 Cnut was accepted by the English as their king.
His dynasty then ruled England until 1042 when the old West
Saxon royal family, in the person of Ethelred's son, Edward
the Confessor, was restored. The kings of Norway and Denmark
both claimed to be Edward's heir and it was not until after the
Norman Conquest that the threat of Scandinavian attacks on
England was finally removed. With the defeat and death of
Harald Hardrada, king of Norway, by Harold of England at
Stamford Bridge in 1066, and the withdrawal of Svein of
Denmark from England in 1070 the period of effective Scan-
dinavian interference in western Europe came to an end. In the
remote and poor northern parts of the British Isles, Vikings and
Norwegian kings were active long after this, but for the greater
part of western Europe the Viking period was over by 1070.

The period takes its name from the Vikings. The origin of
the word 'Viking' has been much debated but as no settled
conclusions have been reached the results of the discussion
have little value for the historian.[9] What is more important
and more certain than the origin of the word is that in the
Viking period it meant a pirate, a robber who came by sea.
Not all Scandinavians at the time were Vikings for some were
traders and others were settlers who only wanted peace, but it
is the Vikings who have attracted most attention. This was the

Viking period and whatever Scandinavian achievements there were in art, ship-building or trade, all are qualified as 'Viking'. This domination of the period by these violent men is not surprising. There is a fascination about the scope and daring of many of their enterprises and our interest is held by the writings of contemporaries who report, often with disgust, the exploits of the raiders. The impressions given by these victims of the Vikings are apparently confirmed by the later Norse writings in which the deeds of Vikings are proudly rehearsed, often with embellishments. Neither the contemporary writings nor the later Scandinavian sources say very much about the settlements or trade and it is therefore difficult to avoid concentrating attention on the violent aspects of the period about which the sources say so much. The study of the activity of Scandinavians who were not Vikings depends on what the historian tends to think of as the 'auxiliary' evidence of archaeology, numismatics and place-names, and it is on these auxiliary studies that the historian has to rely in order to correct the exaggerations and distortions of contemporary writers. It is only when all aspects of Scandinavian activity in the period are considered that it is possible even to understand the raids themselves, for the Vikings were only part of a complex process which left many memorials besides the trail of 'destruction, rape, plunder and murder' which is all too often regarded as the principal Scandinavian contribution to European civilisation at that time.[10] As Marc Bloch put it 'Vus dans leur juste perspective, ils (i.e. the raids) ne nous apparaissent plus que comme un épisode, à vrai dire particulièrement sanglant, d'une grande aventure humaine.'[11]

The historian's problem is not simply that his evidence, and therefore his approach to the subject, tends to be one-sided: there is the additional difficulty that the Scandinavians were active in other parts of the world as well as the Christian West. At the same time as the Norwegians began attacking the British Isles, Swedes were penetrating what is now Russia. They too plundered and destroyed, and they too conquered, settled and traded. This 'Viking' activity in the East was not, like the settlement of Greenland and America, simply a romantic and fascinating extension of Scandinavian enterprise with little or no importance for European history: the Russian ventures are of critical importance for any understanding of the Viking period and their effects on western Europe should not be disregarded. It was, for example, in Russia that Scandinavians acquired vast wealth, some of which seems to have overflowed from the Baltic into western Europe. Moreover, it may be that the renewed raids on England in the reign of Ethelred were the result, not of a cunning Scandinavian appreciation that the English would mismanage their defences, but the consequence of an interruption in the imports of Islamic silver into the Baltic, and it is not unlikely that one of the reasons the Scandinavians were such formidable adversaries at the end of the tenth century was that the remarkable riches of the Baltic had encouraged and sustained organised piracy on a scale unprecedented in northern Europe.

The written evidence for Scandinavian activity in Russia and in Scandinavia itself is far less satisfactory than for western Europe and the auxiliary evidence of material finds and language is, therefore, even more important. This is shown very clearly by the example of Gotland. This island is only mentioned once in the Dark Ages, in a report of a voyage made by an Englishman, Wulfstan, incorporated in the Old English translation of Orosius.[12] Wulfstan had sailed from Hedeby to *Truso** in seven days, and he mentions many of the islands and territories that he passed during the voyage, including, on his left, the island of Gotland, a land belonging to the Swedes. Gotland is not mentioned again until the twelfth century when it clearly occupied an important place in the trading activity of the Baltic. Most surprisingly it is not mentioned by Adam of Bremen, the best authority for the Baltic in the eleventh century.[13] Despite the silence of the historical sources, graves and treasure hoards show that Gotland was unquestionably the richest area of Scandinavia and that its wealth seems to have attracted pirates. The material finds show that Gotland was in contact, directly or indirectly, with the rich fur-producing regions of north Russia, and with Germany and England, and there is no reason to doubt that Gotlanders were

* Words and proper names without modern equivalents are here distinguished by the use of italic type

already active as traders at Novgorod and in the Baltic long before there is any written evidence.[14] The wealth of Gotland and the activity of the Gotlanders must, at least in the later Viking period, have been very important factors in Scandinavian history despite the silence of the historical sources at that time.

The main problem of Viking studies is, therefore, that the evidence to be taken into account comes from a very wide area, is of many kinds and often needs specialised study for its interpretation. It is obvious that no study of the period can claim to be comprehensive unless it is based on all the available evidence, what is not so commonly recognised is that the different kinds of evidence cannot be studied independently. The historian must rely on archaeological discoveries, coin finds and the results of place-name study to help with the interpretation of chronicles, sagas and other writings, and specialists in other fields are equally dependent on the work of others, work that they may often be unable to check. Unfortunately, communication between scholars working with different kinds of evidence has sometimes broken down, not simply because it is difficult to keep up to date, though that is certainly true, but because the nature of the different kinds of evidence, and the limitations which should govern its use, are not always properly understood. Historians, for example, do not always recognise how wide is the margin of error in archaeological dating, and archaeologists and numismatists often fail to realise that written sources require quite as much specialised study as their own material. The failure to understand the nature of the evidence can have most serious results. For example, the discovery of Persian coins of the seventh century in the Baltic region has been taken to prove contacts between Scandinavia and Persia in the seventh century.[15] The commonplace of numismatic study, that coins should be considered in association with the hoards in which they are found, was here overlooked, and the wrong conclusions drawn. In another field, misunderstandings about the nature of linguistic influence have sometimes led to mistaken conclusions being based on the evidence of place-names.

No individual can be expected to master all the specialised

B

techniques needed to study the varied evidence for the Viking
period, any more than any one person can hope to master all
the languages involved. But, as the whole range of evidence
has to be used by students of the period, however limited their
immediate aim, it is important that the general character of
the evidence as a whole should be widely appreciated. Only if
archaeologists, historians, numismatists and philologists all
make an effort to understand the nature of the evidence on
which, however indirectly, their conclusions are based, will
the danger of disastrously mistaken conclusions effectively be
reduced and Viking studies put on a satisfactory basis. This
book has been written as a contribution to such improved
understanding and its first purpose is, therefore, to survey
the main types of evidence for the period.

The second purpose is to examine, in the light of the evidence
thus reviewed, some of the basic assumptions that are commonly made about the Viking period. Some of these are more
often repeated than tested, possibly because there is, for this
subject, such a rich and bewildering variety of sources. Scholars
with a critical approach to evidence in their own field seem,
occasionally, prepared to accept and use evidence, and conclusions, from other fields quite uncritically. The result is that
some assumptions about the Vikings are accepted, used and
given the stamp of authority by repetition when they ought to
be rigorously tested. There are, for example such assumptions
as that Viking armies numbered thousands of warriors,[16] that
the ninth-century raiders took large quantities of loot home to
Scandinavia,[17] that the ninth-century settlements in England
were so dense that in the eleventh century about half the
population of Lincolnshire was of Scandinavian descent[18] and,
in the East, that Scandinavians maintained lively contacts
between the Baltic and Byzantium by way of Kiev.[19] These
and most other hypotheses about the Viking period involve
many different kinds of evidence but underlying them all is
the basic assumption, whether or not consciously made, that
the written sources are a reliable guide to the period, that the
chronicles and other writings, both of the time and later, give
a reasonably correct idea of the scale and character of Scandinavian activity and that they accurately represent the

attitudes and reactions of non-Scandinavians to the invaders. It is only in recent years that the auxiliary studies of archaeology, numismatics and place-names have developed sufficiently to be used, except in the most restricted way, as a check on these written sources, and the statements of contemporary writers and others have for too long been accepted by historians and others almost at their face value. This has had most unfortunate consequences, for most contemporary writers were extremely hostile to the Vikings, and they concentrated almost exclusively on the violent aspects of Scandinavian activity. The hostility of the sources is not surprising; they were mostly written by ecclesiastics who were mainly concerned to record and complain about the activities of these heathen men who regarded the holy places of Christendom simply as treasure houses fit only to be plundered. The bias is often obvious and the exaggerations blatant; they are part of the reaction that historians seek to understand. It is, however, unfortunate that this bias and these exaggerations should have so thoroughly infected historical writing about the Viking period as a whole. Their too ready acceptance has resulted in distortions that make the subject wellnigh incomprehensible. It is too easy to succumb to the judgement of these contemporary writers and, for want of anything better, to accept their estimates of the size and destructiveness of Viking armies. One may recognise that chroniclers are very unreliable in their reports about the size of fleets and armies and that they are likely to exaggerate the destruction wrought, but, unless there is independent evidence, it is too easy to use their figures. Gradually the qualifications with which individual scholars may hedge chroniclers' accounts and the reservations that may be felt are lost in the general impression that is reinforced with each repetition.

The greatest obstacle to a balanced judgement of the Viking period, of the motives and consequences of Scandinavian activity at that time, is this lack of independent evidence that can serve as a check on the admittedly biased Christian sources. Muslim sources are of little use for this and Scandinavian and Russian writings only begin in the eleventh century. The historical value of the Icelandic sagas is slight, but being the most colourful and detailed of all our sources they continue to attract attention. As historical evidence they are most valuable for the periods in which they were written but they present in vivid terms a picture of Dark Age society that seems to fit in with what we learn from contemporary chronicles and other writings. They are largely concerned with exploits of Vikings, with the deeds of heroism that are the stuff of legend and which are presented with great technical skill, powerfully reinforcing the impressions gained from the primary sources. Even though the sagas are now widely recognised to be at best a guide, they continue to be one of the most effective barriers to seeing in the Viking period anything more than battle, murder and sudden death.

The historian, in attempting to study the nature, causes and consequences of Scandinavian activity at this time is therefore in danger of being imprisoned by what are obviously partisan attitudes. The effects of this limitation are cumulative; once it is accepted that the Vikings came in fleets of hundreds of ships and that their armies numbered thousands of warriors, it is easy to recognise in this outpouring of terror the explanation of happenings that are otherwise not fully understood and for these, in their turn, to be treated as consequences of the Viking raids and therefore evidence of their destructiveness. The collapse of the Mercian kingdom, the disappearance of monasticism and the decay of learning in England,[20] the disintegration of Charlemagne's Empire, are all complex processes but there is a temptation to simplify matters by giving the Vikings more than their true share of responsibility, and so to confirm contemporary judgements of Viking violence.

Unfortunately the only evidence available to check and test the written sources is that provided by the auxiliary studies. This is principally unfortunate because the evidence of place-names, archaeology and numismatics is often not readily comparable with the written evidence. The chronicles of western Europe present a particular Christian viewpoint. Archaeological discoveries, place-names and coins themselves have no bias, they do not yield a Scandinavian point of view. The bias is imposed by those working with the material. And here lies the great difficulty for the historian who seeks a more balanced view of the Viking period. This auxiliary evidence is often studied in the light of the historical evidence and its value as an independent check is diminished. This may be seen very clearly in discussions of the density of Scandinavian settlement in England in which the evidence of personal- and place-names and of the sokemen and freemen of Domesday Book has been taken to prove a dense Scandinavian settlement largely because of the basic assumption that the Viking armies consisted of thousands of men.

This uncritical and traditional acceptance of the judgement of contemporary writers has led to the Viking period being considered as in some special way inexplicable. One distinguished historian has, indeed, complained that 'the attacks from Scandinavia have never been adequately explained'.[21] The third, and final, purpose of this book is to offer an explanation not simply for the causes of the Viking attacks, but for the changing patterns of Scandinavian activity throughout the Viking period.

2. The Written Sources

THE most important written evidence for the Viking period is not Scandinavian but Christian and Islamic. The only surviving Scandinavian writings of the time are runic inscriptions and until the eleventh century there were few of those. The traditions of the Vikings were first written down long after the conversion of Scandinavia to Christianity and are preserved in such texts as the sagas of medieval Iceland which are far more valuable as sources for the period in which they were written than for the Viking age. Fortunately for the historian the Scandinavians came into contact with other, literate, societies and the writings of western Europe are particularly valuable sources of information about their activities and the reactions they provoked. In Russia as in Scandinavia the art of writing followed the conversion to Christianity, and the first Russian Chronicle was not compiled until the eleventh century; but for the ninth and tenth centuries there are, fortunately, Byzantine and, even more important, Islamic sources that refer to Scandinavians in the East. Islamic sources are also valuable for the information they give about Viking raids in Spain.

These written sources are not easy to use. The most obvious difficulty is that they are written in a great variety of languages: Norse, Irish, English, Latin, Russian, Greek, Persian and Arabic. There are also the textual problems that always have to be faced with written material. Whenever a text is copied it may be altered, either by mistake or by deliberate omissions or insertions, and when texts are only preserved in late copies and have been transmitted through many stages it is often difficult, if not impossible, to determine what was originally written. Some texts, like the eleventh-century Russian Chronicle or the twelfth- and thirteenth-century Icelandic sagas were themselves compiled late, and the recognition of reliable clues to the Viking period among the distortions of misremembered tradition and artistic adjustment in such works is a delicate and intricate undertaking. The interpretation of the written evidence for the Viking period is, therefore, a difficult business requiring techniques that are quite as specialised as those needed for the elucidation of the more obviously difficult archaeological, numismatic or place-name evidence. The difficulties need to be emphasised because they are so easily overlooked. The meanings of chronicles, sagas and even charters often appear to be obvious and it is easy, in using printed texts, sometimes in translation, to forget that they are based on manuscripts that are themselves almost always copies, if not copies of copies, and that in their transmission there will have been many opportunities, not always missed, for omissions and additions. Whenever a copy is made mistakes may occur. Moreover, while being delighted with the antiquity of a source, or with the colourful details that it may give, it is very easy to forget that it was written with a purpose. All the written evidence on which we draw was written for some purpose, if only that of whiling away the time, and one of the most important parts of the historian's business is to determine what that purpose was: if the intention of a writer is not understood his words may easily mislead.

These commonplaces of historical investigation can conveniently and usefully be illustrated in the Anglo-Saxon Chronicle which is, in many ways, the best of all the chronicles for the Viking period, paradoxically, because it is, for the critical reigns of Alfred and his son, Edward, quite unlike any other chronicle. Chroniclers were not normally historians; their purpose was not to write history, to study and trace a process of change that they had witnessed or wished to explain. It was, rather, to provide a series of landmarks to the past. Medieval chroniclers were almost always members of religious communities and they wrote in order to help their fellows distinguish the years that had passed by recording important happenings. Such chronicles served as the collective memory of the community. The accession of a new king, the death of a bishop or abbot, a Viking raid, heavenly portents or a wet summer were all noteworthy. As Charles Plummer put it, 'that which to us seems a lean and barren sentence was to them the text for a winter evening's entertainment'.[1] In their choice of significant or memorable events the chroniclers naturally betray their interests and concerns. Their writings are valuable not only as a record of events but because they reveal a choice of events to be recorded: what chroniclers left out, if that can be known, is as interesting as what they put in. The Anglo-Saxon Chronicle for the reigns of Alfred and his son Edward is particularly interesting in this respect because the writer has clearly concentrated almost exclusively on the Danish raiders. Most chroniclers of the time, whatever their special interests, mention a wide variety of happenings; the Anglo-Saxon Chronicle does not. From 865 to 920 it is little more than the record of the struggle of the West Saxon rulers against the Scandinavians. This gives the work a unique place among contemporary writings.

There are really four vernacular Anglo-Saxon Chronicles and they are preserved in seven manuscripts.[2] Other versions that once existed have been lost and are now only known through the use that was made of them by other writers. All were based on a compilation produced at the end of the ninth century somewhere in the western part of Wessex. It was formerly thought that King Alfred was himself the compiler but this is now no longer generally believed although he may well have encouraged its production. Several copies of this Chronicle were made at the time and one of them has fortunately been preserved, the 'Parker Chronicle', so called after a former owner. In this manuscript all the entries down to the annal for 891 were written by one scribe and there is no palaeographical reason to doubt that he wrote within a generation of that date. The other versions of this basic ninth-century Chronicle are later copies but all come from one archetype which probably included the annal for 892 although in the Parker Chronicle this was added by a different scribe. In this archetype all the annals from 756 to 842 are consistently two or three years in advance, a chronological dislocation of great importance for the textual history of the Chronicle, but a fruitful source of error.

Despite its early date, the Parker Chronicle has at least one major error, which it shares with almost all other versions.[3] In the annal for the year 885 it describes the arrival of a Viking force at Rochester 'where they besieged the city and made other fortifications round themselves. And nevertheless the English defended the city until King Alfred came up with his army. Then the enemy went to their ships and abandoned their fortification, and they were deprived of their horses there, and immediately that same summer they went back across the sea. That same year King Alfred sent a naval force from Kent into East Anglia. . . .' With one exception all other versions agree closely with this. The exception is a Latin translation made in the late tenth century by a West Saxon noble called Æthelweard. Æthelweard's Latin, unfortunately never very clear, is untranslatable at this point, but it can be seen that he was using a version of the Chronicle in which there were two successive sentences ending with the phrase 'went across the sea'. In the version from which all copies other than Æthelweard's are derived, the scribe must have missed the second sentence and, having written the first 'went across the sea', his eye must have jumped to the second occurrence of the phrase from which he continued copying. This is a mistake commonly made by copyists. It appears from Æthelweard's translation that some of the raiders did not immediately return to the Continent but came to some agreement with Alfred which they broke. Before they in their turn 'went across the sea', they twice raided south of the Thames, and also camped at Benfleet on the Essex coast, the site of another Viking camp a few years later. The passage that has been dropped explains why the Chronicle continues by describing an attack by Alfred's forces on East Anglia. The omission of this sentence, which could not be known without Æthelweard's version, shows that the possession of an early copy of a text is itself no guarantee of correct transmission. Whenever copies are made, errors are possible. The danger that errors may pass unnoticed is of course far greater when only one version is preserved, particularly when that version has been transmitted through many copies. Even in the surviving copies of the Anglo-Saxon Chronicle there may be similar omissions that cannot be detected, but the existence of so many versions gives ground for some confidence that, by and large, a full text of the Chronicle compiled in Alfred's reign has been preserved.

This compiler was probably working in, or shortly after, 892 and may be thought a contemporary witness of the events of the preceding twenty-five years.[4] He seems to have had a fairly detailed knowledge of events since 865 from which date there is an entry for every year, but for his account of the years before this he must have relied on remembered traditions or earlier compilations. The Danish raids on England began in 835 and it is obviously important to have some idea of the reliability of this late ninth-century Chronicle for the middle years of the century. If the compiler of 892 only had memory to guide him, his account of events between 835 and 865 cannot be very reliable, but if he had an earlier set of annals, possibly compiled at the time, his work would be much more trustworthy for those years. It is, of course, not possible to define the sources used by the compiler with certainty but it seems very likely that for the period before about 842 he was using an earlier set of annals but that after 842 he relied on memory.[5] The first indication that the compiler's sources changed after the annals for 842–3 is that for the twenty years before this there are annals for almost every year; between 821 and 843 the only years without entries are 822, 826 and 828, but that between 843 and 865 there are only five annals altogether. Another indication is that the compiler of 892 reckoned years to begin on 25th September but there are annals in the first half of the century that seem to be for years that began at Christmas. The chronological dislocation of two or three years that has already been mentioned ends in 842 and this also suggests that there was some change in the character of the compiler's source at about that time. The reason for putting the change at 842 rather than 843 is that the annal for the latter year is very suspect. It reads: 'In this year King Æthelwulf fought against the crews of 35 ships at Carhampton [in Somerset, on the Bristol Channel] and the Danes had possession of the battlefield.' This sounds suspiciously like a repetition of the annal for 836: 'In this year King Egbert fought against the crews of 35 ships [some versions have 25] at Carhampton and a great slaughter was made there and the Danes had possession of the battlefield.' It is, of course, possible that Æthelwulf was defeated by the Danes near Carhampton in 843, but the unusual verbal similarity between these two annals and the fact that the compiler's source seems to have changed at about this point suggests that the account of 843 depends more on the annal for 836 than on the memory of what happened in 843.

The value of the Chronicle as an authority for the middle years of the century, from 843 to about 865, is therefore less than for the years before or after this and it is for this period that the Continental annals are most useful as a supplement to the English. This does not, of course, mean that the annals between 842 and 865 are worthless; the events they record are likely to have been well remembered, but for these years the Chronicle is not such a complete account of the raids and the details given are less trustworthy. This means that the victory of the English at *Aclea* in 851 need not be doubted, but the size of the invading fleet given by the Chronicle is the sort of detail that is likely to have been exaggerated in the forty years that followed and the statement that there were 350 ships should therefore be taken even less seriously than if it were a contemporary estimate.

The earlier Viking raids happened a century before the compilation of the Chronicle and although the West Saxon sources do not seem to have been very full for this period of Mercian hegemony they did apparently include a detailed account of the first raid on Wessex. The Chronicle account may be compared with the version given by Æthelweard which preserves a number of interesting details.

Chronicle	*Æthelweard*
789 In this year King Brihtric married Offa's daughter Eadburh. And in his days there came for the first	While the most pious King Brihtric was reigning over the western parts of the English . . . A small fleet of

Chronicle	*Æthelweard*
time three ships of North-men [from Hörthaland according to some versions] and then the reeve rode to them and wished to force them to the king's residence, for he did not know what they were; and they slew him. Those were the first ships of Danish men which came to the land of the English.	Danes, numbering three fast ships (*dromones*) came un-expectedly to the coast and this was their first coming. Hearing of this, the king's official (*exactor*), then staying at the town called Dorchester, leaped on his horse and with a few men made haste to the port, thinking they were merchants (*negotiatores*) rather than enemies, and commanding them imperiously he ordered them to be sent to the royal vill, but he and his companions were straightaway killed by them. The name of the official was Beaduheard.

The first Viking raid on Wessex must have been a notable event which would have been long remembered but the details given by the Chronicler are unlikely to have been based on oral tradition alone. Some written account must lie behind this entry but this is unlikely to have been a set of annals otherwise the year of the raid would have been given instead of the general reference to the reign of King Brihtric, who was king of Wessex from 786 to 802. The source may in fact have been literary rather than annalistic, possibly a poem.

The compiler of the 'Alfredian' Chronicle was preoccupied with the Viking raids. Every annal from 865 to 887 is largely concerned with the Vikings, often to the exclusion of all other topics and, with one exception, the opening words of each annal in this period report the movement of what the Chronicler clearly regarded as the main Viking force. Year after year the opening words are almost identical, *Her for se here, Her rad se here, Her cuom se here*, 'In this year the *here*** went, rode, came'.

* An Old English word often translated 'army' or 'host' and generally used for Danish invaders. The reason for not translating it is explained on p. 123.

In some years, the Chronicler reports nothing from England but follows with anxious care the movements on the Continent of the *here* that was to cross to England in 892. His concentration on this particular *here* must mean that it had already reached England when he was compiling the Chronicle for those years. The purpose of the Chronicle seems, indeed, to have been to provide the background to this invasion and to relate the struggle of Alfred against the raiders after 892. The Chronicler's concern not only affected his choice of events to record from his own day, it also guided his treatment of earlier annals. From 835, the first recorded Danish raid, to 842 there are seven annals; all but one of them deal with Viking raids, and five deal with nothing else. It is not simply that the raids are noted with care but that other things normally noted in chronicles must have been left out. Thus, in the first thirty-five years of the ninth century there are five annals reporting the death of ecclesiastics, between 835 and 900 there are only four. Once the compiler of 892 reached the time the Danes began regularly to visit England he concentrated his attention on them. For him, the Danes alone were worth close attention, and in making his selection of annals he seems to have omitted much that was, for him, irrelevant.

This narrowing of interest, this specialisation of the compiler makes his work particularly valuable as a source for the study of Viking activity, but it also tends to exaggerate the importance of that activity. Just because the Vikings were, for the purposes of the compiler, almost the only topic of interest, it must not be concluded that his contemporaries all shared this attitude. The special emphasis on Viking raids and the omission of references to the sort of strife among the English that had been prominent in the annals before 835 has also distorted the picture of the ninth century. The Chronicle appears to represent the English at peace with each other after that year and the contrast with Viking violence seems therefore all the more striking.

The Anglo-Saxon Chronicle is unusual in other respects, particularly in the absence after 835 of any mention of the destruction or even plundering of religious houses. The Irish and Continental chronicles of the time are full of reports of

Viking attacks on churches and monasteries but the only entry of the kind in the English Chronicle for the ninth century is a twelfth-century interpolation in a copy made at Peterborough, which states that the Danes 'destroyed all the monasteries they came to' and that: 'In this same time [870] they came to Peterborough, burnt and destroyed it, killed the abbot and the monks and all they found there, and brought it to pass that it became nought that had been very mighty.' If this report is correct, it is very surprising that the earlier versions of the Chronicle make no mention of any such destructions. The Chronicler reports the movement of armies, battles, and sometimes mentions plundering in general but the destruction or looting of religious houses or churches is not specifically mentioned. The audience for whom this Chronicle was intended seems therefore to have been lay rather than ecclesiastical. The Chronicler was, of course, a Christian and he rejoices at the conversion of some of the raiders, but his interests seem to have been less with the Church than with the West Saxon kingdom and its dynasty. If a chronicle was the collective memory of a community, the community for whom the Anglo-Saxon Chronicle was compiled in 892 must have been a very unusual one. The Chronicle seems, in fact, to have been a work of propaganda, to remind men that it was the West Saxons alone who had successfully resisted the invaders.[6] The achievements of Æthelwulf and his sons are rehearsed and praised while the failure of the Mercians is emphasised. It is a piece of dynastic propaganda produced at a time of great crisis, when the great *here* came to England from Boulogne.

Several copies were made of the compilation of 892 and they may have been distributed although it is not known where. It is sometimes assumed that copies were sent to monasteries or cathedrals but there is no evidence for this and, indeed, the secular character of the Chronicle and its early continuations tells against such an assumption. Had the surviving copies been sent to religious establishments the absence of entries of purely domestic interest would be surprising. Some copies, it is true, were left untouched for a number of years, conspicuously the version on which the Peterborough Chronicle was ultimately based, but some versions were kept up to date after 892. The significant feature of these continuations is that they occur in almost identical form in the different versions and the explanation for this agreement must be that all are based on a common source in which the story and purpose of the compiler of 892 seem to be continued. The annals for the years immediately after 892 deal exclusively with the campaigns against the *here* that arrived in England in that year, the *here* on which the Chronicler's attention had been so narrowly focused, and whose arrival in England seems to have been the occasion for the compilation of the work. Only after its dispersal in the summer of 896 does the Chronicle turn to other subjects, and the annal for 897 is the first for many years that is of normal annalistic type: 'In this year, nine days before midsummer, Æthelhelm, ealdorman of Wiltshire, died; and in this year died Heahstan, who was bishop of London.' After this there is a gap of three years without an entry. It is as though the break up of the *here* in 896 meant that the Chronicler's immediate purpose had been fulfilled. It also means that whoever was responsible for the original compilation of 892 was probably also responsible for the annals for the next few years. It has indeed been suggested that this continuation was produced and issued 'officially', but there is no more evidence for such an assumption than there is for the 'official' compilation of the basic Chronicle. Whoever was responsible, the account of the campaigns against the invaders of 892 makes the Anglo-Saxon Chronicle one of the most remarkable of all the sources available for the Viking period. In these years it springs to life and becomes a vigorous and detailed account of elaborate campaigns by someone who was himself deeply involved and when, in 896, the *here* divided he was able to write 'by the grace of God the *here* had not on the whole afflicted the English people very greatly'.

The Chronicler's relief in 896 is clear, but the dispersal of this *here* still left a large part of England under the lordship of Scandinavians who remained a serious threat to the stability of Wessex. It was against these Danes that Alfred's children, Edward and Æthelfleda, waged a series of campaigns early in the tenth century and the three versions of the Chronicle for the years 900 to 914 describe these campaigns in identical terms. The source of these three versions is likely to have been the same as for the annals immediately after 892 and they were clearly written with the same purpose, to glorify the victorious West Saxon dynasty. From 915 to 920 this series of annals is continued in only one of the surviving versions, the Parker Chronicle. After this none of the Chronicles is very full or detailed and there are many differences between them, differences that sometimes reveal where they were being kept up to date. The annal for 931 in the Parker Chronicle, for example, suggests that it was then being compiled at Winchester: 'In this year Byrnstan was consecrated bishop of Winchester on 29 May, and he held his bishopric two and a half years.' This information is not found in any of the other Chronicles that were being compiled at the time, and points to Winchester as the home of this version. Similarly, another version seems to have been at York, and later in the century there are definite indications that a third Chronicle was being kept up to date at Abingdon. The identification of the centres at which the different versions were being maintained is made difficult by the meagreness of all versions in the middle of the tenth century. For about sixty years after 920 no version of the Chronicle is very full or detailed, and in all there are gaps in which no annals were compiled. There are a few elaborate annals such as the account of Athelstan's victory at *Brunanburh* over an alliance of Scandinavians and others, which is found in three versions in almost identical terms. There are other annals shared by two or more of the surviving tenth-century chronicles, sometimes no doubt because they share a common source or, alternatively, because they have been borrowed and copied.

At the end of the century the Chronicle again becomes a detailed record and the stimulus for this revival was the same as for the original compilation and its early continuations; Viking raids. In 980 the Vikings once again began to attack England and from that year the entries in the Chronicle are almost exclusively concerned with the raids. From 983 to 1019 several versions are in almost identical words and obviously have a common source which has been identified as the Chronicle being written at Abingdon.[7] There are therefore two sections of the Chronicle in which particular attention is paid to the Vikings and the several versions of each are based on a single source. There are, however, important differences between this basic Chronicle for the reigns of Alfred and Edward and the source of the several accounts of Ethelred's reign. The interests of the original compiler and those who continued his work were clearly secular, but in Ethelred's time ecclesiastical interests are more prominent. The earlier section is an account of the successful efforts of the West Saxon dynasty, the later section is the record of the failure of that dynasty, although the writer obviously had some affection for Ethelred. The source of the original compilation is unknown but its character is well indicated by the attempts that have been made to define it as an 'official' compilation; the Chronicle of Ethelred's reign is a far more personal record, written by someone who was, nevertheless, deeply concerned about the disasters. None of the versions of this magnificent Chronicle of Ethelred's reign is earlier than the middle of the eleventh century but there are several indications that it is a contemporary account. The annal for 1012, for example, explains how the body of Archbishop Ælfheah, after his murder by drunken raiders, was taken to London and buried in St. Paul's. It continues 'and God now reveals there the powers of the holy martyr'. As Ælfheah's body was translated to Canterbury in 1023, this annal must have been written within not more than ten years of the event. Such indications of contemporary writing are, of course, welcome but they are almost unnecessary, for the writer's personal involvement is plain. His Chronicle is full of revealing remarks, as in the account of the failure of the English in 1010 'And when they (the raiders) were journeying to their ships, the English *fyrd** should have come out again in case they wished to go inland. Then the English *fyrd* went home. And when they were in the east, the English *fyrd* was kept in the west, and when they were in the south, our *fyrd* was in the north. Then all the councillors were summoned to the king, and it was then to be decided how this country should be defended. But even if anything was then decided, it did not last even a

---

* An Old English word generally used for the English force in contrast to the Danish *here*.

c

month. Finally there was no leader who would collect a *fyrd*, but each fled as best he could, and in the end no shire would even help the next.' This is very unlike the 'lean and barren sentences' of most contemporary annals.

The Anglo-Saxon Chronicle was very largely written in the south of England. The original ninth-century compilation was made in Wessex; the continuations are concerned with the activities of the kings of Wessex, and the account of Ethelred's reign was probably written at Abingdon. There was however a northern version of the Chronicle which has, unfortunately, not been preserved in full, and is known only through the use made of it by other chroniclers. Parts were incorporated in the common ancestor of the Peterborough and York Chronicles and more was used in the twelfth century by the Durham writer, Simeon. The traces that have been preserved in these ways are slight but they are of the greatest value, not only for the light they cast on the obscure history of the north, but because they show a rather different attitude to the Scandinavian invaders than that exhibited in the West Saxon Chronicles. In this northern Chronicle the Scandinavians are seen not as the inveterate enemies of the English, but even as their allies in domestic disputes, allies who were indeed not unacceptable to the Church.

The Anglo-Saxon Chronicle is undoubtedly one of the most detailed and reliable sources for the study of the Viking period but it has certain limitations that should not be disregarded. It may be considered a more or less contemporary record after about 865 and its account of the early years of the ninth century is probably based on some written source, but for the middle years of the ninth century, when the raids first became serious, it should be treated with caution, certainly as a source of detailed information. The Chronicler's concentration on the Vikings has disadvantages and the tendency to omit any information about domestic disputes when the raids were the principal topic can easily give a misleading impression. The Anglo-Saxon Chronicle is the work of men who were deeply committed against the raiders, but their eloquence should not be allowed to obscure the fact that some men welcomed the Vikings and that relations between the kings of Wessex and the Scandinavians were not always hostile, or even potentially so. The topics that interested the Chroniclers were naturally those that concerned them directly or suited their purposes and it is not surprising that so little attention should be paid to the Scandinavian settlements. The fullest account in the Anglo-Saxon Chronicle of any settlement is, indeed, of an abortive attempt to settle in Wessex, near Chippenham. Once the Scandinavians had established themselves in what was later known as the Danelaw, their conquests and settlements were of interest to the Chronicler only as bases for hostile raids against the English. Little is said about the settlements in the east and nothing at all about the settlements in the north-west. If the Anglo-Saxon Chronicle were the only source of information nothing would be known of this important immigration from the west which can fortunately be traced by the study of place-names. This silence of the Chronicle should serve as a warning against the too ready assumption that it tells all. It is, finally, worth emphasising that for much of the Viking period the Anglo-Saxon Chronicle is based on one source and that the agreement between the several versions helps to establish the text, not the reliability of the writers. This English Chronicle is, therefore, in many ways an unusual source but there is nothing unusual about the problems that have to be faced before its evidence can be used with confidence and it illustrates very clearly the often elaborate process of criticism and analysis without which the written sources are likely to mislead. The meaning of chroniclers and other writers may seem obvious and open to all, especially when read in translation, but the appearance is deceptive.

In Ireland several independent chronicles were being compiled in the Viking period but none is preserved in a contemporary copy.[8] The earliest manuscript is about two centuries later than the original part of the Parker Chronicle and some are only known in versions of the seventeenth century. Fortunately the Annals of Ulster, a full and detailed compilation made at the end of the fifteenth century, can be shown to be a reliable copy of annals written in the Viking period. The proof is linguistic. From the end of the seventh century the language of the Annals of Ulster is contemporary and the forms of words and names clearly reflect the important changes that took place in the pronunciation of Old Irish between the seventh century and the tenth.[9] No later compiler could have reproduced these forms unless they had been in his source and their preservation is both surprising and fortunate—fortunate as a proof of the antiquity of the annals, and surprising because most versions of Irish annals are modernised. The same annals were used by other, and earlier writers, including the compilers of the *Chronicon Scotorum* and of the twelfth-century 'War of the Irish with the Foreigners', but the fullest version is the fifteenth-century compilation which, despite its late date, is one of the most valuable of all Irish sources for the Viking period.

Some compilations are apparently fuller and more detailed than the Annals of Ulster, notably the so-called Annals of the Four Masters. This collection was completed in 1636 by Michael O Clerigh and four assistants, who, unfortunately, modernised the language of their sources and so destroyed valuable clues to their antiquity.[10] The 'Four Masters' drew their annals from a great variety of sources including the Annals of Ulster, the Annals of Clonmacnoise, a late compilation now only preserved in a translation made in 1627, the *Chronicon Scotorum* and the so-called Three Fragments. Unfortunately, despite the great variety of their sources the Annals of the Four Masters have little independent value for the Viking period. When the sources they used are known, their annals add little or nothing and when the source is otherwise lost and the 'Four Masters' are the sole authority, little weight ought to be put on their work, certainly for the Viking period.

Among the sources that the 'Four Masters' do not seem to have used are the Annals of Inisfallen.[11] These were being written during the Viking period, probably at the monastery of Emly, about seven miles west of Tipperary, and they have survived in a copy made at the end of the eleventh century, probably for the monastery of Lismore. Until the middle of the tenth century these annals are very brief indeed, and merely record the deaths of kings, abbots and bishops. Important events are seldom mentioned and then very briefly, as in the annal for 796:

'Kalends of January. The heathens in Ireland.
Death of Mael Coba son of Flann Feórna king
of Ciarraige Luachra [a people in the north
of Kerry].
Colla son of Fergus, king of Connachta [the
people of Connacht], dies.'

From 969 the Annals of Inisfallen are more detailed, possibly
because of the increased importance of Munster and its kings,
for this was a Munster chronicle, and possibly also because
the copyist included more material from his exemplar as the
annals approached his own time.

One large-scale Irish source is exclusively devoted to the
invasions of the Vikings and the reaction of the Irish, *Cogadh
Gaedhel re Gallaibh*, 'The War of the Irish with the Foreigners'.[12]
This twelfth-century source has been given far more credit than
it deserves, and many of the misconceptions about the Scandinavians in Ireland are traceable to it. Its popularity as a
source for the Viking period is not surprising; as its title makes
plain its subject is the war between the Irish and the Norsemen, and it is written in an extravagant style that invites
quotation, as for example this description of the miseries of the
Irish: 'In a word, although there were an hundred hard
steeled iron heads on one neck, and an hundred sharp, ready,
cool, never-rusting, brazen tongues in each head, and an
hundred garrulous, loud, unceasing voices from each tongue,
they could not recount, or narrate, or enumerate, or tell, what
all the Gaedhil suffered in common, both men and women,
laity and clergy, old and young, noble and ignoble, of hard-
ship, and of injury, and of oppression, in every house, from
these valiant, wrathful, foreign, purely-pagan people.'[13]

The work is in two parts: the first thirty-four chapters are
devoted to the wars and invasions in general, and are based
on a version of the Annals of Ulster, and add little or nothing
to them; the second and major part deals particularly with
the affairs of Munster and with the events that led to the
Battle of Clontarf in 1014 in which Brian Boromha, king of
Munster, won death and victory. 'The War of the Irish with
the Foreigners' must have been written before 1160 because

part of it is preserved in the Book of Leinster, a manuscript written at about that date, but there are good reasons for believing that it cannot have been written much earlier than that. It can safely be assigned to the middle years of the twelfth century. The source for its first part was a version of the Annals of Ulster to which it adds nothing. The second part, however, is based on both annals and popular traditions some of which obviously developed long after the Battle of Clontarf and this section should be used with very great caution. It is moreover fiercely partisan and gives a distorted impression not only of Brian Boromha but of the importance of the Battle of Clontarf itself.[14]

The greatest difficulty in using the Irish annals is to determine the date of each entry. The annals were originally notes inserted in the margins of Easter tables and the systems used to indicate the year in these tables were also used in the annals. Years are, therefore, distinguished not by the year of the Incarnation but by their ferial number, that is the day of the week on which 1st January falls, or by the Epact, that is the age of the moon on 1st January, or by other variables used in the determination of Easter such as the Concurrent or the Golden Number. Some chronicles lack even these indications and simply mark the beginning of each new year with the symbol K or Kl standing for the Kalends of January as it does in the passage from the Annals of Inisfallen quoted above. When there were several years without an entry copyists might, and often did, omit the blank years and so put the sequence out of phase. The same event may therefore appear to be assigned to different years in different chronicles and when these were conflated by a compiler the same event could easily be repeated. The confusion has been aggravated by the mistaken efforts of some editors to assign annals to their correct year. In the early nineteenth-century edition of the Annals of Inisfallen, for example, the editor gave the ninth-century entries dates that are all at least thirteen years out. The correct dates in the Irish Annals have now been established but care is obviously needed if old mistakes are not to be repeated and given even wider currency.[15]

The greatest variety of written evidence for the Viking period comes from the Carolingian Empire and the Kingdoms that succeeded it.[16] There were, as in Ireland, several sets of annals being compiled at that time and these may be supplemented by such texts as charters, records of councils, saints' lives, poems, letters and collections of miracles in which the power of relics to prevent a Viking raid is, from time to time, reported. The writers were for the most part ecclesiastics and their interests were restricted, not simply to their church, but often to the region in which they lived. Annalists naturally paid far more attention to the events that directly affected their own community than to distant happenings, and the same is true of many of these sources. Even such a rich and varied source as the correspondence of Lupus, Abbot of Ferrières from 840 to 862, fortunately preserved in a manuscript of the ninth century, has relatively little to say about the Vikings unless they approached Ferrières.[17] Only a dozen of 133 letters make any allusion to the Vikings and in most of these the Vikings are only one of the subjects mentioned. The record of Viking activity on the Continent is therefore scattered and reports from one area have to be compared with reports from other areas in order to trace the movements of Viking bands. The ecclesiastical character of this evidence means that the destruction or looting of monasteries and churches plays a much larger part in the written sources of France than in England where the ninth-century Anglo-Saxon Chronicle does not mention the plundering or looting of any church. The difference does not mean that the Vikings treated the Church in England more considerately than in France, or that the Anglo-Saxon Chronicler was favourably disposed towards the Vikings, but that the interests of the English Chronicler were first dynastic and West Saxon and only secondly ecclesiastical while the Continental sources are mostly the work of churchmen whose concerns and loyalties were ecclesiastical rather than secular, provincial rather than dynastic.

One Frankish chronicle, the Annals of St. Bertin, was, however, written by men with wider sources of information than most, men who were concerned with wider issues than the fate of a particular church or district.[18] This remarkable chronicle, a continuation of the Frankish Royal Annals, was

kept up to date until 882. For the period of Viking attacks it
was written by two men. From 835 to 861 by Prudentius who
had been chaplain to the Empress Judith and who became
bishop of Troyes in 843. After his death in 861 it was taken up
and continued by Hincmar, one of the greatest personalities of
the ninth century who was bishop of Rheims from 845 to his
death in 882. These writers were both well informed and give
a very detailed and thorough account of the middle years of
the century. They report happenings all over the Frankish
world and beyond, for they supplement the Anglo-Saxon
Chronicle in the middle years of the century when it is least
satisfactory and are the authority for several raids on England
between 844 and 861. They were also familiar with proceedings
at the Frankish courts, and Prudentius reports the arrival of
an embassy from the Byzantine Emperor Theophilus to the
Frankish Emperor Louis at Ingelheim in the summer of 839.
This was an especially interesting occasion because these
envoys brought with them some people called *Rhos*, whose
king was called *Chacanus*, 'Khaqan'. These men, who proved to
be Swedes, had reached Constantinople but were unable to
return by the same route because of wild and cruel tribes and
were therefore being sent home this roundabout way.[19] In scale
and detail the Annals of St. Bertin are like the Anglo-Saxon
Chronicle at its best but there is a very important difference.
Unlike the English Chronicle it is not exclusively concerned
with the Vikings. Both Prudentius and Hincmar had other
concerns and although Viking raids were reported almost
every year, and were clearly regarded as a serious threat, far
less space and attention is paid to them in these annals than to
other matters which must, in the view of the writers, have been
as or more important.

   This magnificent chronicle is far more detailed and better
informed than most other ninth-century texts and with its
end in 882 the sources for the study of Viking activity in the
western parts of the Frankish Empire suddenly become most
inadequate. This is especially unfortunate for it was in the
three decades after 882 that the Viking duchy of Normandy
was established. The most detailed source for this is the early
eleventh-century account of the Dukes of Normandy by Dudo

of St. Quentin, but this is a most unreliable source and is generally discredited.[20] The best source for the early tenth century is Flodoard, a canon of Rheims who wrote an account of his church to 948.[21] Flodoard's work was used and revised later in the century by Richer, also of Rheims, but neither of these writers was in the same class as Hincmar.[22] Thus the Frankish sources, which are full and detailed for the early stages of Viking activity in the West and a valuable supplement to the less detailed English Chronicle, collapse before the end of the ninth century. The English Chronicle which becomes, for the Vikings, a detailed source in the last quarter of the century, continues to be a full account until 920. After that neither English nor Frankish sources are very satisfactory until the end of the century when, again under the impact of the Vikings, the English Chronicle springs to life. At about the same time the Irish chronicles also become more detailed and in the early eleventh century contemporary Norman writings are available. This means that by the early eleventh century, when Scandinavian sources also have some independent value, the written material for the study of the Vikings in western Europe is richer and more varied than ever before and Viking activity can be studied more closely and the reliability of different texts can be tested more thoroughly than is possible in the ninth and tenth centuries.

During the Viking period there were, therefore, many changes in the number and value of the written sources from western Europe, but almost all have one thing in common; they were written by churchmen. This has given most of the written evidence an easily recognisable bias against the Scandinavians for it was the churches that particularly suffered from the Viking raids. This was not because the Vikings were filled with a ferocious pagan hostility to Christianity, but simply because the treasures of the Church were a rich and often ill-defended source of plunder and when tribute was gathered to buy off the raiders the wealth of the Church was heavily drawn on. It is, therefore, not surprising that in their writings these churchmen regard the Scandinavians in the first place as plunderers. They were naturally not much interested in them as settlers or as traders; the settlements

were, in their eyes, little more than bases for further depreda-
tions. The contemporary writings of the Christian West can
hardly be expected to provide a balanced and impartial
account of the Scandinavians.

The western sources that have so little to say about the
Scandinavian settlements naturally have even less to say about
Scandinavia itself. Before the Danish raids began, and the
Franks were in contact with Denmark through traders and
missionaries, their writings do contain a little information about
the North; but when piracy made trading across the North
Sea increasingly difficult and internal dissension turned the
attention of the Franks more and more to their own troubles
these contacts were weakened, and by the middle of the
century had apparently been broken altogether. The most
remarkable of all the sources that tell of these Frankish dealings
with the Baltic is the Life of St. Anskar written by Rimbert,
his pupil and successor as archbishop of Hamburg-Bremen.[23]
Anskar was a monk of Corbie who went as a missionary first
to Denmark and then among the Swedes. In the course of his
work he made two visits to Birka, one in about 830, the other
in about 850. He died in 865 and within a decade Rimbert
had written his life which is a most valuable source not only
because it describes these early missionary efforts and gives
some information about the trading relations between the
Baltic and the West, but because in explaining Anskar's
dealings with the Swedes, Rimbert provides a glimpse of their
society as understood by a Frank, although there is no reason
to believe that Rimbert himself had ever been to Birka. It is,
however, important to remember that the *Vita Anskarii* was
not written until at least thirty-five years after Anskar's first
visit to Birka and many of the details may reflect more recent
conditions. The *Vita Anskarii* is, moreover, a good example of
the way some sources have been tampered with. There are
two versions. One is longer and represents Rimbert's original
work; in the other, shorter, version all the passages that went
against the claims of Hamburg-Bremen to primacy in Scandinavia have been deleted.

These claims of Hamburg are very clearly seen in the other
main written source for the history of the Baltic, Adam of

Bremen's *Gesta Hammaburgensis ecclesiae pontificum*.[24] Adam completed this great history of the church of Hamburg-Bremen between 1073 and 1075, and as he himself had come from elsewhere in Germany in 1066 or 1067 he was only an eyewitness for a very short time. He used that time well. He based his work not only on the archives of the church, and on such earlier writings as the *Vita Anskarii*, but he also learned much, he claimed the greater part, from 'older men who knew the facts'. Among these authorities there was a certain Danish bishop 'a prudent man' from whom Adam learned of Henry the Fowler's invasion of Denmark a century and a half before, but it is probable that at least some of the information he had from such men as Adalbard, bishop of Sigtuna, and his companions was more reliable. Adalbard of Sigtuna is, admittedly, cited as the authority for Amazons on the shores of the Baltic but, more credibly, it is reported that when he first went to Sigtuna 'as he was on a journey he turned aside to Birka, which now was turned into such a wilderness that scarcely a vestige of the city was visible. On this account the burial mound of the holy archbishop Unni [whose death at Birka in 936 is mentioned by Adam] could not be found.'[25] Adam showed commendable caution in describing Unni's mission. 'Now the Swedes and Goths, who were first grounded in the faith by Saint Anskar and relapsed again into paganism, were recalled by the holy father Unni. This it is enough to know; if we said more, we should be charged with a lying disposition. "For it is better," as the blessed Jerome puts it, "to say what is true crudely than to proffer what is false elegantly." '[26] Adam's most important informant was Svein Estrithson, king of the Danes, who is named as the authority for several statements. Adam himself explains:

'when I came to Bremen and heard of this king's wisdom, I at once resolved to go to him. And he also received me graciously, as he did all, and from his lips I gathered much of the material for this little book. He was well versed in the knowledge of letters and very receptive towards strangers. He personally sent his priests out as preachers into all Sweden and Norway and to the islands that are in those

parts. From his veracious and very delightful discourse I
learned that in his time many among the barbarian nations
had been converted to the Christian faith, that some men
had also been crowned with martyrdom in Sweden as well
as in Norway. . . . What we have said therefore and what
we still have to say about the barbarians, all that we have
come to know from what this man related.'[27]

There are difficult textual problems, for Adam's original work
was revised, partly by himself and partly by others, and in the
several manuscripts in which the work is preserved there are
many variations. Until the relations between these texts have
been established, and this has not yet been done satisfactorily,
it is not always clear what Adam originally wrote. The whole
work is, naturally, biased in favour of the claims of Hamburg-
Bremen and this appears very clearly in the description of the
rival bishops of Skåne.

> 'On the death of Avoco [bishop of Sjælland], King Svein
> divided the diocese of Skåne into two bishoprics, giving one
> of them, that is Lund, to Henry, the other, that is Dalby, to
> Egino. The archbishop [of Hamburg-Bremen], in fact,
> consecrated the latter; Henry had previously been bishop
> in the Orkneys and, it is related, the keeper of King Cnut's
> treasure in England. Bringing this treasure over to Denmark,
> Henry spent his life in voluptuousness. About him it is
> even stated that, revelling in the pestiferous practice of
> drinking his belly full, he at last suffocated and burst.
> We have learned that this was also the fate of Avoco and,
> likewise, that of others. But since Egino was a man who knew
> letters and was remarkable for his chastity, he at that very
> time also directed his every effort ardently to the conversion
> of the pagans. . . . Soon after the gross Henry died, Egino
> received the governance of both the dioceses of Skåne,
> Lund and Dalby.'[28]

This bias against the claims of other churches has to be taken
into account, for, despite Adam and those who revised the
Vita Anskarii, there were other missions in Scandinavia in the
Viking period as well as that directed from Hamburg-Bremen.

One other western source about Scandinavia in the Viking period has to be mentioned. In the Old English translation of the *Universal History* of Orosius, which has sometimes been attributed to King Alfred and is certainly preserved in an early tenth-century manuscript, a section was inserted containing an account of voyages made independently by two men, a Norwegian and an Englishman.[29] The Norwegian, who was called Ottar, or Ohthere in English, said that he lived in Helgeland in the far north of Norway and that no one lived to the north of him except Lapps. He described a journey he had made round the North Cape into the White Sea, and he gave details of his own wealth which consisted mainly of a herd of reindeer. He took part in whaling expeditions but his main source of income was tribute in the form of furs, skins and whale hides paid to him by Lapps. His contribution to the translation of Orosius ends with a description of the journey south from his home to the market of *Sciringesheal* in the south of Norway and beyond to Hedeby. This is followed by an account of a voyage of seven days and nights from Hedeby to *Truso* near the Vistula delta made by Wulfstan, apparently an Englishman. Wulfstan also described in some detail the customs of the Esthonians he encountered. In describing the landmarks on their routes both men gave much valuable information, such as that the people of Bornholm had their own king but that Blekinge, Öland and Gotland belonged to the Swedes, and Ohthere reported that Hedeby belonged to the Danes. These glimpses of Scandinavia and the Baltic at the end of the ninth century are obviously of the greatest value and their preservation in the Old English Orosius, which is fortunately known in a contemporary copy, make this one of the key texts for the study of the Viking period. The fact that Wulfstan could make a voyage in the Baltic at a time when the raids on western Europe were at their height is itself most instructive and the description of King Alfred as Ohthere's lord shows that they were on friendly terms. Even if Ohthere had been a Viking, and there is no suggestion in the text that this was the case, it is clear that relations between the English and the Scandinavians at the time were more complex and could be less hostile than is implied by the Anglo-Saxon

Chronicle. This interpolation in Orosius is a refreshing contrast to most of the contemporary writing about Scandinavians in England and elsewhere.

In the tenth century there is remarkably little to be learned about Scandinavia from contemporary writings and there are certainly no sources to compare with the *Vita Anskarii* or the Old English Orosius. There are a few clues in German sources,[30] for the Germans had some stake in Denmark, but most information about tenth-century Scandinavia comes from later writers. This is, of course, unfortunate because distortions could quickly develop and pass into general currency. Adam of Bremen himself, despite the excellence of his sources, is the 'authority' for a completely fictitious Swedish conquest of Denmark at the end of the tenth century, a conquest that has played a large part in northern historical tradition.[31] Most of the sources that have to be used for Scandinavian history are even later than Adam of Bremen. The first History of the Kings of Norway was written by Theodricus in about 1180, and Saxo Grammaticus, whose *Gesta Danorum* is a large and detailed account of Danish history, died early in the thirteenth century.[32] Best known of all these later sources are the Icelandic sagas which were first written at the end of the twelfth century.[33] These writings of the twelfth and thirteenth century were based on a variety of sources, both written and unwritten. There were oral traditions about the past that had been handed down and there were earlier historical writings many of which have been lost. Writers like Adam of Bremen and Sæmundr Sigfusson whose History of the Kings of Norway was written late in the eleventh century but is now lost, depended in their turn very largely on oral traditions and although a man writing at the end of the eleventh century may have preserved much valuable information about the tenth it is no simple matter to distinguish what is valuable from what is not, particularly when the work is only known through the use made of it in later times. Ari Thorgilsson, known as the father of Icelandic history, wrote several works of which only one, *The Book of the Icelanders*, has survived, but his lost works seem to have been heavily drawn on by later writers about the history of Iceland and Norway. He was, however, only born in 1067 or the year after and the reliability of his information about the tenth century may be doubted. It is true that from the age of seven he was brought up by Hallr Thorarinsson who is reputed to have had a remarkable memory. Hallr claimed to be able to remember his baptism in 998 when he was only three, and as a young man he had served St. Olaf of Norway. He must have told Ari much about his youth and he has been described as 'one of the main channels through which tradition flowed from ancient to medieval Iceland'.[34] He may well have remembered many details of his youth with great accuracy but it is difficult to test his reliability. Old men do sometimes forget and misremember. He was eighty when Ari, then aged seven, first met him, and his memory must have been a very uncertain link with the past. His importance in the transmission of Icelandic traditions need not be doubted, but traditions should not be confused with history.

The Icelandic sagas of the twelfth and thirteenth centuries are full of picturesque detail and it is not surprising that they should have attracted so much attention. Often they are about historical characters and are set in a framework of historical events. The saga of Burnt Njal, for example, written in the thirteenth century, is set in the time of the Conversion.[35] Many historical events are mentioned and play a part in this story and the central episode, the Burning of Njal has an historical basis, but this saga is not an attempt to write history. The writer of Burnt Njal did indeed have a serious purpose but it was related to the times in which he lived not to the times about which he wrote. The details of life in Iceland and elsewhere with which the stories are elaborated have sometimes been treated as though they were a reliable guide to the conditions in the Viking period but these too would have been more easily recognised by men of the thirteenth century than of the tenth. It is easy to feel that in the sagas we are close to the original settlers of the ninth century and their early descendants but it is important to remember that we are at least 200 years away.

Some sagas about the kings of Norway were indeed written as works of history. The most famous and best of these is the magnificent History of the Norwegian Kings known as

Heimskringla, after its opening words, written in the early thirteenth century by Snorri Sturluson.[36] The historical value of these royal sagas can however easily be overrated; some of the confusions in Snorri's own account of St. Olaf's career in England will be mentioned below. These sagas tell not so much what happened as what men believed had happened, they enshrine not history but tradition. The historical sagas do indeed embody the historical traditions of Iceland and Norway but what is otherwise known about the past does more to illuminate them than they do to illuminate the past.

The sagas are not, however, entirely worthless, for the saga writers used and sometimes quoted poetry of the Viking age. This scaldic verse, as it is called, was composed in Scandinavia from the second half of the ninth century and rather later in Iceland and much of it was remembered in the twelfth and thirteenth centuries when the sagas were being written.[37] The non-poetic oral traditions used by the saga writers could easily be changed, but this poetry could not because it was written according to strict rules; if remembered at all it had to be remembered correctly. One of the features of this poetry is the use of kennings or metaphors such as 'swan of the sea-god' for ship or 'troll of the tree trunks' for wind. Some of these poets delighted to evolve extremely elaborate kennings that are by no means easy to disentangle. So, for example, a kenning for sea is 'plain of the ship' and a kenning for ship is 'elk of the fjord'; if the two are combined the sea becomes 'the plain of the elk of the fjord'. As gold was thought to lie in the sea, a kenning for gold was 'fire of the sea' and this could be elaborated with the earlier, already double kenning into 'the fire of the plain of the elk of the fjord' or more correctly 'the fjord elk's plain's fire', *fjarðar elgs vangs furr.*[38]

The effect of metre, alliteration and kennings cannot be conveyed completely in translation but something of the feel is captured in this translation by Professor Hollander of two verses from one of the great poems of the early eleventh century, the *Austrfararvisur*, 'Verses on a Journey to the East', by Sigvat Thordarson.[39] In it several different kennings are used for ship, 'sea-steed', 'keel-bird', 'sea-wethers' and 'Ræfil's horses', Ræfil being a sea-king.

Light my mind was, lord, and
mirthful, when on firth ways
with glorious king the stormy
gales did shake our sailships:
in glee, swiftly, our sea-steeds
o'er sounds of Lister bounded
at will, with the wind bellying
the wings of heeling keel-birds.

Tented, in time of summer,
tethered, our sea-wethers
rode at anchor, floating
before the good land's shore-line:
now, in fall, when on rollers
Ræfil's-horses are coursing,
I, wretch, must ride to Sweden
sans rest, as the king requested.

The historical relevance of much scaldic verse is slight and
the meaning is sometimes obscure but even verses that are most
purely poetical description can have great value for the inci-
dental detail which they may contain, as, in the example
quoted, the references to the tenting of ships in the summer
and their storage on rollers in winter. Details of this kind, in
poetry that genuinely comes from the Viking age, are obviously
of the greatest value.

Not all scaldic verse was written in the Viking period. The
art of writing it lived on until the fourteenth century and
Snorri Sturluson himself wrote a textbook for beginners in the
art of versifying. Some verses are therefore late, and some
saga writers composed verses to fit their stories, but the verses
embedded in the royal sagas seem to be quoted in good faith
and can be accepted as authentic. One of the best tests is in
fact when the writer of the saga misunderstands a verse, or
relates a verse to some inappropriate occasion. Snorri Sturluson himself misused verses in this way, including the following
one by Sigvat Thordarson which he quotes in the saga of
St. Olaf. This prose translation is by Miss Ashdown.[40]

It is true that the sixth attack was where Olaf attacked
London's bridge. The valiant prince offered Ygg's strife to

D

the English. Foreign swords pierced, but there the Vikings guarded the dike. A part of the host had their booths in level Southwark.

In this battle it is clear that Olaf was fighting against the English, but Snorri believed that Olaf was always on Ethelred's side and his interpretation of this verse is a classic misunderstanding that illustrates very well the danger of relying on the prose of sagas. According to Snorri, Olaf and Ethelred joined forces and they made their way to London:

'but the Danes held the city. On the other side of the river is a great market town called Southwark. There the Danes had entrenched themselves strongly; they had dug a great dike and barricaded the inside of the wall with timber and stones and turf, and inside it they had a large force. King Ethelred ordered a great attack to be made, but the Danes repulsed it and King Ethelred made no headway.'

Snorri continues by describing how Olaf took his ships under London Bridge

'wound cables round the stakes which supported the bridge, and, taking the cables, they rowed all the ships downstream as hard as ever they could. The stakes were dragged along the bottom until they were loosened under the bridge . . . and the bridge came crashing down and many fell into the river. . . . Now when the citizens saw that the River Thames was won, so that they could no longer prevent the ships from pressing up inland, they were stricken with terror at the advance of the ships, and gave up the city and accepted King Ethelred.'

Apart from the verse already quoted Snorri also cited two verses by Ottar the Black, another Scald; one which begins: 'And further, O prover of the serpent of Ygg's storms, valiant in war, you broke down London's Bridge', while the other must relate to some occasion when Olaf fought on behalf of Ethelred:

'You came to the land, guardian of the realm, and, mighty in your strength, assured his realm to Ethelred. The true friend of warriors was thus your debtor. Hard was the meeting, by which you brought the kinsman of Edmund back to the protection of his country. The support of his race had ruled that land before.'

There are other sagas about St. Olaf and in all of them there are similar confusions, as the writer of one of them remarked, 'You can accept from this saga whatever you think most likely, for in old sagas many things are confused.' It is the scaldic verses that are the truly valuable historical sources in the sagas.

The verse by Sigvat Thordarson used by Snorri for this episode comes from *Vikingavisur*, a poem that has been called 'one of the best historical documents transmitted to us from the Scandinavian North'.[41] It describes a series of battles fought by St. Olaf and as the first thirteen verses are numbered, the order of the battles is certain and there has been no chance of interpolations. Altogether fourteen verses are known and there seem to have been three more that are mentioned but unquoted. They describe the career of this Viking chief and begin with three battles fought in the Baltic; the fourth was at *Suðrvik* which has been tentatively identified as Søndervig in Jutland, the fifth was off the Frisian coast, the sixth was the attack on London Bridge already mentioned, the next three were also in England. The tenth was in France, the next four apparently in Spain, the fifteenth again in France and the last two in England. The limitations of such verses as an historical source are obvious but the value of such a poem is no less obvious, even if it does exaggerate Olaf's importance in his early battles.

Scaldic verses are not the only Scandinavian memorials of the Viking period. There are also many runic inscriptions, and, especially in Gotland, some stones with pictures carved in low relief.[42] The example of a Gotlandic stone illustrated here in Plate V, also has a runic inscription. The runic alphabet had long been known in Scandinavia and by the ninth century consisted of sixteen letters.[43] Inscriptions in this alphabet were used for memorials, generally on stones raised for the purpose. The most famous of all is the great stone at Jelling in Jutland

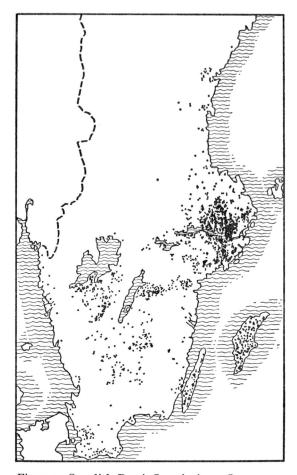

Figure 2 Swedish Runic Inscriptions. Over 2,000
of these are known, mostly of the eleventh century.
See Plates I and V and pp. 41–4. (From a map
prepared by Sven B. F. Jansson and published in
Svenska Turistföreningens Årsskrift, 1949, p. 104.)

set up by Harald, son of Gorm, in memory of this father and
mother and the inscription defines Harald as having won all
Denmark and Norway for himself and made the Danes
Christians. A less famous but more representative stone is

illustrated in Plate I from Fålebro near Uppsala, which, like many others, marks a bridge across a stream. Stones like this, and there are about 2,500 in Sweden, mostly from the eleventh century, do something to compensate for the inadequacy of the more conventional written sources. It is, however, rarely possible to identify the individuals who are mentioned and although there are many references to important events both in Scandinavia and in the outside world, the date of few of these is known.[44] Of the 1,200 inscriptions in Uppland, only twelve refer to events of approximately known date. Five mention the receipt of geld in England—for example a stone from Väsby: 'Ale raised this stone in memory of himself. He received Cnut's geld in England. God save his soul.' Inscriptions like these, and there are others that refer more generally to visits to England, confirm that men from many parts of Scandinavia took part in the raids on Ethelred's kingdom. Some inscriptions are even more important as historical evidence, in particular the stones that stood near Hedeby as memorials to King Sigtrygg, son of Gnupa, erected by his mother, Asfrid, daughter of Odinkar.[45] Gnupa is otherwise known as the man who was defeated by Henry I of Germany in 934 and there is little doubt that these men were members of a Swedish dynasty established at Hedeby at the end of the ninth century.[46]

There are, however, very few 'historical' stones of this kind. One that is often cited is from Hedeby and refers to the time the 'Drengs sat round Hedeby'. It has been pointed out that fighting took place near Hedeby under Gorm, Harald, Svein Forkbeard, Magnus the Good, and Svein Estrithson, and the town was besieged by Swedes and Norwegians, Germans and Slavs.[47] There is no means of telling for certain to which conflict this stone refers. One episode that is well attested in rune stones is Ingvar's expedition to the East, which probably took place in about 1041.[48] There are in Sweden twenty-five inscriptions commemorating men who accompanied Ingvar to *Serkland*, the land of the Saracens, a word used for the Muslim lands of the East. This expedition seems to have been disastrous and was long remembered in northern tradition. The fact that the stones are grouped around Lake Mälar

suggests that this was the area from which men were recruited
for an enterprise that may well have been inspired by the hope
of winning some of the wealth that had formerly flowed so
freely from the East to Birka and thence into the surrounding
lands.

The sources for the earlier Scandinavian activity in what is
now Russia, are far less satisfactory than those for the West or
even for Scandinavia itself. There are later traditions preserved
in Scandinavian and Russian literature but literary tradition
can be a dangerous guide to the past. The main Russian
Chronicle has been preserved in an early twelfth-century
version, but it is based on compilations that were certainly
no earlier than the eleventh century.[49] Its annals may therefore
be accepted as a general guide from the mid-tenth century but
they have little value for the preceding period. They were
probably written at Kiev and their theme is the ruling dynasty
of Kiev, established by Oleg at the end of the ninth century.
Oleg was certainly of Scandinavian descent and many of his
followers, whose names are mentioned in the treaty of 912 with
Byzantium, also had Scandinavian names.[50] Oleg's successor
also had a basically Scandinavian name, Igor (*Ingvar*), but
Igor's son was given a Slavonic name, Sviatoslav; the Scandinavians were quickly assimilated in Russia, as they were
elsewhere. The Chronicler's natural interest in the rulers of
Kiev has emphasised the Scandinavian element not only in
the history of the city but also in his account of what led up
to it.

This early history of Russia must have been based on
traditions which may well have been modified in transmission
and which have certainly been set in an artificial chronology
derived from Byzantium.[51] The first date mentioned is 852,
which is said to have been the year of the accession of the
Byzantine emperor Michael, in whose reign the *Rus* first
attacked Constantinople. Michael's accession was in fact in 842
and the attack on Constantinople is known from Byzantine
sources to have been in 860.[52] The Chronicler has obviously
taken the first mention of the *Rus* in his Byzantine sources as
the starting-point for the activity of the *Rus* in Russia. The
first coming of the Scandinavians, called Varangians, from

across the sea is given under 859, where they are said to have gathered tribute from Slavs and Finns. These tributaries then expelled the Varangians, but the subsequent disorders led them to ask the Varangians to return, which they did under the leadership of Rurik and his two brothers, who established themselves in Novgorod, Beloozero and Izborsk. All this is said to have happened in 860. The chronology is obviously wrong; the Annals of St. Bertin show that Swedes called *Rhos* had crossed Russia by 839, and the coin evidence suggests that the Scandinavian activity in North Russia began very early in the ninth century. If, however, the chronology is disregarded and the emphasis on the dominant group recognised, the account given by the Russian Chronicle agrees very well with what is otherwise known. Particularly convincing is the mention of Rurik's brother at Beloozero, for this lay on the route from the Gulf of Finland to Bulghar. This was the area in which Scandinavians appear to have been active early in the ninth century. Some time in the century, possibly quite early, Scandinavians established their authority in Kiev and collected tribute from the surrounding Slavs which they traded with their richer neighbours in Byzantium, Khazaria or even Bulghar. The relations with Byzantium are described in some detail by Constantine Porphyrogenitus, himself emperor, in a book on imperial administration, which he wrote between 948 and 952.[53] Constantine confirms the Scandinavian element in Russian history by giving the names of the Dnieper rapids in both Slavonic and 'Russian', the latter being clearly Scandinavian in origin.

The Byzantine and Russian sources can fortunately be supplemented by Islamic writings.[54] The great expansion of Islam in the seventh and eighth centuries stimulated an interest in the world and its peoples and many geographical works were written in Arabic and Persian in the ninth and tenth centuries. The basis of all Muslim geography was, indirectly, Ptolemy but these geographers were able to make additions and alterations from their own observation and with the help of such men as merchants and officials who travelled about the Muslim world and beyond. The main interest naturally tended to be in the regions that had been conquered by Islam but some writers also paid attention to people who lived beyond the frontiers of the faith and those who have given some account of the lands between the Black, Caspian and Baltic seas are obviously of first importance for any study of Scandinavian activity in the East.

Unfortunately these writings are often conflations, and many were written by men who had no first-hand experience of this area. The difficulties are aggravated by copying mistakes and there are some very obscure matters. For example, the first writer to mention the *Rus* is Ibn Khurdadhbih, who wrote in the middle of the ninth century.[55] He speaks of the *Rus* travelling on the *Tana'is*, the river of the Slavs (*Saqaliba*). The reading *Tana'is* is uncertain, and although it is commonly taken to refer to the Don, there are good reasons to believe the Upper Volga is intended.[56] Evidence of this sort leads to great confusion, unless it is treated with care and the alternative readings and possibilities taken into account. This is not the only difficulty in Ibn Khurdadhbih's contribution. He calls the *Rus* a sort of *Saqaliba*. This word normally means Slav, but because this conflicts with what is generally believed about the *Rus*, it is in this context sometimes translated as 'Northerner' or 'European'.[57]

The origin and meaning of the word *Rus* itself have been vigorously disputed.[58] It is used by both Slavs and Muslims for one of the peoples living in what is now Russia, and is also used in Byzantine sources in the form *Rhos*, as also in the Annals of St. Bertin. The word originally meant Swedes and although there may have been a Scandinavian form it passed into Slavonic and Arabic from the Finnish. The modern Finnish for 'Swedes' is *Ruotsi* and this could well have led to Slavonic *Rus*, just as the Finnish for Finland itself, *Suomi*, has become *Sum* in Russian. The use of a Finnish word is in no way surprising as Finns then occupied a large part of North Russia and the Scandinavians would have had to deal with Finns long before they encountered Slavs or Muslims. The word was first used for Scandinavians from Middle Sweden, but the *Rus* who established themselves at Kiev were soon Slavicised and it was then used for a wider group, including Slavs as well as men of Scandinavian descent. It is therefore quite wrong

I. An eleventh-century Swedish rune stone of granite, 7 ft. 6 in. (2.35 m.) high, standing at Fålebro, Danmarks parish, about 4 miles (6 km.) south-east of Uppsala. It was probably intended from the first to mark a crossing of the stream, here called Sävjaån, seen in the background. The inscription reads 'Stöding had this stone raised after Arne, his son. He went *hayrt lant*. (The meaning of this is uncertain: "to every land" has been suggested but "to Hörthaland—in Western Norway—" seems preferable.) Tjälve and Orökja cut the runes after their brother.' This does not mean that Arne's brothers did the carving, which may have been done by the great Runemaster Fot, but that they paid for it. See *Upplands runinskrifter,* ed. E. Wessén and Sven B. F. Jansson, no. 948. *(Photo: ATA)*

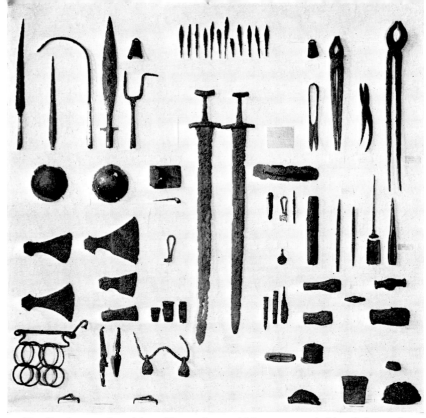

IIa. Equipment found in a Norwegian smith's grave, probably of the tenth century, from Bygland, Kvitseid, Telemark. See Charlotte Blindheim, 'Smedgraven fra Bygland i Morgedal', *Viking*, 26 (1962)), pp. 25–80. (*Universitetets Oldsaksamling, Oslo*)

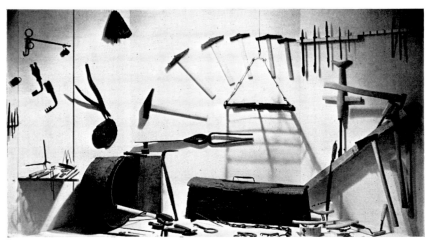

IIb. A Viking period collection of tools found at Mästermyr, Gotland, now in Statens Historiska Museum, Stockholm. See Gösta Berg, 'A tool chest from the Viking Age', *Universitetet i Bergen Årbok* 1955 (Hist.-ant. rekke, 1), pp. 77–83. (*Photo ATA*)

to interpret *Rus* in tenth-century Muslim sources as though it always meant Scandinavians or even men of Scandinavian descent. Scandinavians are undoubtedly sometimes meant, as in Ibn Fadlan's account of his visit to Bulghar in 922, fortunately preserved in the original, for he describes the ship-burial of a *Rus* chieftain.[59] Unfortunately few of these Muslim sources are so well preserved or so explicit as Ibn Fadlan, and, as with all the written sources that have been reviewed here the problems of interpretation should be kept in mind when the evidence is used. If the limitations are disregarded, the conclusions are unlikely to be sound.

3. *Archaeology*

ARCHAEOLOGY, the study of the material remains of human activity, yields some of the most important evidence for the Viking period. It is particularly valuable for such areas as Scandinavia, Russia and Iceland where the written sources are late but it is also making an increasingly significant contribution to our knowledge of the period in the Christian West. No study of the subject can disregard the archaeological evidence or the conclusions of archaeologists. This evidence is, however, subject to important limitations which ought to be reflected in any conclusions based upon it. Unfortunately some archaeologists who are, or should be, well aware of these limitations sometimes disregard them in their anxiety to produce definite results and 'useful' conclusions. Too often the temptation to give a date to an object or a site, or to arrange a collection of objects in a chronological sequence, or to recognise similarities of style and identify origins overcomes the caution that would in many cases be appropriate. This is not to say that archaeologists are by nature incautious; some are very careful and critical in their use of evidence, but there is undoubtedly a temptation to make precise what should be left imprecise and to present tentative hypotheses as though they were established fact. Even when an archaeologist expresses his conclusions with very great care his lay audience, impatient of scholarly hesitation tends to disregard the qualifications and consequently it sometimes happens that a suggestion first made very hesitantly is transformed in a few stages into an assertion proved by repetition if nothing else. The interpretation of archaeological material is not a simple matter and laymen who turn to archaeology for help must beware of accepting archaeological hypotheses too readily. The warning expressed by Thomas O'Rahilly, the distinguished Irish philologist, should be remembered; 'Archaeological facts are often dull, but they have the compensating merit of possessing a permanent value; archaeologists' inferences, on the other hand, are often interesting, but are apt to be precarious and ephemeral.'[1] The evidence of archaeology is important and cannot be disregarded but it is equally important that those who use it should be aware of its general character and the limitations which should govern its use.

It is, in the first place, necessary to emphasise that, as O'Rahilly remarked, archaeological facts are often dull. Pride of place in many museum collections is given to the most spectacular and magnificent finds, to the well-preserved and often intricately detailed objects that are of immediate and obvious interest. It is in many ways appropriate that the ship-burials of Gokstad and Oseberg, among the finest of all Viking period discoveries, should be so well known and so often illustrated in books on the subject, including this one. Such an emphasis on the best finds is not surprising, but it can be misleading, for most archaeological finds are intrinsically neither attractive nor very interesting. The mass of material consists not of gold and silver ornaments or beautifully preserved wood carvings, but of broken pottery, rusty fragments of iron and corroded ornaments. Archaeological arguments, including the interpretation of the spectacular finds, depend on the patient and systematic analysis of all the available material, not just the best.

Much of the material which the archaeologist must take into account has been discovered by scientific excavation in which every effort is made, with the aid of modern techniques, not only to preserve all the finds but to record objects of which only faint traces survive. In such excavations the exact position of each find, however insignificant, is noted, and traces of structure, such as post holes, are recorded so that the history of the site may be more accurately determined. Such a careful approach is nowadays recognised to be necessary, for the very process of excavation destroys much of the evidence. Once the objects have been removed the excavator's recorded observations are the only evidence of their original context and much may depend on his report. Even the best excavators make mistakes and the general, unavoidable, use of unskilled, or at least less skilled labour, multiplies the chance of error. The archaeologist in charge of a dig cannot be everywhere at once, and a moment's carelessness may result in the destruction of a small and delicate find or of faint structural traces such as post holes. It is, in particular, not always easy to be sure that objects found together originally were together, or that objects recorded in the same layer in fact came from that layer. Apart from the hazards of excavation, objects can be moved by roots, animals or even rain, and stratification can easily mislead. Sometimes the layer in which a find was made has to be determined by referring to the sections in adjacent walls of the trench. These sections themselves sometimes owe much to the eye of faith, but even when they are accurately drawn they may be an unreliable guide to the thickness of the layers in the part that has been dug out. An object can therefore appear to have come from the layer above, or below that in which it truly lay. If doubts arise after an excavation has been completed, it is rarely possible to check; they must generally remain unresolved, if not unexpressed, and a new element of speculation is introduced into the interpretation of the site and all that may depend upon it. As a large part of archaeological argument is based on the discovery of objects together or in the same layer of a site, uncertainty about these details is particularly serious. Modern excavations, certainly of important sites, tend to be well supervised and carefully done, and the element of uncertainty is small. Unfortunately the vast majority of Viking period finds in public and private collections were not gathered with the care expected nowadays. All too many were unearthed by enthusiasts interested less in the circumstances of the find than in the objects, and then only in the objects of obvious interest or beauty. As one archaeologist remarked of his predecessors: 'no one seems to have thought a burial which was associated with "rusty pieces of old iron" worthy of careful investigation.'[2] The objects discovered by such digging cannot be ignored. They are an important part of the material, but they are hardly a satisfactory part. Not all early excavations were careless, and some, such as Hjalmar Stolpe's remarkable work at Birka, set a very high standard; but even the most careful of these earlier excavators worked under the serious disadvantage that conservation techniques were then not very well developed. Many of the objects recorded by Stolpe and drawn at the time have disintegrated; for example, the sword found in Birka grave 581, illustrated in Figure 3 no longer exists. Excavation and conservation techniques are now very much better than they were in the nineteenth century but the archaeological investigation of the Viking period will not easily escape the consequences of former mistakes.

The Viking age sites most commonly investigated by archaeologists are graves. Tens of thousands of these are known in all parts of Scandinavia as well as in the areas in which the Scandinavians were then active. There are many kinds, cremations as well as inhumations, some marked by mounds, others flat, some richly furnished, others poor; and in some the dead person was buried or cremated in a ship or boat. These graves, which are the main source of Viking age material, are often grouped together in gravefields associated with settlements, but very few of the settlements have themselves been investigated. This is principally because they are generally still occupied. In the islands of Öland and Gotland, for example, the pre-Viking settlements can easily be studied because they were abandoned in the fifth and sixth centuries, for reasons that are not fully understood, and by the Viking period new settlements had been established on sites that are mostly still occupied.[3] Even when excavation is possible, traces of the Viking period have often been disturbed, if not destroyed, by the foundations of later buildings, or the digging of holes for refuse pits. Only when sites were abandoned in or soon after the Viking period has the archaeologist a good chance of recovering the details of the settlement from that time. The village of Lindholm, in North Jutland, has been well preserved simply because the whole site was covered by a layer of sand in the eleventh century and this has protected it from disturbance.[4] The sand has even preserved the ridges and furrows in a field, and when the sand was removed, cart tracks could still be seen. The chance of discovering traces of the ninth and tenth centuries is greater when buildings were of stone rather than timber and one of the most thoroughly excavated of all Viking age settlements is the Shetland village of Jarlshof.[5] There are also a few very large and important sites like the camp at Trelleborg[6] or the towns of Hedeby and Birka and these have naturally attracted a lot of attention.[7] In considering these imposing monuments and the discoveries that have been made in them it is important to remember that they only form a part, if an important part, of the archaeological evidence. The investigation and interpretation of such a site as Birka itself depends on the results of countless small excavations many of which are not properly recorded, and most of which are rarely considered independently.

These sites and the finds that have been made in them are the raw material with which the archaeologist must work. By a systematic process of comparison and analysis he hopes to be able to offer answers to many different kinds of question. He may attempt, for instance, to trace the fortunes of a particular site or region, to follow migrations, to recognise regional characteristics and so detect imports or alien influences, to study population changes, to compare the wealth and resources of different areas at different times and even to distinguish social classes. In almost all such archaeological investigations the fundamental questions are chronological. One of the first concerns of the archaeologist is to determine, as precisely as possible, the absolute or relative date of his sites and the material that has been unearthed. Like the historian, the archaeologist is interested in a process of change, and for this some understanding of chronology is indispensable. Unless the chronology of a site or series of sites can be established it is obviously impossible seriously to consider any process of change, whether in ornamental styles, building techniques, burial customs or even prosperity. The archaeologist's chronology need not, of course, be absolute: so long as there is no attempt to relate conclusions based on a relative chronology, say of a sequence of styles, to other matters for which that particular chronology is irrelevant, there is no harm. If archaeological material is to be used for the general study of the Viking period it is essential that the historical relevance of archaeological chronology should be well understood. It is also important that historians and others who may have to use material evidence should understand the methods of archaeological dating and these have recently been critically examined by a Swedish scholar, Bertil Almgren.[8]

The chronological questions that have to be considered by archaeologists relate either to the sites or to the objects that are found. The answers are, of course, closely connected; the date of a grave, house or other structure can generally only be determined by the discovery in it of some datable object, and the date of objects is almost always determined, ultimately, by their discovery in some datable context. It is obviously most important that sites should be carefully excavated, for only if close attention is paid to all the circumstances is there any hope of working out the relative chronology of the finds and of asserting that objects found together were buried together. The material from careless excavations and treasure hunts can be worse than useless, and loose finds, turned up accidentally in such operations as road making or ploughing, have little value as dating criteria, for there is obviously no means of telling when they were dropped or buried. The only hope of dating objects that have been found loose or have been excavated unsystematically is by comparing them with others that are datable because they have been more carefully recovered. Unfortunately there are relatively few of these: the bulk of Viking age material was found in circumstances that are not well known, and should therefore, ideally, be disregarded in attempts to determine the historical or absolute chronology of the period.

Coins are the best dating material found in Viking period sites.[9] Some are, admittedly, of uncertain date, but many bear the name of the authority for whom they were struck and their date is therefore known. Islamic coins are even more helpful as they generally give the year they were minted. Unfortunately relatively few graves and other sites have been found to contain datable coins. Of the 4,400 Islamic coins found in Norway and Denmark only thirty were found in a total of ten graves.[10]

The coins used in graves are often fragmentary or badly damaged and their date is often not decipherable. Even when the date of a coin in a grave is known it only provides one limit and that may be misleading. Coins may have been in circulation, or in use as ornaments, for a long time before being used as grave furnishings. The signs of wear are a very unreliable indication of its age when buried; a coin might become battered very quickly or be kept in good condition for a long time. Coins are therefore of only limited value as an aid to the dating of Viking period finds.

The discovery of any datable objects in a find only provides one limit; the other must normally be uncertain. In a few cases some datable alteration or rebuilding gives another limiting date and in one important site the *terminus ad quem* is indicated by the absence of certain objects. This is at Birka where no German coins or coins of the English king Ethelred have been found in all the 1,100 graves that have been excavated or in the material from the town area.[11] Coins of this kind were extremely common in Sweden in the last two decades of the tenth century and their absence from the rich Birka material suggests that the town had been abandoned by about 980. This is an unusual and remarkably valuable guide to the date of the graves and other structures found at Birka. It means, for example, that the grave illustrated in Figure 3 can be dated within uncommonly narrow limits. It contains a silver dirhem that must have been minted between 913 and 933 and being from the Birka gravefield was probably earlier than 980. This is a much closer dating than would have been possible if the grave had been found elsewhere. Sometimes a limiting date is known historically. The settlement of Iceland in the last quarter of the ninth century is a fairly well established starting-point for the discoveries made there. Attempts have also been made to date some sites by their association with particular people or events, but these are less valuable than might be expected and sometimes the association is itself very doubtful, as for example the assumption that Queen Åsa was buried at Oseberg.[12] There are certainly a few sites, and objects, that can be associated with historically known people, such as the Jelling mounds of the tenth-century

Danish kings Gorm and Harald, but such royal burials are unlikely to be a satisfactory guide to the styles and fashions of humbler interments.

There are, therefore, not many sites for which one limiting date can definitely be established and there are very few indeed for which there are two. The graves and other finds that contain some clearly datable material have to serve as the key to the chronology of other finds. The method is simple; objects found in a datable context are themselves used as dating criteria when found elsewhere. The process is obviously unreliable, especially when the starting-points are all too often only furnished with one limiting date, but the method has to be used and some archaeologists claim to be able to date finds with remarkable precision. Professor Shetelig, for example, in discussing the date of some British graves was able to write:

Figure 3 Grave no. 581 in the Grave Field at Birka. See Figure 10 and pp. 54–7, 61. The Kufic coin is marked a. (From the plan published in *Birka I*, p. 189.)

'The corresponding man's grave at Ballinaby contained a sword and an axe characteristic of the first half of the ninth

E

century, and the other man's grave, discovered in the
vicinity of the double interment is dated by an axe from
about 850 A.D. The boat grave at Kiloran Bay must be
considered as being some 20–30 years older, to judge by
the types of the sword and axe that were found there. The
magnificent sword handle from a grave in Eigg also dates
from a time before the middle of the ninth century.'[13]

More recently it has been claimed that the Viking settlement
at Jarlshof in Shetland can be traced back to the early ninth
century.[14] The main reason is that a number of objects said to
be of the early ninth century were found in the earliest occupation level of the first Viking house. The dating of all these
objects can be represented by a

> 'gilt bronze harness mount of Celtic design . . . character-
> istic of the metalwork looted by Viking raiders west-oversea
> at this period. A similar mount occurs in a woman's grave of
> early ninth century date at Gausel, Hetland, in Møre and
> other examples are known in Ireland and in the west of
> Scotland.'

The fact, which may be disputed, that ornaments of this type
are found elsewhere in an early ninth-century context does not,
of course, prove anything about the date of the object from
Jarlshof. But the Gausel grave seems to have been given rather
an early date. It is mentioned in several places by Jan Petersen
in his *Inventory of British Antiquities, found in Norway*, and is
once dated to the ninth century, twice to the second half of
the ninth century and once as 'about 850'.[15] That Jarlshof
was settled in the ninth century need not be doubted but the
claim that it was established early in that century should be
treated with some scepticism, as should most similar claims
that sites can be closely dated by finds of this kind.

The weakness of such dating can best be underlined by
taking an example. The grave in Figure 3 may be dated
913–80. The axe head from this grave is of a kind found
elsewhere, and there are two other examples from the Birka
gravefield.[16] By good fortune both the other graves contain
coins, one of 909–10, the other of the early tenth century.

There is therefore agreement between all three graves, that the axe was available for interment in the tenth century. If this axe head is to be used elsewhere as a dating criterion it is obviously important to know whether, in these Birka graves, it was a new type of axe or an old-fashioned type, and before it can be very much help in dating it is necessary to know in each case whether it was deposited when already old, or soon after it had been made. There is no means of telling this and it would be as hazardous to assume that weapons were always old when buried as it would be to assume that they were always new. There is therefore inevitably a margin of error of at least a generation before and after the limiting dates known for the graves at Birka. In other words, this axe could have been in use, and available for furnishing graves from about 870 to about 1010 and is therefore of little value as a dating criterion. The most that can be said is that axes of this type were in use in the tenth century.

The probability of freak results would be greatly reduced if the objects used for dating purposes were found in large numbers, but there are additional disadvantages in such cases. The existence of large numbers may mean that the object was popular for a long period and is therefore a poor indicator of date. Among the Scandinavian artefacts that are known in large numbers are the oval brooches, sometimes called 'tortoise-shell brooches'. Many different designs are known of these characteristically Scandinavian ornaments and large numbers of some types have been found. The most numerous type is known as Jan Petersen 51, and of this no fewer than 982 examples are known from 676 finds.[17] Unfortunately less than 160 of these have been found along with other objects and only twelve were with coins. The coins range in date from the middle of the ninth century to the end of the tenth century, and there need be no doubt that this style of brooch is characteristic of the late Viking period, but it can hardly be more closely dated than that. The next most numerous of these oval brooches is the type known as Jan Petersen 37, and 535 of these have been discovered in 364 finds in only seventy-eight of which were other objects found. No example of this type of brooch has been found with a coin. This brooch seems to have been an earlier type than the more numerous Jan Petersen 51 but it is obviously impossible to determine its date much more closely than the ninth and early tenth centuries. A study of the associations of these two brooches shows quite clearly that there must have been some overlap because there are ten finds in which both types occur. There are many similar associations of objects that, when found independently, are given different dates. Shetelig himself expressed surprise at such a contradictory association. 'The earliest type of the ninth century, bearing the somewhat heavy decoration termed the Berdal type has come from . . . Clibberswick in Shetland, this last find presenting the surprising association of the Berdal type with a trefoil brooch of the tenth century.'[18] If a brooch of the early ninth century could be buried along with one of the tenth century little confidence can be placed in it as an indication of early date. Dating by association can therefore never be very precise.

Stylistic and typological evolution are themselves unsatisfactory as dating criteria. Changes of type and style certainly took place in the Viking period but old objects may have continued in use for a long time and the rate of change is generally unknown. It may have been different in different areas and with different social groups. There certainly were changing fashions and different styles and these can be traced through the period, but it sometimes happens that apparently different styles or fashions commonly associated with different periods are found together. Among the wood carvings found at Oseberg, for example, the work of ten different artists in at least three different 'styles' has been recognised.[19] Professors Shetelig and Lindqvist have come to completely opposite conclusions about the order in which these artists worked,[20] and Professor Arbman has recently admitted that 'the possibility of distinguishing the dates of the ten artists is very limited'.[21] It is obvious that stylistic arguments of this kind are unlikely to furnish a very sound chronological basis for the study of the Viking period. Bertil Almgren has, indeed, suggested that it is misleading to think of three different Oseberg styles, but that they should rather be considered different facets of one style.[22] His attractive ideas concerning style analysis have not been generally accepted by Scandinavian archaeologists but they should undoubtedly be discussed more generally than hitherto. He argues that styles should be distinguished not by the motifs but by the types of curves used and that the same system of curves was used by all the Oseberg artists. The differences are due in part to different artists and in part to different themes or subjects, but all the carvings belong to one stage or phase of Scandinavian art. The same system of curves is found on many other objects from the early Viking period, notably in the bronzes from Broa in Halla, Gotland, one of which is illustrated in Plate III. Bertil Almgren suggests that the significant thing about this lovely mount is not that it is in the shape of a lion's head with a highly formalised bird in the mouth and elaborate beasts in the neck and body, but that the whole composition consists of curves of constantly changing radius and that the radii are smallest towards the end of the curves. It is also significant that there seems to have been a conscious attempt to avoid right-angles, straight or parallel lines and the whole composition is deliberately asymmetrical. The same type of curves are found at Oseberg, as may be seen in Plate IV. There are certainly differences, notably in the treatment of the frame. At Broa the lines of the composition meet the frame tangentially, they seem to flow into it and the frame merges with the composition. In the Oseberg carving illustrated here the lines of the composition meet the framework of circles at sharp angles and if the eye follows the lines of the birds it is arrested by these frames. Another difference is, of course, that at Broa the frame is itself asymmetrical but at Oseberg it is made of circles. There are also some differences in the pattern of curves, as Almgren points out, not only between Broa and Oseberg but even in Oseberg itself, but these differences do not destroy the essential unity of this early Viking style-phase. The validity of this analysis is demonstrated if it is applied to the ornament of the immediately preceding period, known in eastern Scandinavia as Style D. In this style straight lines are used, as they are not at Broa, the curves are generally regular, but when they have a changing radius the smallest radii tend to be in the middle of the line, and compositions are often symmetrical.

During the Viking period there were many changes in the ornamental styles that were fashionable as may be seen by comparing the designs from Oseberg and Broa with the silver brooches from Jämjö in Öland shown in Plate XI. This is an example of the so-called Borre style of the middle Viking period. A later style in Viking art is represented by the Uppland rune stone in Plate I. The study of the development of these and other styles, and of the influences affecting them is an important part of Viking archaeology but the conclusions that have been reached are neither sufficiently agreed nor well enough defined for arguments from style to have much force outside the world of archaeologists and art historians. It is in any case unlikely that artistic developments had much to do with political or economic changes and the chronology of styles in the Viking period must always be to a large extent relative; even if the sequence of styles could be determined, their chronology would hardly have any relevance to other processes of change. Similarly the detection of particular alien influences in a style or in the art of a region (for example Frankish, English, Irish, Byzantine and Persian influences have been seen in Viking art) is a fascinating pursuit but largely irrelevant to the study of other aspects of the period. Such influences certainly show contact with the art of other regions but it is almost never possible to define that contact. These influences, about which there is in any case much argument, are likely to be a most misleading guide to the political, economic or even personal relations of the time.

Except within very broad limits, absolute archaeological dating can therefore never be established by a study of styles and it is only rarely possible through the discovery of datable objects. The value of such aids as dating by radioactive carbon is less than might at first sight appear, for the margin of error is so large that this method can only hope to indicate that an object belongs to the early or late Viking period, which in many cases would already have been known.[23] For example, the caulking of the ships recently discovered in Roskilde Fjord has been examined and dated, by radioactive carbon, A.D. 910 with an admitted margin of error of a century either side.[24] The best that can be hoped for is therefore dating within wide limits. It is possible to say that certain objects seem typical of the early, middle, or late Viking period, and it may be legitimate to speak in terms of centuries, but closer dating than this is obviously impossible.

Chronological questions are undoubtedly fundamental in the study of Viking archaeology but they are not the archaeologists' exclusive concern. Their interest in the stylistic development of ornamental styles and the external influences that these may display has already been mentioned. They also study the evolution of techniques and the pattern of social customs that can be observed, especially in the burial of the dead. A large number of graves has been unearthed and, although far too few have been carefully enough excavated to permit very refined conclusions, certain facts seem well established. The most notable of these is that in this period the burial or cremation of the dead in a ship or boat is a characteristically Scandinavian habit. The ship- and boat-burials found in Russia and in western Europe are therefore likely to have been for Scandinavians. Unfortunately the discovery of boat rivets in a cremation grave does not necessarily mean that the cremation took place in a boat. If old boat timbers were used to make the pyre, rivets would be found in the burnt remains.[25] There are other kinds of burial that seem to be well defined, including chamber graves of the type illustrated in Figure 3. These are found all over Scandinavia, in Poland, North Germany as well as in South Russia and one Swedish archaeologist has suggested that the type spread into Scandinavia from the south-west and was then taken by Scandinavians to South Russia.[26] This seems unlikely: chamber graves of one kind or another are likely to have been developed independently in any areas with plenty of wood. In all Viking areas except Iceland, cremation and inhumation were alternative methods, and it may be that the custom of inhumation is the result of Christian influence. It certainly seems that cremation was commonest and lasted longest in areas like Finland that were far removed from the Christian West, but it should not of course be assumed that such Christian influence was direct. Inhumations in a gravefield certainly do not mean the visit of a missionary in the area. It is sometimes suggested that graves

without furnishings show direct Christian influence, but they
are as likely to show poverty or inadequate excavation and it
should be remembered that even Christians were sometimes
buried with some of their possessions.

It is therefore difficult to trace the movement of peoples or
beliefs by studying the form of their burials. It is certainly no
less difficult to draw satisfactory conclusions from the contents
of graves. The discovery of swords or brooches of Scandinavian
manufacture in Russian or Irish graves obviously cannot prove
that the people buried in those graves were Scandinavians or of
Scandinavian descent. Objects like these can pass from hand
to hand and are often likely to have been separated from the
people who made or first used them. This may seem obvious
but it is apparently forgotten from time to time. The discovery
of Scandinavian objects, especially in Russian finds, is taken by
some scholars to prove close Scandinavian connections. The
most remarkable example of this is the treatment of the great
chamber grave from Chernigov in which two swords were
found, one Scandinavian, the other of Scandinavian form but
decorated in an alien style. No other objects found in this grave
can with any confidence be associated with Scandinavia, but
a distinguished Swedish archaeologist has recently suggested
that it is the burial of a man of Scandinavian descent.[27] This
is all the more surprising as swords were among the Scandinavian exports mentioned by contemporary Islamic writers.[28]
The argument that Scandinavian objects found in graves prove
the Scandinavian character of the dead has had extremely
unfortunate results in some discussions of the great Viking
period gravefield at Gnezdovo near Smolensk. There are over
3,000 graves at Gnezdovo and the coins and other objects
found there indicate that it was in use in the tenth and eleventh
centuries. Many of the graves were excavated in the nineteenth
century and in the last fifteen years the Soviet archaeologist
D. A. Avdusin has excavated over a hundred more.[29] Among
the finds from the site there are some objects of Scandinavian
manufacture and there are others of Scandinavian type that
were probably made in Russia. The fact that one of the larger
graves was a boat-burial shows that some Scandinavians were
buried here, and there are several other graves that can

reasonably be interpreted as Scandinavian, but the northern element has been greatly exaggerated. Professor Brøndsted is certainly mistaken in claiming that 'most of the contents of the graves are Swedish'.[30] The Scandinavian influence found would be consistent with the theory that the community was dominated by warriors of Scandinavian descent who quickly became slavicised, but there is certainly not enough Scandinavian material to justify Arbman's assertion that it is a Swedish gravefield, the burial place of a Swedish colony. It would indeed be better to recognise this as a gravefield for a community of Russians.[31]

The contrast between Scandinavia and Russia, with their numerous Viking period graves, and western Europe is very striking. In western Europe there are extraordinarily few Viking graves despite the extensive Scandinavian settlements and the prolonged campaigns fought by Viking raiders. In 1925–6 a group of Norwegian scholars made a list of all Viking antiquities then known in western Europe and although some additions would now be necessary to bring it up to date, their work reveals very clearly how few Viking graves have been discovered in the British Isles and on the Continent.[32] For England and Wales the total was 16; for the Isle of Man 11; for Ireland outside Dublin, where a large cemetery has been found, 4; on the mainland of Scotland, 13; and in the isles of the west and north about 60. For the Continent they only recorded three. In England one notable addition has to be made, the cemetery of about sixty mounds found at Ingleby in Derbyshire.[33] Various attempts have been made to explain this remarkable rarity of Viking grave finds in the West. It has, for example, been suggested that the graves are rarely found in England because the Danes were not accustomed to bury their dead in prominent mounds and with rich grave goods, so that the burials are unlikely to have been noted. This may help to explain the few graves in the Danish areas of England (less than ten in the Norwegian Inventory) but it is hardly relevant to the areas settled by men of Norwegian descent. A more satisfactory explanation seems to be that the settlers quickly abandoned their old burial customs, not as Professor Shetelig argued because they had been campaigning

away from home for such a long time,[34] but because they
quickly adopted Christian forms of burial, or at least buried
their dead in Christian graveyards. In several parts of the
British Isles swords, axes and other Viking objects have been
found in churchyards and in the Isle of Man there are some very
prominent Viking burial mounds situated inside churchyards.

Archaeologists are sometimes tempted to associate their
sites and finds with events or places which are known historically. For some of these associations the evidence is overwhelming and there is no need to doubt that the sites at Birka,
Hedeby and Kaupang have been correctly identified with the
trading centres mentioned in ninth-century sources. But not all
of the identifications that have been proposed by archaeologists are so well founded. There is, for example, the recent
claim that a group of graves found at Monkwearmouth were of
the victims of a Viking raid.[35] This depends on the assumption
that our historical and archaeological information is complete, which it manifestly is not. These graves could have been
a result of some other violence in which the Vikings were
not involved. In relating historical and archaeological evidence
it is very easy to accept the most convenient hypotheses and to
treat this as though it excluded all other possibilities, and historians who use material evidence must be particularly careful
of this misleading kind of argument.

The difficulties that have to be faced in using archaeological
evidence have been emphasised not in order to demonstrate
that archaeology is worthless but so that its true value may be
better understood. Archaeology has, undoubtedly, an important contribution to make to the study of the Viking period
but if its limitations are not recognised it may do more harm
than good. Above all it is essential that all who use archaeological evidence, whether directly or indirectly, should recognise that it is generally not possible to give precise historical
dates to material finds, sites or even to styles and techniques,
and that it is consequently very difficult to associate archaeological discoveries in detail with historical events. With this
important limitation on its historical value, archaeology has
much to offer. It makes possible for example, the study of
changes that have occurred in particular places: the growth of

Hedeby from a small trading centre to an elaborately walled town, with a water supply laid on to at least some houses, or the development of the defences at Birka. It is archaeology alone that has revealed the elaborate system of structures that stood inside the large Danish earthworks like Trelleborg.[36] The structural changes on such sites as these can profitably be studied; what is difficult is to relate these changes to each other and to what happened elsewhere. The archaeologist can also draw attention to apparent changes in wealth in different regions, and he can reasonably suggest that the greatly increased number of graves found in many parts of Scandinavia in the early Viking period indicated an increasing pressure of population. In some areas it is, indeed, possible to detect significant local variations in the number of graves, as for example in the hinterland of Kaupang.[37] The archaeologist can also make a valuable contribution to our understanding of the period by studying the distribution of certain easily recognisable objects such as Rhenish pottery,[38] soapstone from Norway,[39] and, above all, coins.[40] He is also able to study the development of techniques and tools, the ships being the most remarkable of all. In these and other ways archaeology is of the greatest value, and it will be drawn on heavily in this study of the subject, but it is always important to remember that it proceeds by hypothesis. In the testing of the hypotheses chance plays as large a part as scientific method. The historian of the Viking period must beware of accepting unproved, and sometimes illfounded, hypotheses and using them as though they were undoubted and incontrovertible fact.

4. The Ships

ALMOST all Viking enterprises depended on ships and many demanded a high degree of seamanship. These ships, and the ability to handle them, were the product of centuries of experience gained among the islands and on the rivers, lakes and fjords of Scandinavia. The environment was ideal for the development of these techniques for, in much of the north, boats were indispensable. Without them life could hardly have been sustained along much of the Norwegian coast; they were needed not only for communications in the fjords and among the islands but also for fishing, and the same was true of the islands of Denmark and the Baltic. Even in mainland Sweden the rivers and lakes were used as routeways through the forest and boats were an important item of equipment, as the rich boat-burials of the Vendel and Viking periods testify. It was in these circumstances that techniques of boat-building and of boat handling were developed which led, eventually, to the production of the remarkable and superbly functional vessels that we nowadays loosely call Viking ships.

The construction of these ships and their development from comparatively primitive boats can be studied in some detail.[1] There are three main sources of information; the remains of the vessels themselves, contemporary depictions of ships in stone or embroidery and, least reliable of all, written evidence. A large number of boats, and parts of boats, of the Viking period and the immediately preceding centuries have been discovered in Scandinavia and along the southern shores of the

Baltic. Many of these were deliberately buried in graves, or deposited in bogs as offerings of some kind. Other boats have been found that seem to have been wrecked, possibly in storms or just left to rot when they were beyond repair, or deliberately sunk, like the five ships recently recovered from Roskilde Fjord, at Skuldelev.[2] In some cases wood, with other organic matter has been preserved almost perfectly and as a result the ships found at Nydam, in southern Denmark,[3] and at Gokstad and Oseberg, on the west shore of Oslo Fjord, can be studied in very great detail. Plates IV and VI show the remarkable preservation of wood in the Gokstad and Oseberg finds. Where soil conditions are not suitable for the preservation of wood, careful excavation has often revealed valuable details. In particular, by recording the position and length of rivets the fairly detailed reconstruction of such vessels as that found in Denmark at Ladby in Fyn,[4] or of the many boats found in the gravefields of Uppland has been made possible. The magnificent series of monumental stones erected in Gotland between the fifth century and the eleventh provide information of the greatest value about ships, especially about their rigging, and one of these stones, from the parish of Alskog, is shown in Plate V.[5] The stone carvings in mainland Sweden have less value for this subject, but there are a few with ships, such as the early Viking period stone at Sparlösa in Västergötland.[6] From the end of the period comes some of the most interesting, but tantalising, evidence in the Bayeux Tapestry.[7] The theme of this elaborate piece of embroidery is the Norman Conquest of England and it was produced within a few years of that event. In it many ships are shown being built, sailed and beached and despite the difficulty of the medium the artist has contrived to represent many details with great accuracy, making this one of the most valuable sources of information about the construction and handling of ships in the middle of the eleventh century. The written evidence for ships and seamanship is in many ways the least satisfactory. There are a few contemporary references to ships in chronicles, saints' lives, letters and in such writings as Ohthere's account of his voyages reported in the translation of Orosius.[8] From these and similar sources something can be learned: Ohthere, for example, describes how the skins of seals and walruses were used for ropes. The most colourful and detailed information is found in the Norse sagas which contain abundant references to ships; indeed our knowledge of the Norse technical terms for parts of ships and for sailing operations is largely derived from them. They must, however, be used with very great caution as sources for the Viking period. They were written for audiences of the thirteenth century or later and should not be used without qualification as guides to the terminology and techniques of the ninth and tenth centuries. Scandinavian law codes should also be used with caution, and for the same reason. The scaldic verses embodied in the sagas are more reliable as guides to the usages of the Viking age but they are, unfortunately so obscure and allusive that they can tell very little, important though that little may be. There are, for instance, references to striped sails, to ships tacking and to the reefing of sails. Expressions such as these confirm conclusions that are based, perhaps more securely, on the material evidence of the ships themselves and of the pictures of them that have survived.

In discussing these ships and their evolution it will be best to begin with a description of the finest of them all in both technical perfection and in preservation. This was the ship found in a large burial mound at Gokstad, by Sandefjord, about 50 miles SSE. of Oslo, excavated in 1881.[9] It had been buried in a trench and a burial chamber constructed amidships for a man who must have been of great wealth and importance. Along with the ship much of its equipment was found, the oars, blocks, the yard and other spars, the gangplank, the frame of a tent that could be erected in the ship, a large pile of cloth and rope that had probably been the sail, and three small boats. Over all a large mound had been thrown up. The ship and the wooden objects found with it owe their preservation to the blue clay in which they were buried; only those parts of the ship that protruded through the blue clay layer, in particular the bow and stern posts, have rotted away.

Apart from the mast and the decking most of the ship, illustrated in Plate VI, is built of oak. It is 76 ft. 6 in. (23·33 m.) long, 17 ft. 6 in. (5·25 m.) broad and from the bottom of the

keel to the gunwale amidships it measures just under 6 ft. 5 in.
(1·95 m.). Its empty weight has been calculated as about 8½ tons
and when fully laden with about 10 tons it drew only 3 ft. Its
seaworthiness was convincingly demonstrated in 1893 when a
copy was made and sailed across the Atlantic in less than a
month. It left Norway on 30th April and made Newfoundland
on 27th May after a stormy crossing. The description of the
voyage written by the captain, Magnus Andersen, reveals
among other things, how very skilfully contrived this ship and
all its equipment was.[10]

The keel consists of a single timber 57 ft. 9 in. (17·6 m.) long
and between 14½ in. (37 cm.) and 16½ in. (42 cm.) deep with
stems jointed to the keel by short transitional pieces. The
planking is in sixteen strakes* and is clinker built, the planks
being rivetted together and caulked with animal hair dipped
in tar. Their thickness varies with their function. The bottom
nine strakes, the underwater part of the hull, are of planks
1 in. (2·6 cm.) thick, the tenth strake, the water-line, is the
thickest of all, 1¾ in. (4·4 cm.); the next three have the same
thickness as the underwater strakes; the fourteenth, in which
the oar holes are cut is thicker, 1¼ in. (3·2 cm.); and the top
two are very thin indeed, only $\frac{7}{12}$ in. (1·6 cm.). The topmost
strake is reinforced by a heavy gunwale, 4¼ in. by 3½ in.
(10·8 by 8·8 cm.).

The hull below the water-line is kept in shape by nineteen
ribs, a little more than 3 ft. (about 1 m.) apart, and further
reinforcement at the water-line is provided by cross beams,
most of which are themselves supported by props. The decking
was laid across these beams. Below the water-line the strakes
are flexibly attached to the ribs by lashings of spruce roots.
The planks are cut to leave cleats on the inside where the
ribs lie and corresponding holes through which the lashings
passed were cut in these cleats and in the ribs. This method
of fastening the planking to the ribs, which is found in other
Scandinavian ships of the Viking period, had the great advantage that the hull could be made both light and flexible. A more
rigid structure would have had to be much stronger and
therefore heavier to withstand the stresses as it passed

---

* Each of the continuous lines of planking in the hull of a vessel.

through uneven water. Apart from this, flexibility in the hull is an advantage in sailing.

The strakes above the water-line are held in place in a way designed to render this part of the structure flexible also. The first four of these strakes are fastened by trenails* to wooden knees that are fixed to the cross beams. The top two strakes, the thinnest in the ship, are similarly fastened by trenails to half-ribs that are attached to the strakes immediately below and butted into the underside of the gunwale. There are only half as many of these supports for the top two strakes and the gunwale as there are cross beams and knees, the result being lightness and flexibility. Magnus Andersen reported that in the crossing of the Atlantic the replica of the Gokstad ship showed great elasticity. In a high sea the gunwale twisted out of true as much as 6 inches. Despite this the ship proved water-tight. As Andersen says, this elasticity with the fine lines of the ship made it a fast sailer and a speed of 10 knots was often made and sometimes more.

The Gokstad ship was steered by a quarter rudder, mounted in a most ingenious way. The rudder, made of oak and measuring 10 ft. 9 in. (3·3 m.) long, was fastened to a large block of wood attached to the outside of the hull and supported by an extra stout rib. This block was called the 'wart'. The fastening was by osiers, knotted on the outside, that passed through both rudder and wart to be firmly anchored in the ship. By this means the rudder was firmly attached to the hull but the flexibility of the osiers allowed it to be twisted in a horizontal plane by the helm, *hjalm*, that slotted into its upper end and projected inboard. The rudder was prevented from rotating on its axis in a vertical plane by a fastening at the gunwale. When the ship was beached, or was passing through shallow water, the rudder could be raised very quickly by undoing the fastening at the gunwale and rotating it on its axis with the help of a rope attached to the lower part of the blade. When in place, the rudder projected about 18 in. (46 cm.) below the keel and was a most efficient steering device. After his Atlantic crossing Magnus Andersen wrote:

---

* Wooden pins used for fastening timbers: also treenail.

'I have thought much about this and have come to the conclusion that this rudder may be considered as one of the
most definite proofs of our ancestors' great understanding
and seamanship. . . . In my experience the side rudder is
much superior in such a ship to a rudder on the stern-post.
. . . I am glad to be able to state that it worked satisfactorily
in every way and had the advantage of never kicking, as a
stern-post rudder would certainly have done. One man could
steer in any weather with merely a small line to help.'

The ship could be rowed and was provided with sixteen pairs
of oars, made of pine, of different lengths so that in use they
would all strike the water at the same time. There were no
rowing benches and the oarsmen may have had some removable
seats, probably their sea-chests. This peculiarity suggests that
rowing was not the normal means of propulsion. The oars
would, of course, have been useful at critical moments when
the ship was becalmed or when it had to be manœuvred in
narrow waters, such as a fjord or haven, but generally it was
sailed: it was designed as a sailing-ship. For long voyages the
crew is therefore unlikely to have been much larger than about
thirty-five men. In hand-to-hand fighting a crowd might be an
advantage, and the levy ships of medieval Norway were supposed to carry several men to each oar, but for crossing the
North Sea a crew of more than about thirty-five would have
made the business of sailing extraordinarily difficult, not to
say hazardous.

The mast was mounted on a very large block of oak called
the *kjerringa*, meaning a 'crone' or 'old woman'. It is about
12 ft. (3·6 m.) long and rests along the keel, spanning four
ribs. The mast rests in a socket designed to ease the business of
raising and lowering it. Above the *kjerringa* is the mast partner,
a massive piece of oak that extends over and is supported by
six cross beams as well as by the upper part of the *kjerringa* itself.
The mast passed through the mast partner, and would have
been pressed by the force of the wind against its solid forward
part. In this way the force produced by the action of wind on
sail was transmitted to the hull. Behind the mast there is a
large cleft in the mast partner, so that the mast could be raised

F

and lowered without having to be lifted vertically out of its
socket. When the mast was in position, this cleft was filled by a
wooden wedge.

The rigging of the ship was first satisfactorily worked out by a
Swedish scholar, Harald Åkerlund, whose reconstruction has
the great merit of explaining all the sailing equipment found
with the ship.[11] Modern discussions of the subject have been
much influenced by Åkerlund's work and new discoveries,
including the ships recovered from Roskilde Fjord, have confirmed many points in his interpretation. The following account
of the rigging of the Gokstad ship and the technique of sailing
it is, therefore, based on Åkerlund's work, with two important
modifications concerning the height of the mast and the system
of reefing the sail.

Åkerlund believed that the greater part of the mast was found
with the Gokstad ship but that it was in two sections. One, the
base, which was about 10 ft. (3 m.) long and 1 ft. (30 cm.) thick
was still in position while the upper part, which Åkerlund
thought had been separated from the base before interment,
was about 25 ft. (8 m.) long when it was excavated. By then a
section of unknown length, including the hole or attachment for
the halyard, had rotted away and Åkerlund therefore concluded
that the mast must have been between 37 ft. 6 in. and 41 ft.
(11·5–12·5 m.) high. This is slightly shorter than the 42 ft.
(13 m.) mast deduced by Brøgger and Shetelig from the
traditional assumption that the mast height would have
equalled the girth of the ship.[12] It has, however, been argued
that such a high mast with a correspondingly high mounting for
the yard and sail, would have made the ship unstable, and it has
also been pointed out that a mast of more than 33 ft. (10 m.)
would, when lowered, have projected beyond the end of the
ship, making it very awkward, if not dangerous, to handle.[13]
It therefore seems likely that the mast was shorter than 33 ft.
(10 m.) and it seems best to accept that the 26 ft. (8 m.) mast
length found with the ship was a spare mast rather than the
upper part of the base which was found in position. This mast
would have been supported by shrouds and their tension maintained by the large blocks found with the ship which were
probably used in the manner illustrated in figure 4. Further

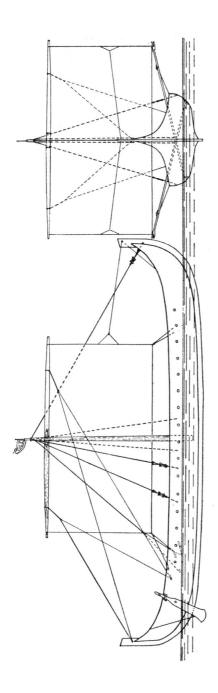

Figure 4 The rigging of the Gokstad ship. This drawing is based on the reconstruction proposed by Harald Åkerlund, *Unda Maris*, 1955–56, p. 81, with a shorter mast. See pp. 73–5.

support for the mast would have been provided by the forestay, the function of backstay being served by the halyard that ran through a hole in the top of the mast or through a block attached to it. The width of the sail is indicated by the T-shaped supports that were obviously designed to hold the lowered yard and sail and so keep the deck clear when it was necessary to row the ship. These supports are 35 ft. (10·7 m.) apart suggesting that the yard was over 37 ft. (11·2 m.) long. More than half this yard was found with the Gokstad ship and it is about 10 in. (25 cm.) thick at the middle and may be compared with the 40 ft. (12·1 m.) yard found intact with the Oseberg ship. The sail area was, therefore, probably rather less than 70 sq. yds. (60 sq. m.). This is two-thirds of the sail area originally deduced by Åkerlund, but a sail of this size would have been quite large enough to propel the ship even in a slight breeze. In the ship was found a large heap of white woollen cloth to which some red cloth had been sewn, the whole being mixed up with the rope. This was probably the sail, which in any case is likely to have been made up from strips of a coarse woollen cloth called wadmal. For strength a double thickness was generally used, and the strips were often interwoven to give a chequered pattern, or the sail may have been strengthened by having a rope net sewn to it, both methods would produce a pattern of squares, familiar in such stone carvings as Plate V. The yard was held to the mast either by a naturally bent piece of wood, as in the Oseberg ship, or by a short but very strong length of rope. The foot of the sail would have been secured by sheets and the yard trimmed by braces. When running before the wind the underyard might be used but an alternative method of spreading the sail when the breeze was slight was to use the two spreading spars, each about 26 ft. (8 m.) long, that were found with the ship. These spars fitted into sockets in a pair of blocks mounted each side of the ship just forward of the mast. These blocks can be seen in Plate VI and their use is shown in Figure 4. When sailing across the wind (i.e. reaching) only one of these spreading spars would have been used. In this case the spar would fit into a second socket in one or other of the blocks, depending on the relative direction of the wind. Each of these blocks has two sockets, with different alignments, and Åkerlund's suggestion that they were used in this way for spreading spars is the only satisfactory explanation of their function. When sailing close-hauled a bowline could be attached to the leech of the sail, in the manner shown in Figure 4. The Gokstad ship would not have needed a bowsprit but the use of these was certainly known in the ninth century.

It is sometimes asserted that Viking ships would normally only be sailed before the wind, but the design of the Gokstad ship and the equipment found with it clearly demonstrate that this was not so. It is well designed for reaching and this capacity has been shown with replicas of it. It is, besides, difficult to understand how the Viking voyages could have been made at all if their ships had been virtually at the mercy of the wind's direction.

There must have been some system for reefing the sail of a Viking ship. References in scaldic verse confirm what common sailing sense demands, that these ships had sails that could be shortened. Unfortunately nothing is known of the method. Åkerlund's suggestion that it was done by means of a system of lines running through loops or rings on the sail is attractive in theory but unlikely to work in practice.[14] It is true that many of the Gotland stones, for example those from Alskog and Stenkyrka reproduced here (Plates V, VII) show members of the crew holding an elaborate network of lines, but a careful examination of these stones shows that the networks in and below the sail are not connected. The pattern on the sails is likely to represent some reinforcement of the cloth while the network of lines shown below the sails is best understood as representing a method of sailing, possibly peculiar to the Baltic at that time, in which the sheets were not attached to the boat but were held by members of the crew. Such manual control would have made it possible, given a well disciplined crew, to change the sail shape very quickly and so gain an advantage when closing on another vessel for a fight.[15] The interlocking network would have reduced the danger of loss of control should any of the crew accidentally lose their grip.

The anchor of the Gokstad ship was found, but its iron disappeared soon after exposure to the air, leaving only the

stock of oak, about 9 ft. (2·75 m.) long. It had the same
design as the better-preserved anchor found with the Ladby
ship. With the ship the remains of three boats were found. These
were most beautifully made and measured 32, 26, and 21½ ft.
(9·75, 8·0 and 6·6 m.) long respectively. Two of them were
equipped with masts, and all could be rowed.

In all its details, the Gokstad ship is beautifully designed and
very well made. It was buried in the middle of the Viking
period, possibly at the end of the ninth century and is then
likely to have been quite old, perhaps as much as fifty years.
This means that the techniques of sailing had been perfectly
understood in Scandinavia early in the Viking period. This has
so surprised one archaeologist that he has suggested that the
Gokstad burial has been wrongly dated and that it ought to
belong to the end of the period, but there is no warrant for
such re-dating and the historian need not be surprised. It was,
after all, the evolution of such vessels as the Gokstad ship that
made the Viking raids of the late eighth century on northern
Britain possible. Already by the end of the ninth century the
crossing to Iceland was being made regularly. The confidence
of the Vikings can be more readily understood in the light of
the technical perfection of their principal instrument.

The Gokstad ship is the largest and best preserved of the early
Viking ships but other finds show that many of its characteristic
features were common in Scandinavia at that time and it is
obvious that these vessels gave the Vikings great advantages in
their attacks on western Europe. Not only did they have the
benefit of surprise, they were also able to operate in very shallow
water and to land relatively large ships on open, gently-
shelving beaches that were generally inaccessible to the boats of
the defenders.[16] The Gokstad ship had a remarkably shallow
draught. With a full load of about ten tons it only had a draught
of 3 ft. and it has been calculated that each additional ton of
ballast would only have increased this by about 1 in. The
rudder which, for efficient sailing, projected well below the keel,
could be raised very quickly and beaching was made less
hazardous by the use of transitional pieces of wood to join the
keel to the stem and stern posts. These, later called *undirhlutr*,
were placed at the normal point of impact when beaching and

if one broke under the strain its replacement would have been a much simpler matter than the repair of a shattered keel. The advantage of having light ships with such a shallow draught was well displayed in the battle described in the Anglo-Saxon Chronicle for 896. In this encounter, which occurred in an estuary, probably on the south coast of Wessex, three Danish ships were on dry land inside the estuary and were opposed by six larger English vessels in the entrance. The English ships seem to have been caught by the ebbing tide and are said to have 'run aground very awkwardly', three on each side of the channel. 'After the water had ebbed many furlongs from the ships' there was a fight between the Danes and the crews of the three ships they could get at and the Chronicler continues, 'then, however, the tide reached the Danish ships before the Christians could launch theirs, and therefore they rowed away out'.

Another advantage of these ninth-century Scandinavian ships was that horses could be landed from them on open beaches. Our sources sometimes describe the Viking invaders landing with their horses and a recent experiment with a replica Viking ship has confirmed that horses can indeed be landed from it on a shelving beach.[17] It has also been pointed out that when William, Duke of Normandy, invaded England in 1066 he too was denied access to a deep water harbour and, as the Bayeux Tapestry emphasises, he built a large fleet of ships that clearly had many points of similarity to the earlier Viking ships. The Tapestry's depiction of the landing of this fleet in Pevensey Bay is well worth close study for it shows many details with astonishing accuracy, notably the lowering of a mast and the landing of the cargo of horses.[18] There could hardly be better testimony to the tactical advantages of Viking ships.

An important question for the historian is when the Scandinavians mastered these techniques of sailing and ship-building. The answer seems to be that although sails may have been used in the Baltic as early as the beginning of the seventh century, it was only in the eighth century that the main advances were made. The earliest sailing-boat found in Scandinavia is the Äskekärr boat, discovered in 1933 not far from Gothenburg.[19] It was carefully excavated and has been dated to the beginning of the Viking period. There are two other boats that have been claimed as earlier sailing boats but neither claim can be seriously maintained. The Kvalsund boat has been dated about a century before the Äskekärr boat but it cannot be shown to have had a mast.[20] It clearly marks an important advance on the Nydam ship and it is just possible that it carried a sail but there is no positive evidence that it did so. The strongest argument in its favour as a sailing boat is that its rudder seems to be designed for sailing as well as rowing, but the evidence is hardly clear enough to invalidate the chronology suggested here. The other claimant is a boat found at Galtabäck, near Varberg in south-west Sweden.[21] This boat, certainly equipped with a sail, was originally dated in the sixth century but this dating has been so seriously challenged that it cannot stand.[22] The Galtabäck boat is post-Viking. The earliest certain sailing boat found in the North remains that from Äskekärr. The chronology implied by this for the evolution of sailing techniques in Scandinavia is confirmed by the stone carvings in Gotland and mainland Sweden. In Gotland there are a few depictions of sailing boats on stones of the seventh century, but in these the sails are always small in relation to the boat.[23] It is only in the eighth century that the sails become larger, and on later stones they are sometimes very large indeed. As far as mainland Sweden is concerned, the earliest carving of sailing boats is no earlier than the Äskekärr boat itself. It seems likely that attempts were being made to equip ships with sails in the Baltic quite early, possibly even before the seventh century, but it was only on the eve of the Viking period that true sailing vessels were developed and this may have first happened in the comparatively sheltered waters of the Baltic. The technical perfection of the Gokstad ship is the product of a long tradition of experience and experiment that first yielded sailing ships adequate for the open sea a century or so before the Gokstad ship was itself constructed.

The significance of this conclusion can hardly be over-emphasised. The Viking activity, both raiding and trading, depended on reliable sailing ships, and without them the long sea crossings would not have been possible. These ships gave bands of raiders their great advantage of surprise and a means of swift retreat. One of the main reasons the Viking raids began when they did was that technical developments only made them possible in the eighth century. The voyages that became a commonplace in the ninth century would have been inconceivable in the first half of the eighth. As Alcuin wrote in 793 when he first heard of the raid on Lindisfarne: 'It is nearly 350 years that we and our fathers have inhabited this most lovely land, and never before has such a terror appeared in Britain as we have now suffered from a pagan race, nor was it thought that such an inroad from the sea could be made.'

The Gokstad ship has been described because it is the best of those that survive. Many others show similar constructional details, for example the Oseberg, Tune and Storhaugen ships.[24] In all these the planking is lashed to the frame, a method of construction that was traditional in the north and of which there are many examples before the Viking period, notably the fourth-century Nydam ship. This was, however, not the only method of fastening the planks to the frame. Trenails were sometimes used but in the early Viking period there seems to have been a deliberate attempt to preserve the flexibility of the hulls despite such rigid fastenings. In the ninth-century boat from Äskekärr in Sweden trenails were used but the ribs are not fastened to every strake, and sometimes there are as many as three unfastened strakes between those that are trenailed. Even more remarkable is the fact that the third and fifth strakes are attached to only two of the ribs on either side. The result of such irregular fastening was, of course, the same kind of structural flexibility gained in larger ships by the use of lashings to join ribs and strakes. The method of construction used in the Äskekärr boat is simpler than that in the Gokstad ship but both were made in the early Viking period and they both clearly belong to the same tradition in which the aim seems to have been to make light, flexible ships that could easily be beached.

The ships recovered from Roskilde Fjord at Skuldelev are rather later and in all of them the planks are fastened to the frames by trenails. Flexible lashings were apparently no longer used but in two of the Skuldelev ships, including the largest, which was probably about 90 ft. (28 m.) long, the keel and two of the strakes were not fastened to any of the frames, a feature that is very similar to that found earlier at Äskekärr. The other Skuldelev ships were, however, more rigidly constructed and do not seem to have been designed for easy or frequent beaching. These heavier vessels reflect a change that apparently occurred in Scandinavian ship design towards the end of the Viking period when heavier, more rigid craft replaced the light, flexible boats of earlier times. This was partly a response to changing needs, for in the eleventh century there was a growing demand for deeper ships capable of carrying relatively heavy loads.[25] The trade of the Baltic and north-west Europe was increasingly in such bulky commodities as corn, timber, cloth, fish and even stone and by the twelfth century the main centres of sea-borne trade in the Baltic had shifted to harbours in which vessels of a deep draught could shelter. The first phase of this change is clearly seen in a comparison of the Äskekärr boat with Skuldelev 1.[26] Both were cargo vessels and they were much the same length, 52 ft. (16 m.), but the contrast between them is striking. The later ship is heavy, rigid and deep, drawing about 5 ft. (1·5 m.) when fully laden. It could carry a much bigger cargo than the Äskekärr boat but it needed deep water and could only have been beached with difficulty.

In ships intended for fighting, the levy ships of medieval Scandinavia, the old type of construction may have survived well into the twelfth century and even later, but the tendency to greater rigidity and weight was strongly reinforced in the eleventh century by the introduction of the saw and the use, for the first time in Scandinavia, of the sawn plank.[27] In the Viking period planks were cut by wedges and adzes, with which it was, and is, possible to make up to 32 separate planks from one oak trunk.[28] Planks prepared in this way are far stronger than sawn planks of the same thickness and the introduction of the saw meant that the planking of ships had to be made noticeably thicker. Later medieval ships, like the thirteenth-century vessel recovered at Falsterbo, in which the interval between the ribs is less than half that of the Gokstad ships, are far heavier and more rigid than the vessels used by the Vikings.[29]

The size of ships built in the manner of the Gokstad ship was to some extent limited by the length of timber available for the keel. A flexible structure of this kind put great strains on the keel, and it is difficult to believe that reliable sea-worthy ships could be built in this way with a keel made of more than one piece of timber. Keels were generally made of oak and the longest known is 20 m.: it is unlikely that many oaks in Scandinavia could have yielded straight timber much longer than this. When the replica of the Gokstad ship was made in 1892 Canadian oak had to be imported for the keel as no suitable timber could be found in Norway. It seems therefore very unlikely that sea-going ships in the ninth century could have been made much longer than that found at Gokstad.

This structural limitation on the size of sea-going Viking ships is often overlooked and it is commonly assumed that the ships normally used by the Vikings for their overseas expeditions were much larger than the Gokstad ship. One of the reasons for this is that the levy ships of medieval Norway generally had 20 or 25 pairs of oars. These may well have been longer than the Gokstad ship but the increase in length is unlikely to have been proportional to the number of oars. The interval between frames could be very much less than the 38½ in. (1 m.) at Gokstad. In Skuldelev 2, for example, the frames were about 29 in. (70 cm.) apart and in this ship 21 pairs of oars could have been accommodated in the same length as the 16 pairs at Gokstad.[30] It is, however, quite wrong to assume that because numbers of such large vessels could be produced in the thirteenth century, ships of that size were used by Viking raiders in the ninth century. The levy ships were generally intended for use in home waters not for expeditions across the North Sea and the number of warriors they could carry is no guide to the number that could have been safely conveyed across the open waters of the north-east Atlantic.

Ships intended for defensive purposes or operating in the comparatively sheltered waters of the fjords, skerries and islands of Scandinavia could be larger, and need not have been so strong as those intended for the North Sea and beyond, because they were not expected to withstand the strains of the open sea for long periods. In ships designed for defence or for fighting other considerations than sea-worthiness might well prevail. The ships built by Alfred in the ninth century for the defence of England are an illustration of this. In the words of the Anglo-Saxon Chronicle they were 'almost twice as long as the others . . . they were both swifter and steadier and also higher than the others. They were built neither on the Frisian nor on the Danish pattern, but as it seemed to him himself that they could be most useful.'[31] In battle, large and high ships had an advantage and this was the reason King Sverrir of Norway decided in 1182 to enlarge his ship *Mariasuden* after the keel and nine strakes had been laid.[32] This decision caused consternation: such lengthening involved the insertion of a central section in the bottom timbers of the ship making it very weak. When the ship was launched some of the joints in the bottom opened and had to be patched up. The decision to enlarge the ship was not, however, a foolish one. The king knew what he was doing: the extra size of the ship gave him the advantage in battle and his reward was victory.

In the thirteenth century the distinction was recognised between the sea-going ship, *hafskip*, and other types like the warship, *langskip*, or the cargo ships of the Baltic, the *austrfarar-knarr*. It was recognised that the voyage to Iceland, the Faroes or even to England could not be made in a *langskip*, because the seas were too rough. The most common *hafskip* for such voyages was called a *knarr*, in the twelfth century and later this term was used for merchant ships, but in the Viking period it had a less specialised meaning. It was in these that the Scandinavians came to Britain and made the crossing to Iceland and the Faroes. It may be assumed that in the Viking period, as in the twelfth century, the *knarr* was more seaworthy than the longship, having a higher freeboard, and being shorter and possibly broader.[33] The size of warships used in Scandinavian waters, whether in the thirteenth century or in the tenth, is no guide to the size of ships used by the Vikings in their overseas expeditions.

It is, therefore, unlikely, that the sea-going ships of the ninth century were much, if at all, larger than the Gokstad ship, with its thirty-two oars. The Anglo-Saxon Chronicle for 896 supports this conclusion. When Alfred ordered the construction of large ships for the naval defence of England they were said to be almost twice the size of the raider's ships. In the words of the Chronicle they were 'almost twice as long as the others . . . Some had sixty oars, some more.' This suggests that the number of oars in the raiding ships was not much more than thirty: and some of the boats used by the raiders must have been very much smaller. Those taken by the Danes 20 miles above London up the River Lea in 895 are more likely to have been on the scale of the boats found with the Gokstad ship than of the ship itself. In 861 a number of ships were carried from the River Seine to the River Epte, a distance of about two miles (3 km.), in order to complete the siege of a rival Viking force on the island of Jeufosse in the Seine.[34] This exploit suggests that the vessels must have been quite small rowing boats rather than ships of twenty oars or more. These smaller boats may very well have outnumbered the large and so made up the main part of Viking fleets. Most boat burials in Norway contained vessels that were less than 33 ft. (10 m.) long.[35] It is, of course, unlikely that the largest ships would be used for burials until, like the Oseberg ship, they were beyond repair, but the fact that only five larger than 66 ft. (20 m.) have been discovered among the many boat burials of Norway hardly suggests that the ships of the Vikings were normally as large as the Gokstad ship. By the end of the tenth century larger ships were undoubtedly being built and used in both Scandinavia and England; the fleet maintained by Cnut and the other Danish kings of England consisted of ships with 30 pairs of oars.[36] It is, however, likely that most craft used by the eleventh-century Scandinavians in home and distant waters were rather smaller than that. Only one of the five ships from Skuldelev was longer than the Gokstad ship and that was clearly a warship, a *langskip* of the kind that was later recognised as being quite unsuitable for distant voyages.

The Vikings had a great variety of ships to suit their varying needs. In later writings, including the Icelandic sagas, several types are named but it has only been with the discoveries at Skuldelev that we have been able to appreciate fully what technical differences lay behind some of them. In Skuldelev 1 we have the type of sea-going ship, *hafskip*, known as *knarr*. This example was probably made in Norway, to judge by the extensive use of pine in its construction. Skuldelev 3 is another cargo-boat and may well be one of those that were specially

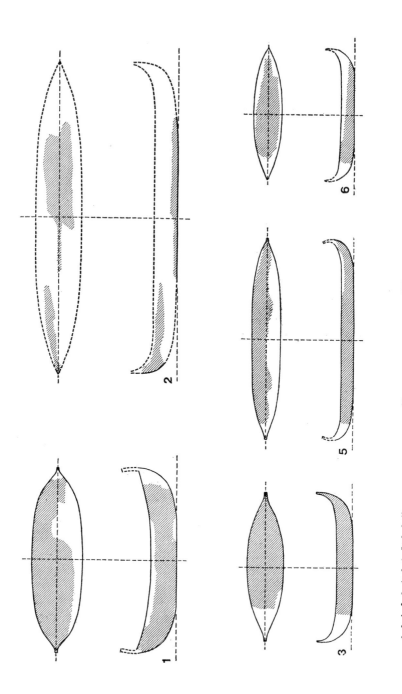

1   2   3   5   6

0 1 2 3 4 5 6 7 8 9 10   20   30 M

designed for traffic in the Baltic, an *austrfararknarr*. There are two warships, Skuldelev 2 and 5, the larger of them being, as already explained, a true *langskip*. The smallest of these ships, Skuldelev 6, is also constructed largely of pine and therefore probably came from Norway, and could well have been a fishing or ferry boat. This variety of purpose and design was no new thing. The differences between the Äskekärr and Gokstad ships show that already in the early Viking period the ship-wrights of Scandinavia had developed very different types of sailing craft to meet different needs. Some were designed to carry cargo, others for fighting, some to work in sheltered or shallow water, others for easy beaching or for portage overland, while others again were well designed to make safe crossings of wide and stormy seas.

The ships used by the Vikings are fascinating in themselves, but for the historian of the period the study of their design and construction and the way they were handled is particularly rewarding. The Scandinavians of the Viking period are seen to have been masters of the design and use of sailing ships, and it was the possession of these cunningly contrived vessels that gave them one of their most important technical advantages in both peace and war. It was, in fact, the development of these ships that made the extended activities of the Scandi-navians both possible and profitable. The evidence also suggests that the ships used by the Scandinavians in the ninth century for their voyages overseas were unlikely to have been much larger than the Gokstad ship, with its crew of less than forty men, and many of their boats must have been very much smaller.

Figure 5 (opposite) The outlines of the five Skuldelev ships. The shaded areas indicate the parts that have been recovered. The dimensions are; 1–16·5 × 4·6 m., 2–28 × 4·2 m., 3–13·3 × 3·3 m., 5–18 × 2·6 m., 6–12 × 2·5 m. See Olaf Olsen and Ole Crumlin Pedersen, *Fem vikingeskibe fra Roskilde Fjord* (1969), p. 101.

5. Treasure

SILVER was greatly coveted in Viking Scandinavia. Wherever Danes, Norwegians or Swedes went at that time, from the rivers of Russia to the farms of Iceland, the value of this precious metal was recognised and one of their main purposes, whether as pirates, traders or mercenaries, was to acquire it. They often wanted other things as well, for many needed land on which to settle, and others looked for adventure and the chance to win a famous name, but all welcomed any opportunity to seize, or to extort, silver. It was for Muslim silver that Scandinavian traders ventured to the Volga, it was for pay in silver that Scandinavian mercenaries served English kings and Byzantine emperors. For some the acquisition of silver, to be hoarded or worn as ornament, may have been an end in itself, but others regarded it as a means of buying other desirable things like food, wine or loyalty. Some worked it skilfully into beautiful things like the brooches in Plate XI while others, caring little for such craftsmanship and artistry, were interested only in the weight of metal and hacked their silver into pieces.

The efforts of Scandinavians to satisfy their appetite for silver, however it was regarded, were remarkably successful. Only a tiny fraction of the former accumulations can have been recovered and recorded in modern times but enough has been found to leave no doubt about the wealth of Viking Scandinavia. Well over a thousand hoards of gold and silver have been found and although, as may be seen in the distribution map on page 107, the greatest concentrations are on the islands and along the coasts and inland waterways, few parts of Scandinavia that were then inhabited have not yielded treasure of some kind. A little gold has been found, but most is silver in the form of ornaments, coin or bullion. Some idea of the quantities involved may be gained from a recent analysis of the silver hoards found on Gotland before 1946.[1] These contained over 570 ornaments, many of native manufacture, as well as 489 fragmentary ornaments, over 2,300 whole or fragmentary pieces of silver in such forms as rods, bars and rings, 93,500 coins and 16,600 coin fragments, all but three of silver. Many hoards are small and contain only a few coins or an ornament or two, but many are large and some are very large indeed. Three of the Gotlandic hoards weighed more than 15 lb. (7 kg.) each[2] and one of these, found in 1936 at Stora Velinge, contained 2,673 Arabic coins as well as an arm ring and weighed altogether over 17½ lb. (7,952 gr.). In contrast the hoard found at Asarve in 1903 contained only two Arabic coins, and one of these was fragmentary, most of its 15½ lb. of silver consisting of bulky ornaments. These are, of course, exceptionally large treasures, and Gotland is richer in silver finds than any other part of Scandinavia, over half the known hoards having been found there, but similar hoards have turned up elsewhere. On the little Danish island of Falster five hoards have been found, one of which contained over 14 lb. (6·5 kg.) of silver and the hoard discovered at Espinge in the middle of Skåne, was heavier even than any Gotlandic hoard, weighing 19 lb. (8·75 kg.), and contained over 8,000 coins.[3]

There were no native sources of silver in Scandinavia being worked in the Viking period and, apart from finds that might have been made from time to time of silver hoarded in an earlier age, all this Viking silver had to be imported. The source of the minted silver can be studied easily, for coins generally bear the name of the authority that issued them and they often also name the mint at which they were struck. The main source of minted silver in the ninth and tenth centuries can be shown to have been the Muslim world. These Arabic coins, sometimes called Kufic because their legends are in a

G

script associated with the Mesopotamian city of Kufah, are particularly valuable evidence for they generally bear the date of issue. Most of the 62,000 so far discovered in Scandinavia were struck for Muslim rulers but a few were issued by their predecessors, and almost all can be shown to have been imported into Scandinavia in the ninth and tenth centuries.[4] There are also a large number of western European coins, including some 70,000 from German mints and well over 40,000 from England, mostly imported in the late tenth and eleventh centuries.[5] The provenance of the unminted silver is often unknown. The many ornaments of Scandinavian manufacture that have been found give no clue to the source of the metal with which they were made. A large number of ornaments were, however, probably made in parts of Russia bordering the Volga, and these are likely to have been made with Muslim silver, and some other objects come from even nearer the Muslim lands. There are a few objects that clearly show Frankish, English or Irish workmanship but there can be very little doubt that the vast mass of silver imported into Scandinavia in the ninth and tenth centuries came from Islamic territory south and east of the Caucasus and the Caspian Sea. The Scandinavian material cannot, indeed, be properly understood unless it is studied along with the finds that have been made in Russia. Some of the Russian hoards are huge. The largest of all was found on the Lovat river near Veliki Luki, about 170 miles south of Novgorod, and was reported to weigh about 2 hundredweight (100 kg.) but it was, unfortunately, dispersed except for a few coins.[6] The report might, in fact, have been thought fanciful but for the discovery in 1868 at Murom on the River Oka of a hoard weighing about 88 lb. (40 kg.) and containing 11,077 Kufic coins, mostly of the ninth and early tenth centuries, as well as coin fragments weighing some 12 lb.[7]

Although most Viking treasure was silver, gold was not unknown and over 400 gold objects of the period have been found in many parts of Scandinavia.[8] One of the most interesting discoveries, illustrated in Plate IX, was found in 1834 at Hon, about 35 miles south-west of Oslo.[9] It contains twenty coins, all adapted to serve as ornaments, and these show that the hoard must have been deposited after 852, the date of the most recent coin, but probably not much later for neither this coin nor the next youngest, a dinar struck in the Muslim year A.H. 234 (between August A.D. 848 and July 849) show much sign of wear. This hoard is remarkable not only because it is unusually early (most gold finds seem to be of the late Viking period), but because it is by far the largest. It contained 5½ lb. (2,500 g.) of gold and the next largest hoard, from Vester Vedsted, near Ribe in Denmark, only weighed a third of this (749 g.).[10] The Hon hoard shows that at least some gold was reaching Scandinavia from western Europe in the early Viking period; the most striking object, the trefoil brooch, was made in a Carolingian workshop and several of the gold coins are also Carolingian. Similar gold imports from the West are suggested by the Frankish influence displayed in early gold work found in Gotland. The West was not, however, the only source of gold. Some must have come from hoards buried centuries earlier in the Baltic's 'Golden Age'. Even in modern times over 500 gold coins deposited in the fifth and sixth centuries have been found on the two Baltic islands, Gotland and Öland, and similar discoveries must have been made in the Viking period.[11] It also seems likely that some gold reached Scandinavia along the same routes as the Muslim silver. These Viking period gold finds are distributed in Scandinavia in much the same way as the silver. Gotland is the richest part with over 130 miscellaneous gold objects, mainland Sweden has yielded about 100 and Norway and Denmark about 70 each.[12] Very little has survived in the form of coin. Only 40 gold coins have been discovered in Viking period finds in the whole of Scandinavia and 33 of these come from two Norwegian hoards, Hon and Strømshaug.[13] This rarity of gold coins is not hard to understand for gold was too valuable to serve, like silver, as a means of exchange. Any gold coins that reached Scandinavia, or were dug up there, were likely to be converted into ornaments, or hammered into leaf for the adornment of other objects, or drawn into fine filaments and threaded through cloth or leather. Gold coins might, like those at Hon, be furnished with loops and worn as ornaments themselves; silver coins were similarly treated, but the temptation to rework the gold must have been great. The rarity of gold coins is, therefore, not surprising wherever they may have come from, and little can be learned about their source from their distribution, especially when 75 per cent. of the known coins are from two hoards.

The gold and silver treasure of the Viking age has been found in graves, hoards and loose finds. Graves are the least important, for silver was too valuable to be much used in furnishing the dead. Some graves contain a little silver, for example the grave illustrated in Figure 3 included a silver dirhem minted in the early tenth century, but such finds are not common; less than a tenth of the graves excavated at Birka contained coins and many of these were fragmentary.[14] Graves might be richly furnished with iron, weapons and perishable goods like food and cloth but silver was rarely used and then only in token amounts. To have used more would have been to tempt grave-robbers.

Treasure hoards are far more important as a source of Viking age silver. The custom of hoarding treasure, of hiding valuables in some secret place is not peculiar to Scandinavia; it is known all over the civilised and uncivilised world. Men naturally attempt to protect their valuables, their portable and convertible wealth, from the covetousness of others and, in simpler days than ours, the best way was often to hide it. Many kinds of hiding-place were used; banks, ditches, field walls, ruined buildings, and tumuli as well as holes in the ground. One enterprising Gotlander even went so far as to hide his valuables in a recent grave.[15] When the owner of such hidden treasure was unable to recover it, and had kept his secret well, it could lie for centuries until discovered by chance. Accidental discoveries of treasure from the Viking period are frequent in Scandinavia, often made in the course of farming operations, such as ploughing, ditching and potato picking, or when building foundations are dug, roads made or quarries excavated. One hoard of about 4 lb. of silver was unearthed in Gotland in 1739 by a dog trying to bury a bone,[16] and the great hoard of Stora Velinge was found as recently as 1936 by two small boys playing in a quarry.[17] Occasionally the pot in which the treasure was stored is also found but often a bag of leather or cloth must have been used and these have rarely left any trace. Sometimes the treasure was a single precious object, a brooch or a bracelet, and at least 312 such loose finds of Viking period treasure were recorded in Gotland up to 1946.[18] Loose or single finds of this kind cannot be treated in quite the same way as hoards for the chances that they were dropped accidentally or were hidden at a later date are much greater than with hoards. Even a hoard may have been deposited long after the period indicated by the style and date of the contents, but in general the presence of several objects provides a more reliable indication of the period of deposit than a single datable object. If an object was deposited after the period indicated by its style, it may have only reached the area in which it was finally hidden or lost at a late date. Travellers and antiquaries have been responsible for the movement of many old valuables and the discovery of Persian or Celtic ornaments of the eighth century in Scandinavia ought not to be regarded as itself sufficient evidence for contact with those areas before the Viking period. On the other hand hoards have sometimes been dispersed accidentally, for example by ploughing, and the objects from the hoard are then found from time to time as single finds.

New finds are reported every year. On the island of Gotland alone, at least fourteen new hoards were found in the decade after 1946 and these contained over 4,200 whole and fragmentary coins as well as ornaments and hacksilver.*[19] Gotland is, indeed, rich in such treasures, but similar finds are made elsewhere in Scandinavia every year.[20]

The treasure that has been discovered and recorded in modern times can only be a small part of the total once hoarded in this way. Much remains buried in the earth, possibly to be discovered in the future, and very large quantities must have been found and dispersed without any record. The discovery of buried treasure must, indeed, have been as common in the Middle Ages as it is today. Occasionally treasure discovered in this way was rehoarded; for example the small hoard from

* Silver ornaments and other objects that have been hacked into pieces regardless of their original shape. The purpose was probably to obtain a certain weight of the metal.

Blädinge in Småland contained ten German coins of the eleventh century along with six coins of the sixteenth century, and probably represents the reburial of at least part of a hoard discovered in the sixteenth century.[21] It is, of course, as impossible to estimate the number of hoards that have been unearthed as it is to know the number still awaiting discovery, but the quantities that are known, and the frequent discovery of new finds, suggests that we are only able to study a tiny fraction of the treasure left in the earth of Scandinavia at the end of the Viking period. This large but unknown quantity itself represents only a small part of the total that had been in circulation in Viking Scandinavia, for the hoards left in the earth in the twelfth century were those that the owners had been unable to recover. Thus, although the total weight of silver in circulation in the Viking period cannot be calculated, the quantity must have been very great. This was indeed the Silver Age of Scandinavia.

It is fortunate for the historian that so much of the silver that has been found is in the form of coins, for the study of ornaments and hacksilver,[22] although both interesting and rewarding, can rarely lead to conclusions so precise as those that may reasonably be based on numismatic evidence. It is, in fact, the coins that provide the only sure chronological basis for the study of the hoarded material. The general character of this coin evidence can be illustrated by two examples: one a hoard of the ninth century containing only Kufic coins, found in Uppland, the other a hoard of hacksilver and coins from many parts of western Europe as well as from the Muslim world, deposited about two centuries later in Gotland.

In 1873 a collection of 117 whole coins and 22 coin fragments was discovered at Fittja in Uppland.[23] The total number of coins represented in this hoard is 136, coming from many parts of the Muslim world and ranging in date from 613 to 863. The earliest coin is pre-Muslim, a drachma struck by the Sassanid king Chosroes II. Another coin is similar but has a bilingual inscription, Pehlevi and Arabic, showing that it was issued after the Arab conquest of this kingdom in 641. All the other coins are of the eighth and ninth centuries. Nine were struck for Umayyad caliphs between 705 and 746 at various

mints between Damascus and Isfahan and eighty-six were
struck between 751 and 853 by their successors, the Abbasid
caliphs. These Abbasid coins were minted in many parts of
the Caliphate, including Egypt and Africa, but most were
minted in the central parts, thirty-five coming from Baghdad
and twenty-four from *Muhammidijah*, an important town
south of the Caspian Sea. There is also a coin struck at Cordova
for an Umayyad caliph of Spain in 777. The remaining decipherable coins were all issued by the Tahirid rulers of
Khorasan. In 822 Tahir I proclaimed himself independent
ruler of Khorasan, a province over which he had earlier been
appointed governor by the caliph. He died later that year but
his son succeeded him as virtually independent ruler of
Khorasan and Transoxania, acknowledging only the nominal
overlordship of the caliphs of Baghdad and his dynasty lasted
until about 873. Some fourteen coins in the Fittja hoard were
struck between 821 and 864 for members of this dynasty at such
places as Bukhara, Merv, Samarkand, and Tashkent. The latest
coins in the hoard come, therefore, not from the heart of the
Abbasid Caliphate but from the rebellious north-eastern
provinces. The Fittja hoard is, in this, typical of the ninth-
century hoards of Scandinavia.

The minting place of the latest coins in hoards is significant
for they provide the best clue to the area from which the
coins were exported.[24] At this period coins of the Caliphate
were legal tender everywhere in it irrespective of the mint at
which they were struck. The coins in circulation in any part
of the Muslim world might include some struck in the
most distant provinces as well as those produced locally.
Coins of Damascus might be found in Samarkand, just as
coins struck at Tashkent might be used in Baghdad. The
extraordinary mixture of Kufic coins in the Swedish hoards is
therefore not surprising; whatever region or regions exported
them they were likely to be a mixed collection. But the coins
minted locally in the exporting region or regions were likely
to be more recent than those minted elsewhere in the Caliphate.
The fact that the mid-ninth-century hoards found in Sweden,
like that from Fittja, have as their latest coins those struck by
the Tahirids in such mints as Merv, Samarkand and Tashkent

suggests that it was from this area that the silver was exported ultimately to the north, which means that this silver probably reached Scandinavia by the caravan route from Khiva south of the Aral Sea to Bulghar on the Volga.

This ninth-century hoard from mainland Sweden may be compared with one deposited about two centuries later in Gotland. It was found in 1952 under a large stone at a place called Gandarve, and contained a small quantity (167 gr.) of hacksilver of no particular interest and 693 coins and coin fragments.[25] The coins represented in this hoard came from many parts of the world. Fifteen were from the Caliphate, including 3 copies, 432 from Germany, 2 from Bohemia, 212 from England, 2 from Dublin, 9 from Denmark and 21 are copies of Anglo-Saxon coins that were probably made in Scandinavia. The few Kufic coins are remarkably varied. The earliest is a fragment of a seventh-century coin, either struck for Chosroes II or copied after the Arab conquest, and the latest coins were struck in Iraq, probably at Mosul, by the Uqailid dynasty between 996 and 1003. Here, as at Fittja, most Kufic coins are of the Abbasid caliphs; there are five or six of these struck between 772 and 938 at Basra and al-Rahbah. There are no Tahirid coins, their place being taken by two coins struck in 909 and 938 at Tashkent and Samarkand by the Samanids, a dynasty that established its authority over the area that had been ruled by Tahir I. The German and English coins at Gandarve are also very varied. Most German mints that were operating in the first half of the eleventh century are represented and the English coins come from thirty-nine mints and were struck between 979 and 1046. The thirty coins that were probably minted in Scandinavia mostly show strong English influence but two of the Danish ones, in contrast, show Byzantine influence. The date the hoard was deposited is suggested by the German and English coins. The most recent German coins were struck at Metz and Trier in or after 1047 and the most recent English coins are of a type issued between 1046 and 1049. The absence of the next English issue and of certain coins commonly found in Scandinavia that were minted at Mainz and Corvey in 1051 suggests that the hoard was deposited sometime between 1047 and 1050.

The interpretation of such coin hoards depends, in the first place, on the identification of the coins themselves; when were they issued, by whom and where? The issuing authority is generally clear, although there is sometimes doubt, especially with barbaric copies, and the mint is often indicated. The main problem is to determine the date of issue of the west European coins. Arabic coins are, fortunately, dated after the *Hijra*, the 'emigration' of Mohammed from Mecca to Medina that took place, according to Christian reckoning in 622, but western coins are not so helpful. It was for long possible to date these Christian coins only broadly, by the reign of the ruler in whose name they were struck. The most recent English coins at Gandarve, for example, are of Edward the Confessor and must therefore be of the period 1042–65. Fortunately for the historian of the Viking period, recent work on these coins has revolutionised our knowledge of the English currency and it is now possible to date many of these coins within much narrower limits. It has, in fact, been demonstrated that at the end of Edgar's reign, probably in 973, there was a major reform of the English coinage and that thereafter new types were issued from time to time. The first new types were issued at intervals of six years but later they were changed more frequently.[26] The different types of coin have, of course, long been known; what is new is the recognition that they were issued in a sequence. It has been shown, for example, that the ten types of Edward the Confessor were issued at intervals of two or three years. These changes of type did not mean simply that new coins were added to the stock of old coins in circulation. To judge by the evidence of English hoards, the old types tended to disappear from circulation and it is probable that some time after the issue of a new type, the preceding type was demonetised. There is no evidence to show that the old types were officially called in and reminted[26a] but it is probable that after a change of type the old coins acquired by the king's government in taxes and renders of various kinds would have been reminted in the new type.

The English coin hoards containing this reformed currency show how effective the control was. At least thirteen hoards containing this coinage have been found that were, to judge by the dates of the most recent coins in each case, deposited between about 975 and about 1042, in areas then under the authority of English Kings.[27] In none of these hoards are more than two coin types present and eight of them are 'single-type' hoards. Had the changes in type only been partly effective, and coins of old types remained in circulation, the hoards of the period might reasonably be expected to contain a greater variety of coin types. Such strict control had powerful motives, of which the Crown's profit was not the least. According to Domesday Book, in the middle of the eleventh century each of the seven moneyers of Hereford paid 38 shillings every time the dies were changed.[28] It was moreover the Old English custom to alter the weight standard from time to time; it was only with the Norman Conquest that a standard-weight penny was introduced and it was this that was distinguished as 'sterling'.[29] These changes of weight meant that the amount of silver being paid out by the government, for example as *heregeld*, could be adjusted and the crown apparently compensated itself for any consequent loss of revenue by demanding at least some of its dues at the rate of 20 pence for 16.[29a] The variation in weight could also work to the advantage of the English government when converting foreign silver, brought by merchants, into English coin.

The recognition of the sequence of English coin types after 973 has allowed far closer dating of English coins than was formerly thought possible. The date of the latest coins in a hoard can be determined within limits of at most six years, and the most recent English coins at Gandarve are seen to be of the period 1046–8. It is also possible to study the chronological structure of hoards containing English coins far more closely than when dating could only be broadly by reigns. For example, the 212 English coins found at Gandarve may all be dated by their types and the composition is seen to be as opposite.[30]

Over half the English coins in this hoard were minted after 1023, that is after the last payment of tribute to Danish raiders which, according to the Anglo-Saxon Chronicle, took place in 1018. It is not surprising that English coins continued to reach Scandinavia for many years after this, for both Cnut

Type	*Approximate period of each type*	*Number of coins of each type*
Ethelred, 978–1016		
First Hand	979–85	1
Second Hand	985–91	1
Crux	991–97	13
Long Cross	997–1003	29
Radiate Helmet	1003–1009	9
Last Small Cross	1009–1016	19
Cnut, 1016–1035		
Quatrefoil	1017–23	36
Pointed Helmet	1023–29	55
Short Cross	1029–35	27
Interregnum		
Jewel Cross	1035–37	7
Harold I, 1037–1040		
Fleur de Lys	1037–40	5
Harthacnut, 1040–1042		
Arm and Sceptre	1040–42	3
Edward the Confessor, 1042–1066		
Pax	1042–44	3
Radiate	1044–46	2
Trefoil Quadrilateral	1046–48	2
	Total	212

and his sons retained the services of Scandinavian mercenaries who were paid with money raised in England by a tax called the *heregeld*, the army tax. This tax continued to be levied by Edward the Confessor until in 1051 the last of these Scandinavian mercenaries was sent home.[31] Hoards like that found at Gandarve are effective reminders that not all the English coins in Scandinavia were tribute extorted by raiders; many of them are from the pay of soldiers in the service of English kings. The association between the levying of *heregeld* and the occurrence of English coins in Scandinavia is remarkably close.

With the ending of this tax, the number of English coins in Scandinavian hoards was drastically reduced, and after 1051 there was only a trickle of English coins into Scandinavia.[32]

The English not only prevented the circulation of their own old coins, they also re-minted any coins that might be imported from abroad. It had been English policy long before the reforms of Edgar not to permit the circulation of foreign silver and the success with which this policy was enforced is indicated by the rarity of such foreign coins in English hoards. Foreign coins minted in the tenth and eleventh centuries are found in the British Isles but not in the areas under the control of English kings.[33] The fact that foreign coins were not legal tender in England and that the English exercised a very effective control over the currency means that English hoards are a very unreliable guide to the source of the silver used in English coins. The absence of Kufic coins, for example, from tenth century hoards in Wessex and Mercia cannot be taken to prove that such coins were not imported. Indeed, for reasons to be discussed below it seems very likely that Kufic coins were imported into England in the late ninth and early tenth centuries, but that all this silver was re-minted.[34] There is, unfortunately, little hope that the provenance of the silver can be determined by the detection of trace elements in proportions that can be recognised as characteristic of any particular source. Apart from the problems of analysis, it appears that the proportion of at least some of these trace elements is much affected by the methods of mining and the processes of refining and re-smelting the silver.[35]

Other European currencies were not managed so thoroughly as the English, nor were they so centralised, but modern studies are allowing many of these Continental issues to be dated with much greater precision than was formerly thought possible. It is, for example, studies of this kind that have allowed the relatively close dating of the latest German coins in the Gandarve hoard.

The work of identifying and dating the coins of the Viking period whether they are Arabic, German, English or Scandinavian, is the essential basis for the study of the Scandinavian material. Much remains to be done but already enough is known to show how critically important this numismatic evidence is for the study of the period.[36] Some characteristics of the material are already clear and must be taken into account in any discussion of the processes at work at that time. Future work will certainly make a far more refined analysis of coin distributions and of hoards possible but is unlikely to disrupt the main outlines of the pattern that can already be observed. New coin hoards will certainly be discovered but these are unlikely to invalidate the main hypotheses for, to judge by past experience, new hoards tend to fit into the patterns already established.

One of the most interesting and remarkable characteristics of the Scandinavian material is the scarcity of ninth-century western European coins. This was a century of raids on western Europe, large areas of which had long been familiar with coin. According to contemporary chroniclers the raiders extorted large sums of tribute as well as taking much plunder. In 845 Charles the Bald is reported to have paid £7,000 of silver to Viking raiders as the price of freeing the Seine valley; in the course of 861 the Franks paid two sums reported as £5,000 of silver and £6,000 of gold and silver and in 877 the Seine Normans were bought off with £5,000 of silver. These are only a few of the payments recorded in contemporary Frankish sources and the total for the period has been worked out as 685 lb. of gold and 43,042 lb. of silver. These chronicles may exaggerate but there is no reason to doubt that large sums were paid to Scandinavian raiders at this time.[37] The same sort of thing was happening in England although the English Chronicle does not give the same details. In 865 the people of Kent made peace with raiders and promised them tribute but, 'the raiders stole away and continued raiding' because, according to Asser, 'they knew that they would seize more money by secret plunder than by peace'.[38] In the light of these contemporary sources the rarity of English and Frankish coins of the ninth century in Scandinavia is extraordinary. In the whole of Scandinavia there are only 125 English and Frankish coins of the ninth century, distributed in some fifty finds, many of which are certainly much later deposits.[39] One explanation for this scarcity of English and Frankish coins at a time when, by all accounts, large sums were being extorted, is that the early raiders were unused to coin and therefore quickly converted any coins they may have acquired into ornaments or ingots. This seems very improbable. If the raiders were only interested in the weight of their silver, it would not matter much to them if the silver was coined or bullion.

There is, in any case, ample evidence to suggest that the ninth-century Scandinavians had no aversion to coin. While western European coins of the ninth century are rare in Scandinavia, Arabic coins are not. These are, it is true, found in Gotland and eastern Sweden rather than in Norway and Denmark, but the reaction of the Swedes and the Gotlanders to the coins they acquired is at least a clue to the probable reaction of the Danes and Norwegians. If the Swedes used and hoarded Kufic coins, Danes and Norwegians are likely at the same time to have used and hoarded any Frankish and English coins they might have acquired. There are, in fact a few ninth-century hoards of Kufic coins in western Scandinavia; their relative scarcity in Norway and Denmark compared with eastern Scandinavia is due, not to the custom of melting down coins, but to the fact that very few reached western Scandinavia at this time.[40] It was only at the end of the ninth century that these oriental coins reached western Scandinavia in large quantities. The explanation for the similar scarcity of European coins at that time must similarly be that very few coins reached Scandinavia. The rarity of English and Frankish coins is, in fact, only surprising if it is assumed that the tribute levied by the raiders was taken back to Scandinavia. There is, however, good reason to believe that, by the end of the ninth century, the raiders did not take their winnings home, but rather used them as a sort of capital with which to settle. The Anglo-Saxon Chronicle describes, in 896, how Hæsten's army broke up, 'the Danish army divided, one force going into East Anglia and one into Northumbria; and those that were moneyless got themselves ships and went south across the sea to the Seine'.[41] The implication is clearly that those who settled in East Anglia and Northumbria had money; it was to win such wealth that they had joined the raiding band, but having won it they did not return home to Denmark, they settled. It was just at this time that the Viking rulers of York started issuing a silver coinage[42] and it may well be that some of the silver used in these coins had been accumulated in the preceding years by those raiders who were allowed, apparently at a price, to settle in the north of England alongside the first generation of Scandinavian colonists. As one leading authority has remarked,[43] 'the whole flavour of this York coinage of the last years of the ninth century is Carolingian and not English' and it seems likely that the same is true of the metal from which the coins were made. The coin hoards of the late ninth and early tenth century found in those parts of Britain that were then under Scandinavian control contain a number of Carolingian coins and some of these had doubtless been stolen or extorted as tribute during the Viking raids on the Continent.[44] The largest of all these hoards was deposited early in the tenth century at Cuerdale near Preston in Lancashire. It contained over 7,000 silver coins, mostly of Viking issues, but 1,000 came from Frankia.[45] Before the Danes began to winter in England their bases were not in Scandinavia but on the Continent, especially in Frisia and it is possible that some of the ninth-century hoards found in Frisia[46] are of the same type as the later hoard from Cuerdale and represent the accumulated wealth of an earlier generation of Viking raiders. The absence of English coins in these hoards is a difficulty, but the objection is not insuperable. We have no means of telling how many English coins we should expect to find in the hoarded wealth of the Danish Vikings in the first two decades of their attacks on England; it is only in the second half of the century, after 865, that we can be confident that the Vikings were gathering English coins in any quantity and by then their bases were in Britain, where we also find their hoards.[47] If the raids are seen as a preliminary to settlement, the contrast between the evidence of the chronicles and that of the coin hoards no longer seems inexplicable.

The study of general coin distributions is interesting and rewarding, but the numismatic evidence is most valuable when the coins are found and can be studied, in hoards. Unfortunately many hoards have been broken up, for until relatively recently the interest was not in the hoard so much as in the individual coins, and museums were prepared to exchange or sell coins without keeping an adequate record of the original composition of the hoards from which they came. When, however, the structure of a hoard is known, either because it was carefully recorded, or better still because the hoard is preserved intact, it is possible to learn far more than is conceivable from the individual coins themselves. For one thing, even when a coin can be dated, this provides only one limit; a coin found loose may have been dropped at any time after its issue, and even when found in graves there is a wide margin of chronological uncertainty. It is, however, possible in many cases to determine the date a hoard was deposited within fairly close limits. It is, for example, important to note that some of the apparently ninth-century European coins found in Scandinavia were in eleventh-century hoards.[48] Moreover, hoards often give a reliable indication of the general character of the coin stock in circulation at the time of deposit, and by comparing hoards from different periods it is possible to study changes in the coin stock in an area, just as by comparing hoards from different areas it is possible to demonstrate the routes along which coins were carried. The evidence of the coin hoards is therefore critically important for the study of the Viking period.

Hoards are valuable in the first place because their date of deposit can be determined within fairly close limits. One date limit is obvious: a hoard cannot be older than its latest coin. The other limit depends on the time the latest coin in the hoard was in circulation. Sometimes the signs of wear, or lack of them, may be suggestive, as in the Hon hoard, but this can never be a very reliable test. A coin might be kept a long time with little wear or it might have a very rough handling and quickly look battered. Fortunately there is no need to depend on such unreliable and inexact indications as there are good reasons for believing that Viking period hoards in general were deposited soon after the date of the latest coins in them. The argument is, briefly, that hoards generally represent the coins in circulation in the area and at the time of deposit and that the latest coin in a hoard is therefore likely to be the latest coin available for hoarding. As coins seem to have reached Scandinavia fairly soon after they were minted, the date of the latest coin in a hoard is generally a reliable guide to the date of deposit.

The representative character of most hoards is shown by the remarkable similarity of hoards found in the same area with end coins of the same period. Professor Bolin's analysis of five Russian hoards of Kufic coins in which the latest coins were of the period 850–75 has revealed that the proportion of coins of the same age, or minted in the same regions of the Caliphate, is very much the same in all of them.[49] Figure 17*a* and *b* shows the chronological composition of two of these hoards, one relatively large, over 200 coins, the other small, only 32 coins; both show very similar characteristics and both correspond closely to the curve for all five of these hoards in Figure 17*c*. The similarity of the curves in these graphs means that the chronological composition of all these hoards is very similar and that each hoard could be taken as representative of the others. The only satisfactory explanation for such similarities is that the coins for all these hoards were drawn from a common stock available for hoarding in Russia at the time they were hidden, and that they are all therefore representative of that coin stock.

This is not a peculiarity of Russian hoards. Much the same thing can be observed in hoards from other areas. The composition, shown in Figure 18*a* of the Fittja hoard from Uppland, with an end date of 863–4, is clearly very similar to the chronological composition of four other Swedish hoards with end coins of the period 857–68, shown in Figure 18*b* on the basis of Professor Bolin's analysis.[50] Nor is this similarity between hoards only found in the ninth century; other examples could be given from other periods and all support the argument that hoards, in general, represent the stock of coins available for hoarding. The representative character of Scandinavian hoards in the late tenth and eleventh centuries, when coins were imported from many areas, is further shown by the fact that no hoards consist exclusively of coins from one area; all hoards are mixed, thus showing that the available coins were dispersed widely and so generally available for hoarding. This dispersal can also be seen in the distribution of Byzantine coins. Until 1946 only 410 Byzantine coins had been found in

Gotland but these were spread through the coin material of
the island and were found in eighty-three hoards.[51] Only one
of these was large, the Oxarve hoard with ninety-eight Byzantine coins and six Byzantine coin fragments;[52] almost all the
others are in small groups of two or three. It would, of course,
be quite wrong to assume that any one hoard represents the
coin stock of its time, for there are some exceptional hoards,
such as that from Oxarve just mentioned, but most hoards
seem to reflect the general character of the coins current when
they were deposited.

In order to determine the date of deposit it is, therefore,
necessary to know how long coins took to reach the area of
deposit. With the purely Kufic hoards there is no means of
telling how long the delay may have been, but there are
indications in the middle of the tenth century that it is unlikely
to have been very great. The latest purely Kufic hoards in
Denmark are those from Bovlund and Rørdal in Jutland, in
which the latest coins are dated 942–54 and 961–70 respectively.[53] As German coins appear regularly in Danish
hoards after about 950,[54] the latest coins in these two hoards
are unlikely to have arrived in Jutland long after they were
struck. In Sweden the latest purely Kufic hoard contains a
coin dated 969–70 and similarly this cannot have been slow
in reaching the north, because other foreign coins play an
increasingly important part in Swedish hoards after that
year.[55]

When hoards contain coins from several areas it is possible
to compare the date of the latest representatives of each, and
in many cases these correspond quite closely. Such a correspondence may be seen in two of the hoards that have already
been mentioned: at Hon the latest Kufic coin was dated 848–9
and the most recent Byzantine coin was issued in about 852;
and at Gandarve the latest German and English coins were of
about the same date. There are many similar cases as may
be seen from the list of mid-tenth-century Danish hoards
opposite.[56]

The generally close correspondence between the dates of
the latest coins from widely separate areas circulating in Scandinavia suggests that they must all have reached Scandinavia

Name of Hoard	No. of coins	Date of the latest coins		
		Kufic	German	English
Terslev	1,751	940–4	936–62	949–52
Rø, Bornholm	36	954	936–73	—
Jyndevad, S. Jutland	146	954–5	936–73	946–55
Gravlev	263	952	936–73	—
Sejrø	143	942	953–65	946–55
Aalborg Klostermark	43	970	—	958–75
Tarup	112	965	962–73	—
Bødstrup	124	967	976–82	—
Kongens Udmark	124	968	965–91	—

fairly quickly. There is therefore no reason to doubt that in most cases the latest coin in a hoard is unlikely to be more than about three years earlier than the date of deposit, and in the eleventh century the time lag was even less.

Before the development of reliable banks men must often have concealed their hoarded wealth in secret places indoors, away from curious eyes. To hide such valuables out of doors was a risky business, only to be resorted to in case of great need as, for example, when marauding bands of robbers threatened or when the owner had to leave his home for a while. These hoards were buried for safety, and only those that were not recovered by their owners have been left for discovery in modern times. They are more likely to have been left unrecovered in times of trouble and there is some correspondence between concentrations of hoards and local disturbances. This is well established for historical times both in Scandinavia and elsewhere and one explanation for the large number of hoards from certain periods seems to be that those were unusually disordered. It has long been recognised that in Norway there are many hoards from the disturbed reigns of Olaf Tryggvason (died 1000), St. Olaf (died 1030) and Harald Hardrada (1046–66) while there are few from the more peaceful reign of Magnus the Good (1035–

47).[57] Similarly in Denmark there are many hoards datable to the period 1050–65 when there was extensive fighting between Harald and Svein Estrithson[58] The same is true of England: the reign of Edgar has yielded very few hoards and the five years that saw the Norman Conquest, 1065–70, produced more hoards than the preceding five decades.[59] Unfortunately these concentrations of hoards cannot be taken as indications of disorder, for some of them, and we can never know how many, were buried by men who failed to return from journeys. The little group of three hoards deposited about 1070 in the Swedish province of Småland, where such hoards are normally rare, may, therefore, indicate some local disturbance or an unsuccessful expedition recruited from that region.[59a] Nor can the occurrence of hoards be used as a guide to the prosperity of different areas or periods. Men with many valuables may have left few hoards if few were concealed, or most were recovered by their owners. Some areas may have been especially vulnerable to attack and so show relatively more hoards than sheltered regions.[60] This may partly explain the concentration of hoards along the coasts and inland waterways of Scandinavia, but it should be recognised that it was in the same areas that the bulk of the population was to be found. The distribution of rune stones in Sweden, by and large of the eleventh century, gives a reasonably reliable indication of the areas then settled and the correspondence between the distributions of rune stones and of hoards of treasure is very close, as may be seen by comparing Figures 2 and 6.

The discovery of a relatively large number of hoards from a particular period may indicate a period of unrest or of great external activity. The hoards of Gotland have been studied more systematically than those of any other area and it has been discovered that although there are at least two hoards from every decade from 840 to 1100, there were some periods when hoards are particularly frequent. One such concentration is in the decade after 860 and there is an even more striking one in the middle years of the tenth century. In the decade 940–9 there are at least nine hoards of more than twenty-five coins and in the following decade there were twice as many.[61] After this the number of hoards declines until the end of the century when there is a remarkable increase, and the number deposited in the first half of the eleventh century is much larger than at any other time, suggesting that this was either a very disturbed time in Gotland or that the Gotlanders were then very active overseas and not always successful.

With remarkably few exceptions the coin material of Scandinavia from the beginning of the ninth century to the middle of the tenth was entirely Kufic. The rarity of western European coins at that time has been mentioned and Byzantine coins were even rarer.[62] The most numerous non-Kufic coins, having legends in Pehlevi, were struck by the Sassanid rulers of Persia and were imported along with the Muslim

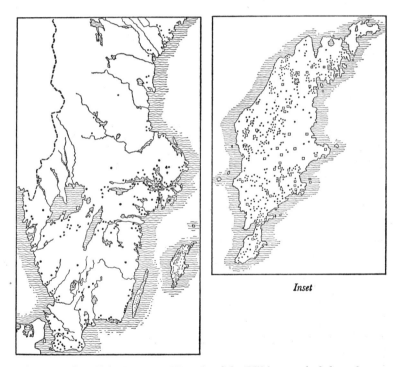

Inset

Figure 6   Swedish Treasure Hoards of the Viking period, based on a map prepared by Professor Mårten Stenberger for Statens Historiska Museum, Stockholm. In the inset map of Gotland, based on the map in *SG* ii, the gold hoards are marked by squares.

silver. The occurrence of these Pehlevi coins in Scandinavia does not, of course, mean that there were contacts between the Baltic and Persia as early as the seventh century. The stream of Muslim silver into Scandinavia, in fact, only began in the early ninth century. There are a few hoards that appear to be very early indeed, two having end coins dated 780 and 793,[63] but these are all small and little weight ought to be put on them. To judge by early ninth-century Russian hoards the bulk of the coins then in circulation were of the period 760–800 and the chance of small hoards having misleadingly early end dates is greater at this period than at any other.[64] By the early ninth century Muslim silver was undoubtedly available for hoarding in both Russia and the Baltic. The quantities were probably small and the average size of the Gotlandic hoards in the first half of the ninth century is very small. The coins circulating in Scandinavia were very similar to those in Russia at the same time. Professor Bolin has convincingly demonstrated that the composition of the Russian hoards in the third quarter of the ninth century is almost identical with the contemporary Swedish hoards.[65] The chronological composition of the hoards of that period from the two areas may be compared in Figures 17*c* and 18*b*. The two groups of hoards are also very much alike in the provenance of the coins, for example 56·3 per cent. of the Russian coins in these hoards were struck at mints in Iraq, while 54·1 per cent. of the Swedish coins came from that area and the proportions from other areas are also almost the same. It is clear that the coins circulating in Sweden at that time, and therefore available for hoarding, were of the same age and provenance as those in Russia. The coin stock of both areas was at that time identical. This does not, however, mean that the Russian coin stock was itself the source of the coins hoarded in Sweden. Had the coins been exported from the Caliphate to Russia and thence to Sweden, significant differences might be expected between the coins circulating in the two areas. The similarity between the Swedish and the Russian material could only be preserved, in that case, if the replacements reaching Russia from the Caliphate were identical with those being exported to Scandinavia. In any case the Russian hoards of Figure 17*c* do not seem to have been imported from the Caliphate by the same route as the contemporary Swedish hoards. The regions exporting coins from the Caliphate are indicated not by the largest number of coins in a hoard but by the latest coins, for the coins minted in or near the exporting region are likely to be more recent than those from distant provinces.[66] Professor Bolin has shown that in this respect the Russian hoards of the ninth century fall into two groups.[67] In one group the most recent coins were minted in regions neighbouring the Caucasus and the southern shores of the Caspian Sea, while the latest coins in the other are from the distant north-eastern provinces and were struck at such mints as Balkh, Bukhara, Merv, Samarkand and Tashkent. This suggests that this Muslim silver reached Russia by two routes, one in the south-east, through the Khaganate of the Khazars on the lower reaches of the River Don, the other along the caravan route from Khiva on the Oxus, south of the Aral Sea, across to the territory of Bulghar on the middle reaches of the River Volga. In the Russian hoards of the period 850–75, however, the more southerly route is indicated. The latest coins in the five hoards were struck in Isfahan, Basra, Armenia, Baghdad and Merv and the last, a hoard from Novgorod, fits as well with the Swedish material as with the more southerly Russian. Had the contemporary Swedish material been derived generally from the coins circulating in Russia, the latest coins in the hoards there would either have been from the same areas, or not particularly distinctive. In fact the latest coins in many Swedish hoards of the mid-ninth century were struck at such places as Merv, Bukhara, Samarkand and Tashkent, by the Tahirid dynasty that ruled this area, which suggests that, at that time, the northerly route by the Volga was more important for Scandinavia.[68] This does not necessarily mean that coins imported into Russia by the more southerly route never reached Scandinavia, but it does show that enough later coins were imported by the northern route to leave their mark on the hoards. As the general composition of hoards in both areas is so similar, the general character of the coins being exported from the Caliphate by both routes must have been very much the same. The hoards in both Sweden and Russia reflect the character of the coins circulating in the Caliphate, and the similarity of the coins hoarded in both areas is, therefore, no reason for assuming that the Swedish coins came from the general Russian coin stock rather than direct from the Volga.

Hoards with end coins earlier than 890 are concentrated in the eastern parts of Scandinavia. There are at least thirty-two in Gotland containing between them over 4,000 whole or fragmentary coins. Other hoards are found scattered along the coastlands of the eastern Baltic (Hälsingland, Gästrikland, Uppland (two), Södermanland, Öland, Åland (at least two), Österbotten, Estoniya, Livoniya, and the largest of all in Småland).[69] In contrast, finds of this period from the western parts of Scandinavia are few and small. The only ninth-century hoard in western Sweden is Kettilstorp, and none is found in Skåne until the tenth century. There are only two in Denmark, one of them possibly deposited *c.* 900, another two in Norway and there are two small finds from Rantrum in Sleswig. There are two possible explanations for this distribution of ninth-century Kufic hoards. Either the coins were, by and large, confined to the eastern part of Scandinavia, or they were generally dispersed but seem more common in the east because more hoards have been found there. It is true that hoards are an indication of disorder rather than of wealth and the absence of Kufic hoards in western Scandinavia may mean that this was a time of peace and prosperity there, but this is unlikely as far as Denmark is concerned. Contemporary Frankish sources indicate that Denmark was then very disturbed and the evidence of other hoards confirms this impression. Dr. Skovmand lists thirteen hoards in Denmark that he considers to be of the ninth century, only one of which contained any coins, and there are other hoards from neighbouring areas.[70] There seems to have been no reluctance to hoard silver at that time in Denmark and the absence of Kufic coins suggests that there were few to be hoarded. This is confirmed by the grave finds. Had there been an abundance of ninth-century Kufic coins in western Scandinavia more might have been expected in graves; many Birka graves contained Kufic coins minted before 890.[71] The absence of such finds in Denmark may be explained by the general poverty of the grave finds there, but this hardly applies to Norway where the graves are numerous and richly furnished, but where only three have been discovered containing such coins.[72] The conclusion must be that Kufic coins were relatively rare in western Scandinavia; that the coins imported into the eastern Baltic tended to stay there. The coin stock was continuously renewed by new imports, as is shown by the tendency for hoards of the period 820–70 to have Tahirids as their latest coins, but few coins left the area. Some were hoarded, and no doubt many were converted into bullion or ornaments, but few were in their turn exported.

In the tenth century, Kufic hoards are spread further afield, although the main concentrations are still in the eastern Baltic. There are nineteen hoards in Denmark from the period 890–970 and these contain between them over 2,500 coins and it is in this period that Kufic coins are found furthest north.[73] They are also found in the British Isles, not, of course, in the areas under the control of the English kings but in the peripheral areas where coins of many kinds circulated without restriction.[74] Kufic coins are not only widely dispersed in this period, the hoards are larger. This is the period of the largest Kufic hoards: in Gotland there are six with more than 1,000 coins each,[75] and two of these have more than 2,000. Denmark's largest hoard of Kufic coins is from Terslev with 1,708 of them, the latest dated 944,[76] and the largest Norwegian hoards belong to the period 925–55.[77]

At the same time there are important changes in the composition of the hoarded material. In the ninth century most coins were issued by the Caliphs whether Umayyads or Abbasids, but in the period after 890 such coins are relatively rare. Most of the coins in tenth-century hoards were struck by the Samanids, the dynasty that was established by the end of the ninth century in the north-eastern parts of the Muslim world, the area formerly ruled by the Tahirids. Samanid coins begin to appear in Swedish hoards shortly after 890 and very soon dominate the find material. At the same time, to judge by the latest coins in the Russian hoards, the southerly route seems to have ceased to have any importance.[78] In the tenth century the Russian coin material, like the Scandinavian, was predominantly Samanid and the latest coins in hoards indicate that they were imported by the Volga route, direct from the Samanid provinces. The source of these increased imports of silver, and the reason for the preponderance of coins from the Samanid provinces, is that rich silver mines were being exploited in that area in the late ninth and early tenth centuries. Ever since the end of the eighth century silver had been mined at Tashkent but in the second half of the ninth century the fabulous mine of Pendjhir in Afghanistan was discovered and worked.[79]

This flood of Samanid silver into Russia and Scandinavia coincides with a very significant change in the character of both the Russian and the Scandinavian hoards. Whereas in the ninth century the coins hoarded had generally been relatively old at the time of deposit by the beginning of the tenth century they had become remarkably young. In a hoard with an end date as late as 882, buried in Poltava province, over 70 per cent. of the coins were minted earlier than 820, and this is very similar to the earlier ninth-century hoards, but in the sixteen tenth-century Russian hoards analysed by Professor Bolin only six have any coins minted before 889 and in five the percentage of these older coins is two or less. The only tenth-century Russian hoard with more than 2 per cent. of its coins from the period before 890 is from Pskov with an end coin of 905 and almost 90 per cent. of its coins were minted after 890.[80] This dramatic change in the character of the Russian hoards cannot be explained by the assumption that the new imports simply overwhelmed the old coins, for more trace of these older coins would then be expected. In Scandinavian hoards coins of the period before 890 continue to occur until the eleventh century, for example at Gandarve. The explanation for the almost complete disappearance of coins minted before 890 from the tenth-century Russian hoards must be that they were removed from circulation. There are three ways in which this could have happened; the old coins could have been hoarded, they could have been smelted to make ornaments or bullion or they could have been exported. Hoarding is an unsatisfactory explanation as the Russian hoards give no indication that there was a sufficiently massive hoarding of coins at the end of the ninth and beginning of the tenth centuries. Smelting would only be satisfactory as an explanation on the further assumption that relatively few, or no, coins were so treated before about 890 or later in the tenth century when older coins again form an important part of the Russian material.[81] The only satisfactory explanation for the disappearance from the Russian hoards of these coins of the ninth century and earlier is that at the end of the ninth century coins were being removed from circulation by being exported. Some were no doubt exported south, to Byzantium,[82] but more may well have been exported north to, or through, the Baltic. Professor Bolin's analysis of the tenth- and eleventh-century Russian hoards is given on page 224. It suggests that the large-scale coin exports of the late ninth century did not continue beyond the first three or four decades of the tenth.[83] The hoards at the beginning of the tenth century consisted almost entirely of coins minted in the three or four decades preceding the deposit, but later in the century the span of time represented by most hoards increased. If coin exports continued after about 940 they cannot have been on the same scale as those of the beginning of the century which so effectively removed the older coins from circulation, otherwise the process of removing older coins would have continued and hoards of the middle years of the century would have had much the same age structure as those deposited in the first decades.

Many of the early tenth-century Swedish hoards show a change similar to the Russian, but there the removal of coins minted before 890 does not seem to have been so complete. There are, indeed, some important Scandinavian hoards of the early tenth century with the characteristics of ninth-century hoards. Figure 19 shows the chronological composition of two of these, Stora Velinge in Gotland and Over Randlev in Denmark, and these curves may be compared with those given for earlier hoards in Figure 18. There is, nevertheless a clear tendency in the Scandinavian hoards for the older coins to disappear from circulation as they did in Russia. Figure 20*a* shows the chronological composition of five Gotlandic hoards deposited in the decade 930–9, in which only twenty-five coins, out of a total of 1,079, or 2·3 per cent., were minted before 890. As in Russia, most coins older than 890 have been removed from circulation and the explanation must be the same; they had been exported. Kufic coins were, after 890, more widely distributed in Scandinavia than hitherto, and there are good reasons for believing that they were also dispersed outside Scandinavia. It is in this period that they are found in the British Isles although not, of course, in the areas under the control of the English kings. Kufic coins found in the British Isles were of the period *c*. 870–950 which agrees well with the hypothesis that their export from the Baltic began about 890.[84]

Professor Bolin has drawn attention to the fact that in Scandinavian hoards deposited after the decade 930–9 the proportion of recent coins drops in a most remarkable manner.[85] The result is that throughout the century the majority of Kufic coins in Scandinavian hoards were of the period 890–930. This may be seen very clearly in Figure 20*b* and *c* in which Professor Bolin's analysis of the Gotlandic hoards in the decade 950–9 and in the period 978–1016 is depicted. The same phenomenon may be observed in hoards from elsewhere in Scandinavia and in Figure 21 the composition of three hoards from Norway, Sweden and Denmark is shown. There are, of course, exceptions such as the hoard from Uggårds, Gotland, in which the most recent coin was of 960 but which contained 101 coins later than 930 and only thirty that were older.[86] Professor Bolin's explanation for these ageing characteristics of most Scandinavian hoards of Kufic coins is that after about 930 the export of these coins from Scandinavia stopped, or was at least relatively restricted, and this explanation seems to be the only satisfactory one. New coins continued to reach Scandinavia until about 970, but not in large enough numbers to counterbalance the preponderance of coins from the first decades of the century. It is, of course, probable that fewer coins were being imported into Scandinavia after about 930, but after that the export must have been at least restricted or the proportion of older coins would have been reduced more quickly. The persistence of these older coins in the coin stock of Scandinavia must mean that relatively few were being removed from circulation and that the conditions which had removed most ninth-century coins from circulation no longer applied.

Professor Bolin has attempted to support this argument by the analogy of Russian hoards after about 970 which then begin to show similar ageing characteristics.[87] This change coincides with a remarkable drop in the number of Kufic coins reaching Scandinavia. So few Kufic coins of the period 965–83 are found in Scandinavian hoards that there must have been an almost complete cessation of imports by about 970. Bolin's argument is that the export of these coins from Russia to Scandinavia stopped at that time and that the Russian hoards then begin to show the same characteristics observed in Scandinavian hoards about forty years earlier. The analogy is not really satisfactory for two reasons. First, it is by no means certain that the Scandinavian coin material came from the coins circulating and being hoarded in central and southern Russia. In the ninth century the indications are that Kufic silver was reaching Scandinavia direct from the Volga, not through the coin stock of Russia generally.[88] Until a lot more is known about the tenth-century Russian hoards it would be dangerous to assume that the situation had changed. It is there-fore by no means certain that the cessation of imports of Kufic coins into Scandinavia is to be explained by the cessation of exports from Russia. The second reason for doubting the value of Bolin's analogy is that the changing composition of the Russian hoards after about 970 could as well be explained by declining imports of Kufic coins into Russia after that date. The reason for the decline was the rapidly developing silver crisis of Islam. In the late tenth and early eleventh centuries the exhaus-tion of the silver mines caused serious economic and political dislocations in the Muslim world, and at the beginning of the eleventh century the export of Kufic coins to Russia and the Baltic stopped altogether; the last Kufic coin found in Russia was struck in 1015.[89] Just as with the Scandinavian hoards after 930, the persistence of older coins in the Russian hoards long after 970 must mean that relatively few were then being exported, but the evidence hardly suggests that they were being exported in the decades before 970 either. Indeed, Professor Bolin's analysis of the hoards, given on page 224 would

agree very well with the hypothesis that the export of coins
from Russia, which must have been substantial after about 890,
had already declined before 950. The fact that this analogy
between the Scandinavian hoards after about 930 and the
Russian hoards after about 970 is unsatisfactory in no way
invalidates Bolin's main argument, that after 930 the export of
Kufic coins from Scandinavia must have been drastically
reduced, if not stopped altogether.

Kufic coins continued to reach the north until about 970, but
the remarkable scarcity of coins minted between 965 and 983,
which has already been mentioned, indicates that in or about
that year these imports stopped. The explanation may in part
be the silver crisis of Islam which led to an apparent drop in
the imports of Kufic coins into Russia, but there must have
been additional factors to explain the almost total cessation of
imports. The Volga route was still open for imports into
Russia,[90] and the failure of these coins to reach Scandinavia
must have been due to the interruption of the route between
the Volga and the Baltic, possibly by the activity in North
Russia of the Kiev princes.[91] This interruption was permanent. When, after 983, Kufic coins were again imported
into Scandinavia they came by a more westerly route, not
from the north-eastern parts of the Caliphate but from mints
in such central provinces as Syria, Iraq and Mesopotamia.[92]
Moreover, the Scandinavian hoards at the end of the century
are connected not with the hoards of Russia, but with those
found in the lands south of the Baltic, indicating that the import
route was then through Poland rather than Russia, along such
rivers as the Vistula.[93] This resumption of Kufic imports into
Scandinavia was not for long. The latest Kufic coins found in
Norway and Denmark were struck in the first two or three
years of the eleventh century, and the latest from Sweden
was of the Muslim year 401, that is A.D. 1012–13, only two
years before the last found in Russia. The silver crisis had
finally ended the great flood of silver that had for about two
centuries poured northwards from the Islamic lands.

Much of this silver reached the Baltic and the Scandinavians
had consequently developed a taste for the metal. After about
970 they had to turn elsewhere to satisfy their demands. Two

sources in particular were exploited when the supply of Muslim silver was reduced; Germany and England. From the middle of the tenth century an important source of silver in the Harz mountains was increasingly exploited, and many of the coins that were minted from this silver found their way into the Baltic. That the English were also rich in silver is suggested by the elaborate currency reform of Edgar that has already been described. Some of this English silver came from sources within the British Isles, and some may very well have come from Germany, but it is not unlikely that a part of the silver current in England at the end of the tenth century had earlier been imported in the form of Kufic coins from the Baltic. It was to England and Germany that the Scandinavians in the second half of the tenth century turned to supplement, and eventually replace, the dwindling supplies of Islamic silver and from the middle years of the tenth century English and German coins play an increasingly important part in the coin hoards of Scandinavia.[94] By the beginning of the eleventh century, when the supply of Islamic silver dried up completely, almost all the silver imported into the north came from England and Germany. The change in the character of the coin hoards is very clearly marked. In Gotland, for example, before 950 the hoards are almost exclusively Kufic; in the second half of the century German and English coins begin to appear and the hoards deposited in the period 990–1020 contained over 40 per cent. German coins and 10 per cent. English. In the following thirty years the proportion of Kufic coins declined to about 5 per cent., most of the coins being hoarded were then German, 56 per cent., or English, 30 per cent.

Some English coins were imported into Scandinavia before the reign of Ethelred; there are, for example, ten English coins among the 1,751 represented in the great hoard from Terslev in Denmark (Sjælland), which must have been deposited in the middle years of the tenth century,[95] but the main stream began with the raids on England at the end of the century. Among the causes for the renewed Viking attacks on England in Ethelred's reign must be reckoned the need to make up for the failing supply of Kufic silver. At first most English coins represent the tribute paid by the English but after Cnut's conquest of the country English coins continued to reach the North as the payments of the Scandinavian warriors retained by Cnut and his successors in their service. According to the Anglo-Saxon Chronicle Cnut maintained a fleet of sixteen ships which were paid at the rate of eight marks for each rowlock, and in 1040 the number seems to have been increased greatly by Harold's successor Harthacnut.[96] The hoard evidence of Scandinavia, such as that from Gandarve already mentioned, at least confirms the main outlines of the Chronicler's report. The connection between the English coins in Scandinavia and these mercenaries is shown by the remarkable drop in the number of English coins found in Scandinavia after 1051, the year in which, according to the Chronicle, Edward the Confessor disbanded the last of these Scandinavian mercenaries.[97] The German coins, which also reached Scandinavia in very large numbers, were in part the loot from raids which Germany also suffered, but in the eleventh century they were increasingly the product of the active Baltic trade in which Scandinavians, in particular Gotlanders, played such an important part.[98]

The Scandinavian coin hoards therefore consist very largely of Kufic, English and German coins, but not exclusively. There are, for example, some Byzantine coins, which are perhaps most remarkable for their scarcity. Only about 500 are known in the whole of Scandinavia and over 400 of these are from Gotland.[99] Less than ten are ninth-century coins and with the exception of the three gold solidi from Hon, the hoards in which they are found are of the tenth century or later; in Sweden the oldest hoard with Byzantine coins was deposited about 950. There are also native Scandinavian issues most of which were modelled on Carolingian types and produced in Denmark not, as was formerly thought, at Birka.[100] Their production apparently began early in the ninth century but it was only towards the end of the tenth century that they seem to have been struck in relatively large quantities. The earliest Swedish attempts of Olov Skötkonung and Anund Jacob (c. 996–1050) to issue a regular coinage failed, like the contemporary Russian one, because of the abundance of silver; but in Denmark and Norway coinages were firmly established in the eleventh century[101] and with their success, and the consequent restriction on the types of coin accepted as legal tender, the hoard material of Scandinavia, although still fascinating, ceases to be such a remarkable indication of the sources of wealth as the hoards of the Viking period are proving to be.

6. The Raids

MANY of the chroniclers and other writers of the Christian West agree in describing the Vikings as brutal and ruthless men who killed and destroyed with a barbarian ferocity in their search for loot and adventure. Abbo, in his poem on the siege of Paris by the Northmen in 885–6, describes these 'Wild Beasts' going 'by horse and foot through hills and fields, forests, open plains and villages, killing babies, children, young men, old men, fathers, sons and mothers. . . . They overthrow, they despoil, they destroy, they burn, they ravage, sinister cohort, fatal phalanx, cruel host.'[1] This is poetry, but a similar vocabulary is used by chroniclers. In 841 according to the Annals of St. Bertin, Danish pirates raided Rouen 'and carrying everywhere a fury of rapine, fire and sword, they gave up the city, the monks and the rest of the people to carnage and captivity. Some of the monasteries and other places near the Seine they devastated, the rest they left filled with terror, having received much money.'[2] These passages are typical of many contemporary descriptions of Viking atrocities. That they contain obvious exaggerations is not surprising for the writers were generally churchmen and the principal victims of Viking attacks were unlikely to have presented a balanced and impartial view of their tormentors. There is no reason to doubt the general reliability of their accounts of the movement of groups of Vikings but there is every reason to suspect exaggeration in their descriptions of the size and destructiveness of the raiding bands. Apart from the natural tendency to excuse defeats and magnify victories by exaggerating the force and violence of the enemy these church-men had a further incentive to represent the raids as an over-whelming disaster. In their eyes the raids were the judgement of God on the wickedness of a generation too ready to dis-regard its obligations to His Church. In their attempts to point the moral and call the laity to repentance they are unlikely to have minimised the severity of this Divinely ordained scourge.

There are, unfortunately, no contemporary Scandinavian sources with which the Christian accounts of Viking exploits may be compared and the general unanimity of contemporary complaints, supported as these seem to be by the well told tales of medieval Iceland, has stifled suspicions that the resulting picture is one sided. Modern writers have been far too ready to accept the estimates of contemporaries. Christopher Dawson's account of the ninth-century raids and their consequences is typical of many: 'Viking expeditions were organised on a large scale with fleets numbering hundreds of vessels and the western provinces of the Empire, together with England were systematically ravaged year by year. For nearly fifty years the invasions went on increasing in intensity until all the abbeys and towns of the west from Hamburg to Bordeaux had been put to the sack and great tracts of country, especially in the Netherlands and in north-western France were converted into desert.'[3] Not all scholars are so sweeping but there is a general tendency to accept contemporary descriptions of the size of Viking fleets. Sir Frank Stenton, for example, accepted the Anglo-Saxon Chronicle's estimate that in 851 Æthelwulf defeated a host of 350 ships' companies,[4] and Abbo's enumera-tion of the force besieging Paris in 885 as 40,000 men has been taken as reliable by many scholars, including the Norwegian archaeologist Haakon Shetelig and the French his-torian Henri Waquet.[5] This willingness to accept contemporary estimates of the size of Viking bands and the devastation they caused has unfortunately affected the interpretation of other evidence, both linguistic and archaeological, and so diminished its value as an independent check on the reliability of the written sources. The Scandinavian place-names of the Dane-law have been treated as proof of the dense and extensive settlement of many thousands of Danish warriors more because the 'armies' that settled are believed to have numbered many thousands than because the place-names themselves prove anything of the sort.[6] Similarly the archaeological evidence is too often interpreted in the light of the written sources; and objects of western European origin found in Scandinavia are normally treated as loot without qualification. When the archaeological evidence conflicts with that of the contemporary writings, as it does in the scarcity of ninth-century west European coins in Scandinavia,[7] the main efforts of historians and archaeologists alike seem to be to explain away the archaeological evidence rather than treat it as a welcome check on the historical. The general assumption of the overwhelming destructiveness of the Viking raids has moreover led some scholars to hold them responsible for happenings of which the causes are obscure. The absence of monasteries, for example, in early tenth-century England has been treated as though it were a consequence of the Viking raids in the ninth century.[8] This is an hypothesis to be examined on its merits, but, unless there is more to support it than an apparent coincidence in time and the belief that the Vikings were very destructive, it would obviously be improper to treat such an assumed 'consequence' of the raids as proof of their devastating character. Nevertheless the temptation to do so is great and many have succumbed to it.

The cumulative effect of contemporary complaints and later legends, the misinterpretations of linguistic and archaeological evidence, and ill-founded assumptions about the consequences of the raids has been that the overwhelming destructiveness of the Vikings is now widely accepted and treated by some as virtually axiomatic. The deeply rooted conviction that the Vikings came in large armies and spread little but desolation with unparalleled savagery seriously handicaps attempts to determine the true nature and extent of the Viking menace. In this chapter the evidence for the size of the Viking bands that campaigned in western Europe, and for the destruction that they caused will be examined in an attempt to determine, as far as possible, the scale and character of the Viking threat. Unless this can be done there is little hope of correctly interpreting either the activity of the Vikings or the reactions of their victims. The important question of the raiders' motives will be discussed in the last chapter of this book.

It is first necessary to consider the size of the raiding bands, and here there are problems of translation. The Anglo-Saxon Chronicle uses the term *here* to distinguish the raiding bands from the English *fyrd*. This word *here* is usually translated 'army' or 'host' but both are misleading. Modern armies are elaborate instruments of war numbering tens, if not hundreds of thousands of men and it is difficult to avoid thinking in such terms when using the word 'army'. 'Host' similarly implies a multitude. The inappropriateness of these translations is shown by a passage in the early seventh-century laws of Ine, preserved in a manuscript copied in the reign of Alfred: 'We call up to seven men thieves; from seven to thirty-five a band; above that it is a *here*.'[9] This definition is, admittedly, over 200 years earlier than the raids but it provides a more reliable clue to what men of the ninth century meant by the word *here* than the modern words 'army' or 'host'. If a *here* could be three dozen men, it would be as well not to call it an 'army'. Sometimes the *here* is distinguished in translations as the 'Danish Army' and when the Chronicle mentions a *micel here* it is sometimes rendered the 'Great Danish Army'. The use of this phrase as though it were the title of a particular *here* is unfortunate. The Chronicle certainly describes the raiders of 865 as a *micel here*, but in later years the same band is described more simply as *here*. *Micel here* is not a contemporary title to be translated 'Great Danish Army', but an indication by the writer that the *here* that arrived in 865 was, in his view, a big one.

Contemporary writers very rarely attempted to estimate the number of men taking part in a Viking raid. The Anglo-Saxon Chronicle never once gives the number of men in a raid and Continental sources only do so rarely. The number of men reported to have died in a battle is occasionally given but the size of Viking bands is more commonly indicated by the number of ships in a fleet.

The chroniclers' figures are interesting but before they are discussed it is necessary to emphasize how unreliable chroniclers' estimates of numbers can be. When, in the later Middle Ages, it is possible to compare chroniclers' reports with such independent and reliable evidence as muster rolls and accounts of pay, some of the exaggerations are seen to be absurd. In the campaign of 1340 the English forces were said to have numbered over 200,000 men when they cannot have been more than 4,000 at the most.[10] A force of some 3,000 men at the Battle of Najera in 1366 was inflated by Froissart to 27,000 men-at-arms and over 40,000 foot.[11] Not all exaggerations were on this splendid scale; some merely involved a doubling of the true figures and some were even less extravagant but without independent evidence it is difficult if not impossible to discover how big any exaggeration is. There is no universal factor by which chroniclers' figures can be divided to restore the truth. And as there is no reason to believe that chroniclers of the Viking period were any more reliable than those of the Hundred Years War, all figures given by contemporaries, whether of the size of an army, the number killed in a battle or the number of ships in a fleet, must be treated with the greatest caution.

The Anglo-Saxon Chronicle reports the number of ships in several Viking fleets before the end of the ninth century. The figures are most instructive and should be considered in detail:

789 3 ships of Northmen in Dorset
836 35 ships; 25 in some versions
840 33 ships; 34 in one version
843 35 ships
851 350 ships; 9 ships captured later that year
875 Alfred fights 7 ships and captures 1
877 120 ships lost at Swanage in a storm (or in a mist)
878 23 ships
882 Alfred fought 4 ships; two captured and two surrendered
885 Alfred's fleet encountered and captured 16 ships but was later defeated by 'a large naval force'

892 The *here* crossed from Boulogne, 'in one
journey, horses and all' in 200, 250 or 350
ships according to different versions of
the annal
892 Hæsten came with 80 ships
893 Northumbrian and East Anglian Danes collected
'some hundred ships and went south round the
coast'. One version adds 'and some 40 went
north around the coast'
896 6 ships
896 20 ships perished along the South Coast

The first reference is to one of the very early landings but it
may well be a reliably reported incident, as may the entries
for 836 and 840, which come, as has been explained, from a
section of the Chronicle that was probably based on an early
set of annals.[12] The entry for 843 is probably a duplicate of the
annal for 836, and the fleet of 851, the largest ever reported by
the Anglo-Saxon Chronicle, is from a section of the Chronicle
that was compiled about forty years later and the number
given, 350 ships, is hardly trustworthy.[13] It looks suspiciously
like the result of multiplying the largest fleet previously mentioned by ten, and it should in any case be treated as meaning
simply a large number of ships. The remaining ninth-century
fleets are all mentioned in what may be considered a contemporary part of the Chronicle and they fall naturally into two
groups; six small fleets of between four and twenty-three
ships and four large ones of more than eighty. The small fleets
are numbered exactly and in most cases additional details are
given that encourage confidence. The battle of 896 seems to
be described from an eyewitness account and the details
mentioned in connection with the fleets of 875, 882 and 885
all suggest that they were based on reports that may well have
been reliable. The contrast between these small fleets and
the large ones is striking. Apart from the forty ships that,
according to the Parker Chronicle, sailed north around the
island in 893, all are more than eighty ships and all are
expressed in round numbers while the numbers of the smaller
fleets are given exactly. The largest fleet of all, that crossed

from Boulogne in 892, is variously reported as 200, 250 and 350 ships, and although the figure of 350 from the Annals of St. Neots may reasonably be dismissed there is no good reason for preferring the 250 of the Parker Chronicle to the 200 given by three other versions. In any case these figures cannot be regarded as more than an attempt by the Chronicler to indicate large fleets. The figures given should not be treated as though they were an accurate enumeration. The evidence of the Anglo-Saxon Chronicle therefore suggests that while many Viking raids were undertaken by small fleets, like the six ships that in 896 did so much damage along the South Coast between the Isle of Wight and Devon, larger fleets were sometimes assembled. Unfortunately the figures given by the Chronicle for these larger fleets cannot be considered such accurate reports as for the smaller ones.

These fleets, large and small, must have included ships of various sizes. Abbo confessed that he did not count the small ships in his total of 700 vessels at the siege of Paris, and although the figure is ridiculous his remark underlines the fact, discussed above, that small ships were used as well as big ones.[14] It is also worth repeating that at least in the ninth century ships are never likely to have been much bigger than the Gokstad ship with its 32 oars.[15] When a raiding fleet arrived the presence of such smaller vessels must have added greatly to the appearance of numbers without adding much to the number of men being transported. There is also uncertainty about the number of men carried by a Viking ship. It has been suggested that the largest of them could carry as many as 100 men, but there is little evidence to support such an assumption. The ships of medieval Norway may sometimes have been manned by as many as five men per oar, but there is great difference between fighting battles in home waters and venturing across the sea to fight abroad. It is, indeed, doubtful if a ship like that found at Gokstad ever carried more than about thirty-two men on raiding voyages.[16] Certainly that was its complement of shields. That the maximum number of warriors in ninth-century Viking ships was of this order is, moreover, confirmed by the Anglo-Saxon Chronicle in its account of the battle of 896.[17] In that year nine of Alfred's ships fought against six of the enemy.

It was perhaps a small encounter but the Chronicler seems to have had any eye-witness account to go on and he describes the affair in detail. In this battle the crews of two Viking ships were killed and of a third only five escaped alive. The crews of the remaining three ships were fought on land until the tide enabled them to get away. The Danish dead are said to have been 120 which must represent the crews of two ships, all but five of the crew of another and an unknown number killed in the land fight. If the figure of 120 for the Danish dead is accepted, and it looks suspiciously like a doubling of the 62 who died on the English side, these ships can hardly have had crews of more than about thirty.

If horses were carried as well, as they were in 892, the total number of men per ship must obviously have been greatly reduced. The Bayeux Tapestry was embroidered shortly after the Norman Conquest, and in its depiction of William's fleet crossing the Channel the largest number of horses in any one vessel is ten. The Tapestry has a remarkable reputation for accuracy but it is, of course, in such details as these that least weight can be put on it. Nevertheless, its evidence agrees very well with what seems to be a trustworthy account of the shipment of mounted warriors in the twelfth century. According to William of Malmesbury, a contemporary keenly interested in these proceedings, in 1142 Robert earl of Gloucester recruited and embarked more than 300 but less than 400 horsemen on board fifty-two vessels for shipment to England.[18] The reputation of William of Malmesbury as a careful writer and the unusual precision of the details in this passage encourages confidence in the figures he gives and indicates an average of seven or eight horsemen per ship. Had the *micel here* that crossed from Boulogne in 892 consisted exclusively of warriors and their equipment, including horses, the Anglo-Saxon Chronicle's figure of 200 ships would, in the light of William of Malmesbury's evidence, have conveyed between 1,200 and 1,500 men, or rather more if the Parker Chronicle's figure of 250 ships is insisted upon. When allowance is made not only for the probable exaggeration of the Chronicler but also for the fact that this fleet brought women and children as well, the probability is that this *micel here*, the largest force ever described in detail in ninth-century English sources, was well under 1,000 men. There is nothing in the ninth-century sources to suggest that the Viking armies were ever larger than this and the probability is that most, if not all, the raiding bands were about three or four hundred men. This figure is suggested by the one detailed account of a battle against Vikings in Hincmar's Annals of St. Bertin.

In September 866 a party of 400 Normans and Bretons rode from the Loire to Le Mans and devastated it.[19] On their way back at a place called Brissarthe they encountered Robert the Strong, marquis of Neustria, Rannulf, count of Poitou and Geoffrey and Hervey, counts of Maine. In the ensuing battle, Robert died, Rannulf and Hervey were wounded, Rannulf mortally, and the Frankish force was defeated. Hincmar certainly detested Robert and Rannulf as disturbers of the wealth of the Church and he regarded their downfall as the judgement of God. He may even have exaggerated the adequacy of the Frankish forces, but he is hardly likely to have seriously minimised the Norman force. That an army of 400 could take and devastate Le Mans and then defeat a force commanded by some of the leading nobility of western Frankia suggests that behind all the exaggerations of the chronicles, the true size of the 'armies' or 'hosts' of Vikings that campaigned in Frankia as well as in England, were on the same scale.

Some scholars however, notably Ferdinand Lot and Sir Frank Stenton, have argued that these ninth-century armies ought to be numbered in thousands of men, and Lot suggested that they may sometimes have been about 5,000 strong.[20] There are many reasons, as well as those that have already been discussed, for rejecting such a figure. For one thing it is inconceivable that an army of that size could have been kept in being through one, let alone through ten winters. Sir Frank Stenton has himself commented on the remarkable achievement of William the Conqueror in maintaining an army in being for a few weeks.[21] This army, recruited for the invasion of England is believed by Stenton to have consisted of about 5,000 men, many of them landless knights 'who joined William for pay because they had heard of his generosity. The maintenance of such an army during weeks of idleness on Norman soil would have defeated most commanders of the age. . . .' Viking armies were, however, kept together for years at a time. William's achievement was indeed remarkable, but if the ninth-century Viking armies had really been as large as William's the achievement of their leaders in keeping them together, sometimes for more than a decade, would have been little short of fantastic. Apart from problems of control and discipline there would have been many difficulties to overcome in feeding and mounting such large numbers of men. The prolonged existence and occasional rapid movement of the Viking bands in the ninth and early tenth centuries would not have been possible had they contained more than a few hundred men at the most. Their successes were largely due to surprise and mobility and once they lost the initiative they might allow themselves to be bottled up on some island for long periods, and they then showed a strange reluctance to fight. Strange, that is, if it is believed that there were thousands of them.

The little that is known about ninth-century Viking encampments supports the argument that their armies were small. At first, Viking bases in England, as elsewhere, were on islands like Sheppey and Thanet in the Thames estuary but the raiders who arrived in 865 spent their winters at such places as York, Nottingham, Thetford, Repton, Cirencester and Wareham. Nowhere is there any suggestion that they fortified these places and it is possible that some already had defences. The first Viking fortification in England mentioned by the Chronicle was near Rochester in 885 but this was quickly abandoned and it was not until 892 that the main series begins. In the four years after 892 the raiders who then crossed to England built several fortifications. The first were at Milton Regis, near Sittingbourne, in Kent and at Appledore, on the edge of the marshes between Rye and Ashford. No trace of either survives. In the following year they constructed fortifications at Benfleet and Shoebury on the Essex coast and at Buttington on the Severn. Nothing survives at Benfleet or Buttington but at Shoebury there are traces of a large earthwork measuring about 500 yards from north-east to south-west.[22] The identification is not proved and the argument that 'as there are no

traces of other earthworks, it may be assumed that those fragments which remain on the coast are of Hæsten's construction'
is weakened by the complete absence of equivalent earthworks
at other places where the Chronicle states the Danes built
forts. Even so the Shoebury ramparts may well be part of the
camp of 893. The sea has eroded some away, but the size seems
to be similar to the contemporary English fortifications built
against the raiders. A camp on this scale would not have been
surprising for a base intended to shelter the women, ships and
property of the raiders during campaigns and, no doubt, between
campaigns the men and horses as well. In 894 these raiders
built two other fortifications, one by the River Lea about 20
miles above London, the other at Bridgnorth on the Severn,
but no trace of either has been identified. Before the development of modern earth moving techniques prehistoric banks and
ditches were not easily destroyed, and the difficulty of identifying these Viking forts suggests that they may not have been
very formidable.

Apart from Shoebury there is one other earthwork that has
been identified with a Viking fortification mentioned by the
Chronicle. In 917 the *here* 'came from Huntingdon and East
Anglia and made the fortress at Tempsford, and took up
quarters in it and built it and abandoned the other fortress at
Huntingdon, thinking that from Tempsford they would
reach more of the land with strife and hostility'. At Tempsford
there is an earthwork called Gannock's Castle, a small rectan-
gular construction with a rampart now about 11 or 12 feet
above the bottom of the outer ditch.[23] In one corner there is a
small circular mound about 20 feet across at the top, and the
enclosure measures about 120 by 84 feet within the ramparts.
Sir Cyril Fox has argued that as it would only provide defence
for about 270 men, allowing two men to each yard of rampart
'it certainly would not have accommodated the large army from
Huntingdon and from East Anglia mentioned in the Chronicle'.
There is, of course, no reason to think that the *here* mentioned
by the Chronicle was much larger than this, and there is
certainly no suggestion of a *micel here*. Whatever its size, it was
defeated later that year by the men of Bedford. Sir Cyril
Fox may well be right when he also argues that it is *a priori*

unlikely that citadels of this type would be built by the Danes, but its size is certainly no objection. If Gannock's Castle is, as Sir Cyril Fox suggests, a structure of the eleventh or twelfth centuries, the problem of locating the fortification of 917 remains.

The raiders often preferred to shelter, if they could, not behind fortifications but on islands where they could conveniently beach their boats. The camp at Benfleet was proved vulnerable in 893 and possibly because of this in 894 they used as their base, in the words of the Chronicle, 'an island called Mersea, which is out in the sea'. The Isle of Mersea is large and gives no clue to the size of the base, but at least one of the islands on which ninth-century raiders sheltered was fairly small. In 893 the *here* that had been at Appledore, came out and plundered the eastern parts of Wessex before being intercepted at Farnham. According to the Chronicle the Danes abandoned their booty and fled across the Thames to shelter on an island in the River Colne. The name of the island, or rather eyot, is given by Æthelweard as *Thornige*, and it has been identified by Sir Frank Stenton with the island of Thorney near Iver on the border of Buckinghamshire and Middlesex.[24] It is rhomboidal in shape and from point to point measures about 300 by 100 yards. On this small island the *micel here* that landed in the Lymne estuary in 892, that constructed and sheltered in the lost fortification at Appledore, was besieged. It would, however, hardly have afforded very comfortable shelter for a month or two for an army of 5,000 with their horses.

There are, therefore, good reasons for thinking that the ninth-century Viking armies were relatively small, numbering, at most, a few hundred men. In contrast, the armies that attacked England at the end of the tenth century appear to have been much larger. The Anglo-Saxon Chronicle reports the arrival of Olaf Tryggvason in 991 with a fleet of 91 ships and three years later he returned with Svein Forkbeard, the Danish king, and 94 ships. These precise figures may be doubted, but later entries in the Chronicle suggest that such large fleets were, at that time, by no means impossible. In 1012 Ethelred recruited a Viking leader, Thorkel, who came with 45 ships and Cnut, after his conquest of England, sent part of his fleet back to

Denmark, keeping 40 ships with him. The standing fleet was
later reduced to 16 ships but Cnut's son aroused the hostility of
the English by increasing the fleet to 60 ships or more. The
figures given by the Chronicler indicate that these ships had
crews of at least 60 men. In 1041 it is reported that 11,048
pounds were paid for 32 ships and as the stated rate was 8 marks
per rowlock these ships must have had at least 30 pairs of oars.
The Anglo-Saxon Chronicle, therefore, furnishes evidence that
the fleets with which Svein and Cnut conquered England could
well have consisted of 60 or more ships each with a crew of at
least 60 men.

There is some confirmation that Svein and Cnut did indeed
command military resources on that scale in the remarkable
camps or barracks that have been recognised at Trelleborg and
three other sites in Denmark.²⁵ In the first edition of this book
it was argued that these camps could not be dated more closely
than within the broad limits 950–1050 and that, as there were
no good reasons for dating them before rather than after Cnut's
conquest of England, they were worthless as evidence for the
armies with which that Conquest was achieved. In the past few
years more material has become available from these sites and
they have been thoroughly discussed, notably by Olaf Olsen,
who has demonstrated that they can be dated with some confidence within the limits 970–1020 and that they are, therefore,
good evidence for the size and organization of the Danish royal
armies in the reign of their principal victim, King Ethelred.
The extraordinary problems that Ethelred had to face are much
easier to understand in the light of this evidence and the camps
consequently merit detailed study.

They are widely distributed in Denmark. The largest is
Aggersborg on the shore of Limfjord in the north of Jutland.
there is another called Fyrkat a little further south; the third,
Nonnebakken, is in the middle of Odense in the island of Fyn
and the fourth, Trelleborg, is on the island of Sjælland close
to the Great Belt that divides it from Fyn. They have all
been at least partly excavated and the plans of three may be
compared in Figure 7. The similarities are obvious. They
are all surrounded by circular ramparts each with four
openings at regular intervals through which two roadways

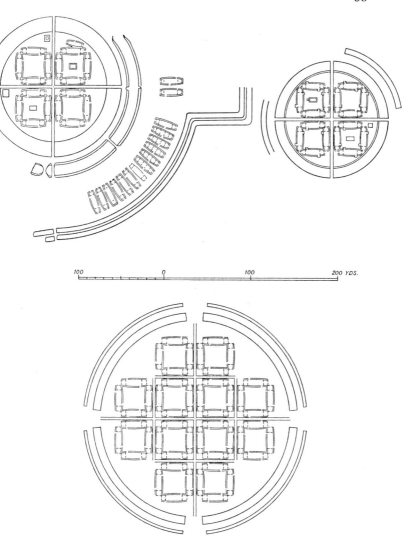

100   0   100   200 YDS.

Figure 7   Three Late Viking period camps in Denmark: Trelleborg, *top left*, Fyrkat, *top right*, Aggersborg, *bottom*. (From the plans published in J. Brøndsted, *Danmarks Oldtid* (1960), iii, p. 363.)

passed. They are different sizes, at Fyrkat the internal diameter
of the rampart was 131 yds. (120 m.), at Trelleborg 148 yds.
(136 m.) and at Aggersborg, 240 m. The ramparts were
also on different scales; at Trelleborg it was 59 ft. (17·6 m.)
thick, but at Fyrkat only 40 ft. (12 m.). Excavation has revealed that the Fyrkat rampart, which was probably about
10 ft. (3 m.) high was originally an elaborate timber structure
filled with earth or turves. Inside the circular ramparts the
roads, which at Fyrkat and Trelleborg were paved with wood,
intersected at right angles, dividing the interior into quadrants. In each of these quadrants there were a number of large
houses arranged in groups of four. The houses were all of the
same design, with a central area partitioned off from smaller
rooms at each end, but there were structural differences. The
Trelleborg houses had walls of wooden planks set vertically,
but at Fyrkat the houses were timber framed, with wattle and
daub covering on the long, curved sides and horizontal planks
at the gable ends. The roofs seem to have been supported by
the walls, by an outer row of posts and by large posts inside
the buildings. The houses were of slightly different sizes. Those
at Fyrkat were 31 yds. (28·5 m.) long and 8 yds. (7·5 m.)
across at their widest point. At Trelleborg the houses inside the
circular rampart were about a metre longer and at Aggersborg they were even longer still, 38 yds. (34·5 m.). At Fyrkat
there were remains of a weak and unfinished ditch but Trelleborg was better defended. On the landward side of the peninsula
on which it stood there is a well formed ditch immediately
outside the circular rampart and another bank and ditch
protects the fifteen slightly smaller houses that were built
radially outside the inner rampart. The rectilinear extension
of this outer ditch at Trelleborg was to accommodate the
gravefield, in which the graves of some 150 people have been
discovered. They were all poorly furnished inhumations, but
the skeletons were not well preserved, so it is difficult to determine the sex of many and there is no warrant for the assertion
often made that there were few women buried here. Of the
eighty-seven skeletons that could be examined, the sex of
only forty could be determined and of these nine were women.[26]
The larger number of men is partly explained by the fact that

the two large common graves containing between them fifteen male skeletons were well preserved. As the sex of so many could not be determined it would be unsafe to generalise from this sample. There was less difficulty in estimating the ages of the people buried there, and sixty of the eighty-seven were younger than forty, but it should not be forgotten that almost a third were older than this. The fact that only one child of less than six was identified has been taken to prove the unusual character of the settlement. In the gravefield of Fyrkat, which was joined to the camp by a wooden roadway, twenty-three graves have so far been excavated, but unlike those at Trelleborg some were richly furnished.

The most remarkable feature of these camps is that they were laid out with great precision and in all of them the same unit of measurement was used, the Roman foot of $11\frac{1}{2}$ in. (29·3 cm.). Measured in these units the houses at Fyrkat were 96 feet long, those inside Trelleborg's circle were 100 feet long, and at Aggersborg 110 feet. The precision of the surveying is shown in many ways, including the fact that the internal diameter of the circular rampart at Trelleborg is exactly the same (234 Roman feet) as the distance from the centre of the circle to the nearest gables of the outer houses. The builders must have had very sophisticated surveying techniques which seem to belong to the world of Rome rather than to the Dark Ages. There has been a lot of speculation about the source of the surveying methods and of the unit of measurement, but no generally acceptable answer has yet been found.

The similarities between these camps suggest that they were all built at much the same time and for the same purpose. The objects that have been found point to the end of the tenth century and the beginning of the eleventh and, as there are no signs of any rebuilding, or of the replacement or repair of any of the wooden posts, we can be fairly confident that these structures had a life of little more than a single generation, after which the wooden posts would have rotted in the ground. These encampments give the impression of having been intended to keep men together as much as to keep others out, and they may very well have been built as barracks. The evidence of rune stones in several parts of Scandinavia shows that Danish kings

K

in the late tenth and eleventh centuries used mercenaries from far afield and it is not improbable that camps of this kind would be used to house the warriors before campaigns. Unfortunately, relatively few traces of occupation have been found in these camps, possibly, as Olaf Olsen has suggested, because, like modern barracks, they were kept scrupulously clean. The scarcity of weapons is remarkable but not, perhaps, surprising, for such equipment was too valuable to have been lightly discarded. The whetstones needed to sharpen sword and axes were, however, not so precious and at Fyrkat well over 200 have been found.

Each of the main buildings in the camps could comfortably have housed about 60 men, but not all were used as living quarters. At Fyrkat, where half the buildings were used as workshops, particularly for metal working, or stores, the remainder could have accommodated between 500 and 600 men. All 16 houses within the circular rampart at Trelleborg seem to have been used as living quarters, the workshops and stores were probably in the buildings outside, so that its complement of men could have been about double that of Fyrkat. Nonnebakken cannot be studied in detail but the absence of external buildings suggests that it was much like Fyrkat. The purposes served by the 48 buildings at Aggersborg have not yet been determined, but on the assumption that the proportion devoted to auxiliary purposes was much the same as at Fyrkat, it could have housed some 3,000 men. The date and distribution of these camps shows that they must have been royal, no rival power could have been responsible, and the king in question was almost certainly Svein Forkbeard. The fact that these four camps could, between them, have accommodated 5,000 men is some measure of the formidable force at his disposal.

All these camps were close to navigable water. Trelleborg, for example, was originally on a promontory projecting into a lake that has since disappeared, although the outline of its shore can be traced in the aerial photograph on Plate XIII. The approaches were certainly shallow, but that would not have been a difficulty for Viking ships with their characteristically shallow draught. It has, indeed, been suggested that the houses in these camps were each intended to accommodate the crew of one ship. If so, three of the camps were originally designed for fleets of 16 ships, the size of the fleet normally maintained in England by Cnut and his successor Harald and it may be that this was the size of a customary unit of the Danish fleet at that time. The enlargement of Trelleborg and the conversion of some of the houses to other purposes at Fyrkat and, probably at the other camps may have resulted from the discovery that an efficient fleet needs more than ships and living quarters.

The material recovered from the camps does not suggest that they were exclusively, or even particularly connected with the raids on England. Their location seems to have been dictated by internal needs; only Aggersborg is conveniently placed for the voyage to England. The Danish leaders needed warriors to fight campaigns in many parts, in Scandinavia and the Baltic as well as across the North Sea. The camps are, however, striking testimony to the size and the organization of the armies commanded by the Danish king at the end of the tenth century. The problems of an English government threatened by such a force are easy to understand. It is tempting, and probably right, to see in these camps evidence that the armies they housed were well trained and disciplined. This would certainly be consistent with other evidence showing that the Danish attacks on England in the reign of Ethelred were marked by a remarkable degree of discipline. There does not seem to have been much pillaging, the monasteries suffered little material damage[27] and Svein was apparently able to restrain his troops from plundering friendly territory.[28] The murder of Archbishop Ælfheah was notable as an exception, and was blamed by the English Chronicler on drink.[29] The extraordinary scarcity of coin hoards in England for the last ten years of Ethelred's reign, a time when Danish armies were ranging widely throughout the country cannot be because of any scarcity of coin; it must mean that the Danes did not plunder indiscriminately.[30] Their concern was to extort tribute, 'protection money', and the Chronicler complained that they were never offered tribute in time.[31] The English government was incapable of organising an effective defence against these armies but to the people of England, peasants, landowners, merchants and possibly even monks, these armies were not a threat of the same kind as that faced by the English and the Franks in the ninth century when, in Alfred's famous phrase 'everything was ravaged and burnt' and when, in contrast, coin hoards provide abundant evidence of the fear the raiders then inspired.[32]

When all reasonable allowances have been made for the exaggeration of contemporary writers and of later commentators there is no doubt that the Vikings of the ninth century did a great deal of damage. Churches were undoubtedly plundered, damaged and destroyed, towns were looted, and many men were killed. It was the churches especially that suffered, not because the raiders hated Christianity but because they found the loot they wanted in large and often accessible quantities in the monasteries and churches of western Europe. They were sometimes prepared to leave a church unharmed, at least for a while, on payment of what would nowadays be called protection money, but if some tribute was not offered it would be taken. In order to escape these visitations some communities uprooted themselves with their relics and treasures and fled. Many returned when the danger had passed but some migrations were permanent. The most famous of all these removals was that of the monks of St. Philibert who abandoned their exposed island of Noirmoutier and eventually found safety and a new home at Tournus in Burgundy.[33] The raiders were undoubtedly feared and many must have prayed for deliverance although the often quoted addition to the Litany, 'From the fury of the Northmen, O Lord, deliver us', is certainly apocryphal.[34]

It is very difficult to assess how much damage was actually done. It may be suspected that contemporaries spoke of destruction or utter ruin when in fact the damage was slight and soon repaired. When Ermentarius wrote his account of the miracles and translations of St. Philibert he not only gave a precious account of the migrations of his community but he also described in vivid terms the terror and devastations that made flight necessary. The long journey is unquestioned, but not his assertion that the Vikings took and destroyed the towns of Angers, Tours and Orléans. Towns as well as monasteries undoubtedly attracted the Vikings; both were likely sources of loot, and they were often badly protected, but the Vikings

Figure 8 Map of Western Europe

seem to have been more interested in plunder than in destruction for its own sake. Dorestad, a trading centre in Frisia, was
particularly vulnerable to Viking raiders. The Annals of
St. Bertin describe the sequence of attacks, in 834 it was
plundered, in 835 wasted, in 836 depopulated, and in 837
tribute was exacted from its wasted and depopulated inhabitants. According to the same Annals it suffered three more
attacks before 863 when it was finally destroyed, not by the
Vikings but by the River Rhine which changed its course and
flooded the town. It may well be that Viking threats prevented
its recovery but that is not quite the same as destruction by
the Vikings. For many years Dorestad in its exposed position
had suffered Viking demands but it survived, and the fact
that Frankish mints continued to produce coins throughout
the ninth century, apparently without interruption, suggests
that Dorestad was not the only town to suffer Viking attacks
and survive.[35] Soissons was attacked by Vikings in 886 and,
according to one source, the Abbey and church of St. Médard
together with the royal palace were destroyed by fire. In the
following year St. Médard served as the burial place of Henry,
Duke of Saxony. There is, however, no independent evidence of
any reconstruction before the twelfth century and it is more
likely that the report of destruction was exaggerated than that
Henry was buried in a gutted ruin.[36] The scale of the attacks
and of the consequent destruction is obviously exaggerated in
some sources, particularly late ones, but even contemporary
and generally reliable sources can err, as, for example, the
entry for 859 in the Annals of St. Bertin which reports the
burning of the cathedral of Noyon by the Vikings and their
murder of Bishop Immo, despite Immo's survival in the following year.[37]

Many Viking raids, on churches must have been little more
than violent acts of robbery. That the raiders were more
interested in treasure than in destruction is shown very clearly
by what happened at St.-Germain-des-Prés in 858.[38] A Viking
band arrived to find that most of the monks had fled with their
relics, treasures, archives and library. Deprived of their hopes
of riches they provisioned themselves, and are said to have
killed a few serfs and to have set fire to a store and then retreated

disappointed. The few monks who had remained behind came out of hiding and, with the help of the people of Paris, put out the flames which threatened the church. This fairly well described incident probably gives a good idea of what many Viking visitations must have been like. The raiders came, demanded tribute, or took what treasure they could find and withdrew to the safety of their island refuges. That the damage done by the raiders was not always as serious as some contemporaries and modern writers would have us believe is suggested by the Anglo-Saxon Chronicler. When in 896 he is able to close his account of the wars that the West Saxons had fought against the *micel here* that came in 892 with the news that the enemy had dispersed, he commented 'By the grace of God, the *here* had not on the whole afflicted the English people very greatly; but they were much more seriously afflicted in those three years by the mortality of cattle and men, and most of all in that many of the best king's thegns who were in the land died in those three years.' The Chronicler does not say that these men were killed by the Danes, indeed he implies the contrary. No doubt those who had suffered directly at the hands of the Vikings, in particular churchmen, would have put it differently but this passage in the Anglo-Saxon Chronicle shows that at least one Englishman who was deeply committed in the struggle against this enemy did not rate the damage they did too highly. Such a statement as this is especially valuable for a time when the historian's evidence comes almost entirely from men whose concern was to report, often in strident terms, their own sufferings. One independent indication of the extent of Viking raids is provided by the coin hoards which have been discovered in areas in which coin was normally available. It is significant that the ninth-century coin hoards in England confirm the judgement of the Chronicler that the invaders of 892–6 did not 'on the whole afflict the English people very greatly'.[39] Only three coin hoards that could have been deposited at that time are known from the whole of England, found at London, Erith and Leigh on Sea. In the decade 865–75 no fewer than 36 have been found, 7 south of the Thames and 7 between the Thames and the Trent. That must have been the time when 'everything was ravaged and burnt'.[40]

Figure 9 English coin hoards concealed *c.* 865–*c.* 875. See R. H. M. Dolley, *Hiberno-Norse coins in the British Museum* (1966), pp. 48–9 and map 2.

It is sometimes suggested that the more extreme contemporary accounts are confirmed, and the overwhelming destructiveness of the Vikings demonstrated by a study of the consequences of the raids. Because there is, in many cases, no evidence to prove that these assumed consequences were the sole responsibility of the Vikings, this kind of argument is hazardous and often circular. The Vikings may reasonably be held to have contributed to the collapse of the Carolingian Empire and of the kingdom of Mercia, but these were complex processes and other factors have to be taken into account. These happenings cannot properly be used to prove anything about Viking violence. There is a similar temptation to blame the absence of monasteries in England in the early tenth century on the Vikings and then to argue that the destruction of English monasticism by the Vikings proves that they were as violent as some contemporaries claimed. There is no doubt that when Alfred died there were in England no monasteries in the sense understood by the reformers of the tenth century, but there is certainly no evidence to show that the Vikings wery responsible for this situation. On the contrary Asser, in his Life of Alfred, favours another explanation:

'For at first he had no noble or freeman of his own nation who would of his own accord enter the monastic life—apart from children who by reason of their tender age could not choose good or refuse evil—for indeed for many years past the desire for the monastic life had been utterly lacking in all that people, and also in many other nations, although there still remain many monasteries founded in that land, but none properly observing the rule of this way of life, I know not why; whether on account of the onslaughts of foreigners, who very often invaded by land or sea or on account of the nation's too great abundance of riches of every kind, which I am much more inclined to think the reason for that contempt of the monastic life.'[41]

The generalisation that the Scandinavians destroyed monasticism has many local applications. The old monastery of Much Wenlock in Shropshire, for example, had to be refounded after the Norman Conquest and its disappearance has been blamed on a Danish raid, probably of 874, when they were active in the area.[42] The force of this explanation is reduced by a charter of 901, fortunately surviving in a contemporary copy, which shows that the community of Much Wenlock was then still in existence.[43] What seems to have happened at Much Wenlock and elsewhere is that what had once possibly been a monastery had become a community of secular canons, and this agrees very well with what Asser wrote. What is most remarkable is that the evidence for the extinction of English monasteries in the ninth century by the Danes all comes from a much later period. The only reference to such destruction in the Anglo-Saxon Chronicle, for example, is a twelfth-century interpolation.[44]

King Alfred's famous complaint about the state of learning in his day has been used as evidence for the destruction wrought by the Vikings. There are good reasons for believing that the condition of learning was not as bad as Alfred claimed and, in any case, he did not himself blame the Vikings. On the contrary, he treats the invasions as the judgement of God on the English for their laxity. 'Remember what temporal punishments came upon us,' he wrote, 'when we neither loved wisdom ourselves nor allowed it to other men; we possessed only the name of Christians, and very few possessed the virtues.' His complaint was that 'before everything was ravaged and burnt, the churches throughout all England stood filled with treasures and books, and likewise there was a great multitude of the servants of God. And they had very little benefit from those books, for they could not understand anything in them, because they were not written in their own language.'[45] The increasing use of the vernacular confirms Alfred's comment on the declining latinity of the age but he did not blame the Vikings for this. The decline is, in fact, evidenced in charters long before the Vikings were a serious menace in the south of England, and Sir Frank Stenton has pointed out that 'the decay is already evident in a solemn charter recording a grant to archbishop Wulfred by King Ceolwulf I of Mercia on the day of his consecration in 822'.[46]

The habit of blaming the Vikings has deep roots. Medieval

historians were no less eager than their modern successors to see in Viking raids the explanation for the disappearance of monastic discipline or buildings and many of the twelfth- and thirteenth-century references to Viking destructions depend less on the memory of such happenings than on the traditional recognition, particularly among churchmen, that the Vikings were the scourge of Christendom. If the Viking menace is to be measured by its consequences it is important that only those that can be proved should be taken into account. Arguments based on hypothetical or illusory consequences can only mislead. As far as England is concerned neither the decay of learning nor the collapse of the monastic order seems to have had much to do with the Vikings. On the Continent, however, the disappearance of monasteries from what later became Normandy is more likely to have been a direct result of Viking activities although even there it should not be assumed that the disappearance of a monastery meant its physical destruction. The threat of attack was enough to persuade some communities to move away and under the same threat others may have just failed. The interruption of some episcopal successions in both England and Normandy has been cited as evidence for the disruption of the ecclesiastical order by the Vikings.[47] These breaks do not, of course, mean simply that the bishops were killed. Bishops were certainly killed by the Vikings, some of them in battle, but others were chosen in their place. The failure of a line of bishops, like the migration of a monastery, meant a withdrawal. Not all the clergy deserted their flocks: the archbishops of York, for example, stayed and came to terms with the Viking rulers of their cathedral city, but some obviously did. Such withdrawals do not seem to have been prompted by the raids so much as by the settlements, and it is as a consequence of the Scandinavian settlements that these breaks in episcopal succession, like the collapse of monasticism in Normandy, should be considered.

The emphasis on the Vikings as raiders, whether this is in such sources as the Anglo-Saxon Chronicle or in modern discussions of the period can have the unfortunate result of concealing the fact that the Vikings came into a world that was itself torn by strife. Some scholars have indeed gone so far as to claim that, despite the references to wars and battles in the sources before the Vikings came, western Europe was relatively peaceful. An extreme statement of this view is given by Miss Francoise Henry.[48]

> 'The hundred years or so which preceded the Viking invasions in Ireland . . . seems to have been a period of comparative peace. The Annals speak of "wars", but these were only cattle raids or skirmishes between chieftains involving little damage and disturbance except for those immediately concerned. The ban put by the Church on the piratical expeditions which had been the chief pastime of the pagan kings seems to have affected deeply the life of the country.'

In contrast, when the Vikings came they brought 'swift and terrible destruction'. This is a most subjective interpretation of the annals and one which it would be difficult to sustain. It has recently been pointed out that the habit of burning and plundering Irish churches was a native one, well documented before the Viking raids began.[49] The Vikings doubtless aggravated the disruption but they can hardly be held responsible for undermining Irish respect for the church and for ecclesiastical sanctions; these were already seriously threatened long before the Vikings reached Ireland.

If there is any difference between the native violence of the Christian West and that brought by the Vikings it is because those who were 'immediately concerned' were different. The English, Franks and Irish generally, if not always, respected the Church in their wars; the Vikings regarded the churches as their main source of wealth. The wars of the Christians are described in the Christian annals in terms of the kings and other leaders taking part, the killing of men and the destruction of property is rarely described. Occasionally there are revealing glimpses of the beastly reality beneath, as in the Anglo-Saxon Chronicle for 1006: 'in spite of it all the Danish *here* went about as it pleased, and the English *fyrd* caused the people of the country every sort of harm, so that they profited neither from the native *here* nor from the foreign *here*.' The Chronicler used the word *here* for both the English and the Danish forces although it was normally reserved for the enemy. The

Vikings brought little that was new in the way of unpleasant-
ness, and some men were even prepared to welcome them as
allies. Alfred's nephew, Æthelwold, deserted to the Danes and
was accepted by them as their king, and he was joined by at least
one other highborn Englishman, Brihtsige, son of the atheling
Beornoth, names that suggest membership of the Mercian royal
house, who fell alongside Æthelwold at the battle of the Holm
in 902 while fighting on the Danish side.[50] Members of the
Frankish royal family similarly changed sides.[51] If some of the
West Saxons were prepared to submit to the Danes in 878, they
must have appeared even more attractive to the men of East
Anglia and other areas that had suffered under the Mercian
hegemony. Churchmen apart, in the eyes of most men the
Vikings were but a complication and for some a welcome one.

7. *The Danish Settlements*

IN the last quarter of the ninth century the Anglo-Saxon Chronicle reports the settlement in Northumbria, Mercia and East Anglia of two bands of Scandinavian invaders. In 865 what the Chronicler called a *micel here* arrived and campaigned for ten years before beginning to find permanent new homes. In 876 one group, under the leadership of Healfdene 'shared out the land of the Northumbrians and they proceeded to plough and support themselves'. In the following year another group, apparently from the same *micel here* 'went away into Mercia and shared out some of it' and very early in 878 the remainder 'came stealthily to Chippenham and occupied the land of the West Saxons and settled there and drove a great part of the people over the sea and conquered most of the others; and the people submitted to them except King Alfred'. In the spring and early summer of that year Alfred rallied the West Saxons to his support and the intruders were defeated in battle at Edington. Forced to leave their new homes they retreated to Cirencester where they stayed for a year, and then in 880 they 'went from Cirencester into East Anglia and settled there and shared out the land'. For the next ten years the Chronicler had very little to say about either these settlers or new bands of raiders; his main concern was with the movements of another Viking *here* in the lands south of the English Channel. This *here* made two short visits to England in 879 and 885 but it was only in 892 that it crossed in force from Boulogne and stayed. For the next four years Alfred fought these invaders and his efforts proved successful when, in the

Figure 10   Map of the British Isles

summer of 896, 'the Danish *here* divided, one force going into
East Anglia and one into Northumbria; and those that were
moneyless got themselves ships and went south across the sea
to the Seine'.

Long after they had found new homes in the north and east
of England these settlers continued to trouble the English of
western Mercia and Wessex. Settlement did not mean that these
invaders abandoned their warlike ways, and they continued
to venture on plundering expeditions in the south and west.
There is nothing surprising in this; the English had been
accustomed to behave in much the same way among themselves before the Vikings came. Nor is there anything surprising
in the reaction of the West Saxon Chronicler who continues to
speak of the settlers as a *here* or, strictly, in the plural as *hergas*,
which it can be misleading to translate as 'army' or 'armies'.
These Danes, who had shared out a large part of England,
appeared from time to time in English Mercia or in Wessex
in raiding bands, and for the Chronicler there was perhaps
little to choose between a *here* of raiders without permanent
homes and one that had. So in 896 the Chronicler reports
that 'the *hergas* in East Anglia and Northumbria greatly
harassed Wessex along the south coast with marauding bands,
most of all with warships they had built many years before'.
It was against such threats that Alfred attempted to provide
some defence by building a fleet of ships. The raiders also came
by land. In 903, for example, the *here* in East Anglia was
induced 'to break the peace so that they harried over all
Mercia until they reached Cricklade. And they went across
the Thames, and carried off all they could seize both in and
around Braydon, and turned then homeward.' The best
answer to such attacks was the system of strongpoints established by Alfred and his children. They fortified many places
with ditch and bank, probably topped by a palisade, and made
the manning and maintenance of these defences a responsibility
of the local population. Some of these 'boroughs' were well
established centres, but some places seem to have been newly
chosen as suitable sites for strongholds. These fortifications
were generally strong enough to protect the inhabitants and
their possessions from the raiding bands, who in any case

III. A gilded bronze harness mount from Broa in Halla, Gotland, now in Statens Historiska Museum, Stockholm. The original is about half the size. See p. 59. (*Bertil Almgren*)

IV. A panel from the so-called 'Fourth Sledge' found with the Oseberg ship,
now in the ship museum, Universitetets Oldsaksamling, Oslo. See pp. 59, 67.
Haakon Shetelig described this as one of the finest pieces of wood-carving
in the Oseberg find, *Vestfoldskolen* (Osebergfundet III, 1920), p. 101.
(*Bertil Almgren*)

V. A picture stone of the Viking period from Tjängvide in Alskog parish, Gotland, now in Statens Historiska Museum, Stockholm. See pp. 41, 67. The runic inscription shows that it was raised for a man called *Iurulf* by his brother. Similar mythical scenes are found on other stones. See Sune Lindqvist, *Gotlands Bildsteine* (KVHAA, 1941–2), i. 15–17, ii, Figures 137–38.

(*Photo ATA*)

VI. The Gokstad ship, now in the ship museum of Universitetets Oldsaksam-ling, Oslo. See pp. 68–76. The oars are in the foreground, the gangway and spars to the left. The tubs beyond the mast were probably for food and drinking water. The sockets for spreading spars are clearly visible either side of the mast, cf. p. 74 and Figure 4. The T-shaped erections were for storing the yards and spars while the ship was rowed. See Harald Åkerlund, *Unda Maris*, 1955–6, p. 52 and note. (*Ernst Schwitters, Oslo*)

VII. Detail from the great picture stone Smiss I, from Stenkyrka parish, Gotland, now in Gotlands Fornsal, Visby. (*Photo ATA*)

VIII. Detail from the Bayeux Tapestry. (*Phaidon*)

IX. A horse disembarking from the *Imme Gran*, a modern replica of the Ladby ship. (*Olaf Olsen*)

X. Two of the blocks from the Gokstad ship. The larger is 57 cms long. The accompanying diagram shows Harald Åkerlund's reconstruction of the manner in which such blocks could have been used to tighten the shrouds. See *Svenska Kryssarklubbens årsskrift* 1959, pp. 68–9. (*Universitetets Oldsaksamling, Oslo* and *Harald Åkerlund*)

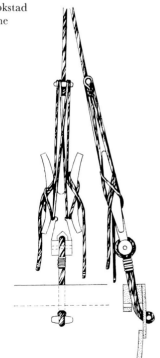

XI. Silver brooches found in a silver hoard at Järnjö in Gärdslösa parish, Öland, now in Statens Historiska Museum, Stockholm. See p. 60. The hoard also contained 5 spiral rings, see *Fornvännen*, 1908, p. 275. (*Bertil Almgren*)

XII. A gold hoard from Hon, Eiker parish, Buskerud, now in Universitetets Oldsaksamling, Oslo. The hoard weighed 5½ lb. (2,549 g.). The largest ring has a diameter of 10 in. (26 cm.) and weighs 2½ lb. (1,106 g.). The beads are of coloured glass, green, dark blue, white and yellow. (*Aslak Liestøl and Universitetets Oldsaksamling, Oslo*)

XIII. The camp of Trelleborg, see pp. 132–37. The foundations are marked and a reconstructed house stands outside the outer ditch. The camp's position at the confluence of two streams, Vaarbyaa and Tudeaa, is clear. The open waters of the Great Belt lie about 2 miles (3 km.) beyond their confluence. The extent of the lake that formerly protected the camp is indicated by the flood line. (*The National Museum, Denmark*)

XIV. Two faces of one of the crosses at Middleton, near Pickering, Yorkshire.
(*Alan Binns, The Viking Century in East Yorkshire,* 1963)

depended more on speed and surprise than on overwhelming
force for their successes. So, in 917, the raiders who went to
Bedford were put to flight by the defenders and in the same
year a larger *here* went to the newly constructed fort or borough
'at *Wigingamere* and besieged and attacked it long into the day,
and seized the cattle round about; and yet the men who were
inside defended the borough', and the enemy had to abandon
their assault.

In the shelter of such defences counter-attacks could be
prepared and these boroughs were soon turned to offensive
use. The extension of the authority of the West Saxon kings
largely depended on the extension of this system of boroughs
year by year deeper into the Danish-held lands. From the
Chronicle it is possible to study the way Alfred's children,
Edward the Elder, king of Wessex, and Æthelfleda, lady of
the Mercians, co-operated in the construction of a chain of
these forts across England.[1] It was from the security of these
that counter-attacks were launched and new forts, like that at
Wigingamere mentioned in 917, were built in Danish areas,
and by 920 Edward had been acknowledged as overlord
throughout the greater part of southern England. North of
the Humber the situation was more complicated. The native
Northumbrians seem to have been very reluctant indeed to
acknowledge the overlordship of a southerner and with the
help of allies from the Viking kingdom of Dublin they resisted
the claims of the West Saxons until Eric Blood-Axe, the last of
the Scandinavian kings of York was deposed in 954 and
Northumbria finally became part of the united kingdom of
England.[2]

The first evidence of the extent of the Danish conquests is the
treaty agreed between Alfred and Guthrum, a Danish leader,
possibly in 886. The boundary between their kingdoms is said to
be 'Up the Thames as far as the river Lea, then up the Lea to its
source, and then straight to Bedford, and then up the Ouse to
Watling Street'.[3] It seems probable that Watling Street
marked the boundary for some 50 miles although the treaty
says nothing about such a continuation, possibly because
this lay well beyond Alfred's kingdom at the time. The area
to the north and east of this line was later called the Danelaw.[4]

L

This word first occurs in the eleventh century and is used to distinguish that part of the country in which Danish custom prevailed in contrast to the areas of English Law, also sub-divided into Mercian and West Saxon Laws. In one of Ethelred's law codes, for example, the method of denying an accusation of plotting against the king's life is defined as the most solemn oath or the triple ordeal in districts under English law, and in those under Danish law, *on Dena lage*, in accordance with their laws. The three laws are only defined in later texts, according to which the Danelaw consisted of fifteen counties from Essex, Middlesex and Buckinghamshire in the south to Yorkshire in the north, but there is not much that is specifically Scandinavian in the place-names and administrative nomenclature of the southern counties of the Danelaw as it was defined in the twelfth century and the inclusion of such areas as Middlesex, Hertfordshire and Buckinghamshire is probably the result of a misinterpretation of the treaty between Alfred and Guthrum. The boundary agreed there only joined Watling Street at the Bedfordshire Ouse; the later definitions of the Danelaw seem to assume that Watling Street was the boundary as far as London. In fact, in one of these texts, the Laws of Edward the Confessor, the southern part of this area is stated to be Northamptonshire as far as Watling Street and also eight shires beyond Watling Street. The area under Danish law, that is the area in which the law was administered by a predominantly Danish aristocracy, would naturally tend to be much larger than the area of dense Danish settlement. As Sir Frank Stenton remarked, 'the prevalence of Danish custom within a particular district does not mean that it had been colonised in force by Danish settlers. The establishment of a Danish aristocracy which controlled the course of business in the local courts would be hardly less effective than the settlement of an army in imprinting a Danish character on the law of a shire.' There is, however, no evidence, other than such definitions of the Danelaw, to suggest that the customary law observed in the shire courts of Middlesex, Buckinghamshire, Hertfordshire and Bedfordshire had ever been Danish, or that these counties had ever had a Scandinavian aristocracy, and they should therefore be excluded from realistic definitions of the Danelaw.

The heart of this Danelaw lay where Scandinavian settlement was densest, in Leicestershire, Lincolnshire, Nottinghamshire and Yorkshire. It is probable that in this region, between the Welland and the Tees, Scandinavians or men of Scandinavian descent ruled locally for a long time after they had accepted the West Saxon overlordship and it is not surprising that they have left their mark on both the legal and administrative nomenclature of the area. In Domesday Book's description of the counties of Lincoln, Nottingham, Derby, Leicester and in the North and West Ridings of Yorkshire the local administrative divisions were called 'wapentakes', a word of Scandinavian origin that comes from an Old Norse word, *vapnatac*, meaning the flourishing of weapons at an assembly.[8] It occurs in its Old English form *wæpentac* in the middle of the tenth century as a name for an administrative division with a court and one of Ethelred's early law codes, which seems to lay down procedures for an area under Danish law, includes the clause, 'and a court shall be held in every wapentake, and the twelve leading thegns along with the reeve shall go out and swear on the relics which are given into their hands, that they will not accuse any innocent man or shield any guilty one'.[9] The equivalent in English areas was the 'hundred' and as Sir Frank Stenton has remarked 'there seems to have been no essential difference of function between the courts of the wapentake and hundred'.[10] The difference is one of terminology and in some areas the terminology seems to have been unsettled. In Domesday Book, the East Riding of Yorkshire is divided into hundreds, but one of these is also called a wapentake; in Northamptonshire one area is sometimes called a wapentake and sometimes a hundred. A few Scandinavian legal terms have also survived in the Danelaw as, for example, in a tenth-century memorandum from Peterborough Abbey where sureties for land transfers are called *festermen*, a Scandinavian word,[11] which, according to Sir Frank Stenton, proves 'that even in the southern Danelaw the transfer of land was carried out in accordance with Scandinavian practice'.[12] It is indeed likely that Peterborough lay close to the southern limits of the Danelaw proper, for it is not far from the southern boundary of Lincolnshire; it is, however, less certain how distinctively

Scandinavian this system of sureties was. The Anglo-Saxon laws say extraordinarily little about land transactions, but they provide abundant evidence for the use of sureties in the buying and selling of goods, and like so many other apparently distinctive Scandinavian features of the Danelaw, including the wapentake and the *sacrabar*,[13] the use of *festermen* may well be a difference more of name than of substance.

Attempts have been made to determine the extent and character of the Scandinavian settlements, inadequately described by the Anglo-Saxon Chronicler, with the help of place-names and archaeological evidence. Unfortunately grave finds are too rare to be much use,[14] but there is a large number of stone carvings which show Scandinavian influence and the way in which these help our interpretation of the settlement will be discussed below.[15] Hitherto most discussions of this topic have been largely based on the study of the Scandinavian influence on place-names,[16] for the Scandinavians brought with them, and used, a distinctive stock of words and personal names which they used to describe farms and villages and features of the landscape such as hills, streams, woods and fields. Where the English would call a farm or village a *tun*, the Scandinavians used their own word *by*, which similarly means farm or village. The names Stanton and Stainby mean very much the same thing, but one is English and the other Scandinavian. When the Scandinavians used their own personal-names the contrast is sometimes even more marked, as between Aismunderby in Yorkshire, '*Asmund's by*' and Osmondiston, in Norfolk, '*Osmund's tun*'. In using this place-name evidence for the Scandinavian settlements it is very important to recognise that settlement names, that is names of farms and villages, are not given by the people who live in the farms and villages but by their neighbours. The men living in, say Aismunderby, when talking among themselves would call it simply the *by*, it is the people who lived nearby who called it 'Asmund's *by*' to distinguish it from other settlements. In doing so they not only show that this particular settlement had once been named after Asmund, probably sometime an owner and possibly its founder, but they also show that they used the word *by* for settlements. A name like Ingleby, which may well have meant 'village or farm of the English' suggests that to be English was itself distinctive, and this would be consistent with the use of the Scandinavian word *by* among the name-givers.[17] The use of this word *by* does not, however, mean that the name-givers were Scandinavians or even of Scandinavian descent. This can be seen very clearly in such names as Denby or Danby meaning the *by* of the Danes or the Dane. These names imply that Danes were distinctive; as Dr. Cameron has said of a Derbyshire example 'Denby . . . must have been in a region where Danes were an unusual feature of the population'.[18] The names Denby and Danby are indeed generally removed from the main concentrations of Scandinavian names and although they obviously indicate some Scandinavian settlement this was unlikely to have been very dense, especially if the name meant '*by* of the Dane' rather than 'of the Danes'. Nevertheless the surrounding non-Danish, indeed non-Scandinavian, population used this word *by*. It did in fact pass into English and was used by both English and Scandinavians, its most striking survival being in the word 'by-law', the law of the village. The use of this word, then, is no guarantee that the speakers were of Scandinavian descent, but 700 or more English place-names that include this element *by* prove beyond doubt the importance of Scandinavian influence on the nomenclature of England.

This influence was not limited to one element. There are many other characteristically Scandinavian place-name elements such as *thorp* that generally means a secondary settlement, and is used both on its own and in names like Newthorpe in Nottinghamshire and Yorkshire, or Danthorpe in the East Riding, a name like Danby. Other Scandinavian elements are *both*, 'a booth or temporary shelter' as in Boothby or Oozebooth; *lundr* 'a small wood, a grove', as in Lound which occurs in Lincolnshire, Nottinghamshire and in Suffolk or in Toseland in Huntingdonshire; *bekkr*, 'a stream, a beck', as in Caldbeck or Whitbeck in Cumberland. There are many different kinds of Scandinavian name elements that were used in England but the most numerous and distinctive are *by* and *thorp*. The Scandinavians not only brought their own names and words for places; they also had a distinctive pronunciation and this has left its mark. For example, what the English call Shipton, 'sheep village or farm' was pronounced then as now with a soft initial *sh.* Scandinavian influence has altered the pronunciation of this name in Yorkshire to Skipton. The same change occurred in the Nottinghamshire name *Scirgerefantun,* 'the *tun* of the sheriff', which has become Screveton instead of Shrewton as it did in Wiltshire. In such ways the newcomers transformed many English names.

The Scandinavians also brought a distinctive stock of personal-names, many of which were used in the formation of place-names. Some of these personal-names were current in England for a very long time. Sir Frank Stenton worked out that the Lincolnshire Assize Rolls for 1202 contained 215 Scandinavian names and only 194 English.[19] Scandinavian personal-names were not, of course, confined to the Danelaw, but it is there that the largest numbers are found. In Domesday Book, for example, there are at least 350 different Scandinavian personal-names in use among pre-Conquest tenants, ninety of which are only found in Lincolnshire and Yorkshire, and thirty-five were exclusively recorded in East Anglia.[20] It is tempting, but it would be wrong, to assume that men with Scandinavian names were the descendants of Scandinavian settlers. Professor Ekwall drew attention to several cases that show how different members of the same family might have Scandinavian and English names.[21] He quotes the case of the four brothers in the Lincolnshire Domesday, *Ingemund, Oune, Edric* and *Eculf,* and remarks, '*Oune* is certainly, *Ingemund* probably Scandinavian, while *Edric* is certainly English and *Eculf* probably so'. It is only rarely that the names of several members of the same family are known, but there are enough to demonstrate the danger of assuming that Scandinavian names were reserved for descendants of Scandinavians. Name-giving fashions change and are affected, among other things, by the example of the socially dominant class. So, in the thirteenth century a large number of the names in use among the small landowners and peasantry in all parts of England were those introduced by the Normans and their Continental friends. Professor Whitelock has demonstrated from the *Liber Vitae* of Thorney Abbey how quickly Continental names became popular in the class of people whose names are recorded in such a work.[22] She has calculated that the lists, which were drawn up from the early eleventh century to the thirteenth, are made up of 2,133 entries with about 660 different names, 'of which about 272 are of Continental origin in 1,221 entries, 185 Old English names in 548 entries and 123 Scandinavian names in 236 entries, not including those names, originally Scandinavian, that occur in a form showing Continental influence'. The changing proportions in these lists after the Norman Conquest are as follows, expressed as percentages:

	Scandinavian	Old English	Continental
Early post-Conquest	10	45	45
Early twelfth century	7	26	67
Second half of twelfth century	3	16	81
Late twelfth or very early thirteenth century	1	4	95

Changes like this do not, of course, mean that the bulk of the population was directly descended from men who arrived in or after 1066; they show, on the contrary, that the name-giving habits in England had been profoundly affected by the example of the ruling class. In the same way, the Scandinavians who conquered and colonised large parts of England in the ninth century, effected great changes in the personal names current in those parts, a change that may have been reinforced in the eleventh century by the example of Cnut and his Scandinavian followers.[23] These names were used along with English names, and the recent study of this topic by Gillian Fellows Jensen has shown that there are about as many cases of fathers with Scandinavian names giving their sons English names as there are of the reverse process.[24] A Scandinavian name is, therefore, no guarantee of Scandinavian ancestry: what can be said is that Scandinavian invasions deeply affected the personal nomenclature of large parts of England, a change that is only paralleled by the effects of the Norman Conquest. In neither case can conclusions about the number of colonists be

drawn from the popularity of the names they introduced.
Place-names can sometimes help determine the provenance
of the settlers for some words and names can be recognised as
distinctively Danish or Norwegian. So, for example, *thorp* seems
not to have been used in Norway during the Viking period and
its use in England indicates Danish influence; on the other hand
slakki, 'a small shallow valley, a hollow in the ground' was
brought by Norwegians. Similarly some personal-names
were distinctively Danish while others were Norwegian. Not
all names and words are recognisably Danish or Norwegian;
there was a large common element, but the differences are
clear enough to show that most of the settlers in the eastern
parts of England were from Denmark and that the settlers in
the north-west were predominantly of Norwegian descent.
The names in this north-western group have other characteristics showing that the settlers came from Celtic areas. In this
area Celtic names are sometimes compounded with Scandinavian elements, and there are some names in which the
elements are Scandinavian but the method of formation is
characteristically Celtic, with the defining element second
where in Germanic languages it would be first. Examples of
such 'inversion compounds' are Brigsteer in Westmorland,
'Styr's bridge' and Aspatria in Cumberland 'Patrick's Ash'.[25]
Scandinavian influence continued to affect English place
nomenclature long after the original settlements, not only by
affecting pronunciation, but also by the formation of new
settlements that were given Scandinavian names. The continued use of Scandinavian personal-names and words to
describe places certainly shows how persistent Scandinavian
influence was, but it makes it very difficult to determine the
extent of the original settlements. The first evidence for most
English place-names is in Domesday Book, a survey undertaken
in 1086 in which most of the places then existing in England are
described by name. This is a remarkable record but it should
not be forgotten that it is some 200 years later than the original
Danish settlements. In that time there had not only been many
opportunities for Scandinavian influence to affect English
names, but many new settlements were formed and some of
these were given Scandinavian names. This process of name-

formation can be seen clearly in Domesday Book where at least thirty places seem to be named after very recent owners or tenants.[26] So for example, *Blæcmann* held an estate in Kent in 1065 that was called in 1086 *Blachemenestone*, now Blackmanstone, no doubt after him. Some of the names formed at this time were Scandinavian, such as Ormesby in the North Riding of Yorkshire, apparently named after a post-Conquest tenant called *Ormr*. The formation of names continued after the Norman Conquest, and although it would be wrong to assume that all the 150 names in *by* for which the evidence is later than Domesday Book were only formed after the Norman Conquest, some were undoubtedly late formations, including Baggaby in the East Riding of Yorkshire, named after a post-Conquest tenant called Bagot. If Scandinavian names were being created in this way after the Norman Conquest, it is likely that they were also being created in the tenth and eleventh centuries, and that the Scandinavian influence to be observed in Domesday Book is the result of a long and continuous process of settlement and name-giving. So long as new settlements were formed and Scandinavian personal-names and words were used to describe them, the Scandinavian influence on the place-names of England grew.

There can be little doubt that new settlements were being formed in the tenth and eleventh centuries. This is shown by the common use of the element *thorp*, which means a secondary settlement. The large number of these *thorp* names in Domesday Book suggests that the area of settlement had been greatly enlarged in the preceding two centuries.[27] Not all the new settlements of the tenth and eleventh centuries were called *thorp*; other Scandinavian words were undoubtedly used, including *by*. The number of *by* names was further inflated by the translation of such elements as *tun*, and in some cases it is possible to detect the transformation of other elements as, for example, at Rugby in Warwickshire which was *Rocheberie* in Domesday Book, and means 'Hroca's *burh*', but had by the end of the twelfth century been turned into *Rokebi*. At least some of the *by* names in Domesday are therefore late formations or transformations.

These place-names with the element *by* are among the most

distinctive signs of Scandinavian influence and there are over 550 of them in the Domesday descriptions of the counties in which Danish settlement was preponderant.[28] There are 217 in Lincolnshire and 207 in Yorkshire.] Leicestershire comes next with 56, Nottinghamshire and Norfolk each have 21, Northamptonshire has 22, while there are only 9 in Derbyshire and 3 in Suffolk. Some scholars have accepted that the distribution of these *by* names defines the main areas of Scandinavian settlement. This assumption has been questioned and one of the crucial points in the discussion has been whether it is possible to date the formation of these *by* names with any confidence. Some attempts to demonstrate their early date are not entirely satisfactory, as, for example, the claim that many of them are compounded with personal-names that are otherwise rare or unknown in England or Scandinavia.[29] Our knowledge of personal nomenclature at this time is too inadequate to allow the assumption that personal-names only found in place-names cannot have been current after the early years of the tenth century. Even if we allow that it is possible to distinguish some personal-names that are more likely to have been current at an early stage of the colonisation than later, it is significant that under 22 per cent. of the *by* names in Lincolnshire and Yorkshire are compounded from such 'older' personal-names.[30] There is, however, one good reason for accepting that *by* names are, as a class, early rather than late, namely the relative rarity of names in which *by* is compounded with an English personal-name. Of the 303 *by* names in the counties of Derby, Nottingham, Lincoln and Leicester, Professor Cameron has shown that 207 have a personal-name as the first element and 192, or 92 per cent. of these are Scandinavian.[31] The proportion in Yorkshire is identical. In that county 119 Domesday place-names in *by* have a personal-name as the first element and 109 (92 per cent.) are Scandinavian as against 7 Old English and 3 Old Irish personal-names.[32] Had *by* passed into general currency and continued in active use as a place-name element in the Danish areas of England, we could reasonably have expected more of the place-names in *by* to have been compounded with English personal-names. The same conclusion is suggested by the relatively few

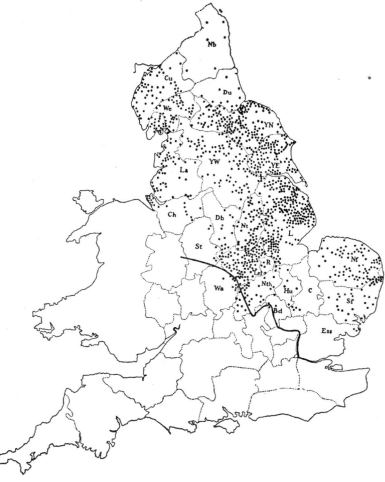

> .   Parish Names of Scandinavian Origin
> ──   Boundary of Alfred and Guthrum's Treaty.
>   see p. 149
> ....   Modern County Boundaries

Figure 11 Scandinavian Place-names in England. (From A. H. Smith, *English Place-name Elements* (English Place-name Society, vols. xxv–vi, 1956), map.)

names in *by* that seem to have been formed in the Danish areas of England after the Norman Conquest. The element *by* certainly continued in active use in the Norse area but in the East Riding of Yorkshire, where Norse influence is slight, only four of the 42 names in *by* are not found in Domesday Book.[33] A comparison with the place-name element *thorp* is instructive for this word was undoubtedly used to describe secondary settlements and was in active use after the Norman Conquest in the Danish areas as, for example, in the East Riding of Yorkshire where 12 of the 68 *thorp* names are not recorded in Domesday Book.[34] Of the 109 place-names incorporating *thorp* in the Domesday account of the counties of Derby, Nottingham, Lincoln and Leicester, 71 have a personal-name as the first element and of these only 71 per cent. are Scandinavian as against 92 per cent. for place-names in *by*.[35] The proportion in Yorkshire is slightly higher, 84 per cent. with Scandinavian personal-names, out of a total of 83 *thorp* names having a personal-name as the first element.[36] [This contrast between names in *by* and *thorp* suggests that the former are, as a class, relatively early.]

[Another early group of names are the hybrids in which Scandinavian personal names are compounded with English elements. Foston in Derbyshire is an example compounded of the Scandinavian nick-name *Fotr* and the English element *tun*,] but this type of name is generally described as a 'Grimston hybrid' because the most commonly used personal-name is Grimr and, although other English elements, such as *feld*, *ford* and *leah* occur, the most frequent is *tun*.[37] The use of such English elements suggests that these names were given by English speakers and although it is possible that some of the personal-names were borne by men of English descent it seems probable that most of them were the names of Scandinavians. There are significant differences between the distribution of these hybrid names and of the more purely Scandinavian names, such as those in *by* and *thorp*. This is shown clearly in the following table of Domesday place-names based on figures kindly supplied by Professor Kenneth Cameron, in which the hybrids are names in *tun* with a Scandinavian personal-name as the first element.[38]

County	Hybrids	by *names*	thorp *names*
Derbyshire	10	9	4
Nottinghamshire	19	21	16
Leicestershire	21 (one doubtful)	56	18
Lincolnshire			
North Riding	1	52	1
South Riding	0	86	20
West Riding	1	28	17
Kesteven	8	51	28
Holland	1	0	0
Rutland	1	0	5

The differences between the distributions is also brought out in Figures 12a, b and c based on maps prepared by Gillian Fellows Jensen. Figure 12a showing the hybrid names of Lincolnshire and Yorkshire may be compared with Figures 12b and c which show the names in *by* and *thorp* that also incorporate Scandinavian personal-names.[39] The fact that these hybrid names are generally found on good settlement sites that were unlikely to have been left vacant by the English, together with the use of English elements, strongly suggests that, as a class, these names represent an early stage of the Scandinavian colonisation when the invaders were seizing the best estates they could find. The hybrid names therefore seem to represent an earlier stage of the conquest and colonisation than the names in *by*, which are generally not on such good land,[39a] and the names in *by* are themselves earlier, as a group, than the names in *thorp*. The difference in the distribution of these names may therefore be taken to reflect different stages of the Scandinavian settlement.

It is possible that the hybrid names come from the very first stage of the Scandinavian colonisation, but for that stage we are fortunate in having additional, independent evidence in the form of stone carvings that show Scandinavian influence. There are in the north of England a large number of stone carvings by English craftsmen in the English tradition in which attempts have been made to satisfy Scandinavian tastes.[40] Some of these monuments, like the stone from Middleton near Pickering, Yorkshire, shown in Plate XIV, are undoubtedly early and a

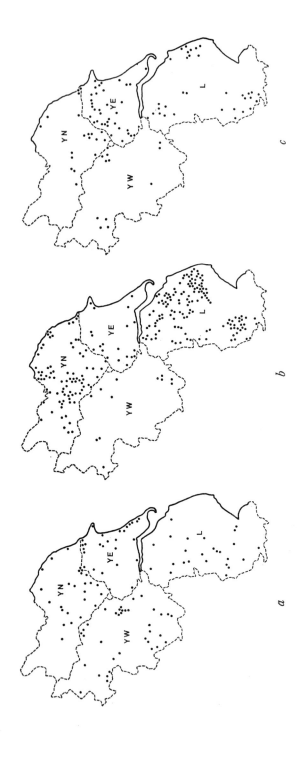

Figure 12 (above) Sketch maps showing the distribution of place-names in Lincolnshire and Yorkshire, based on Gillian Fellows Jensen, *Scandinavian Personal Names in Lincolnshire and Yorkshire* (1968), pp. xxxiv, xxxix, xliii and xlviii.

a Place-names consisting of a Scandinavian personal name and an English element.

b Place-names consisting of a Scandinavian personal name and *by*.

c Place-names consisting of a Scandinavian personal name and *thorp*.

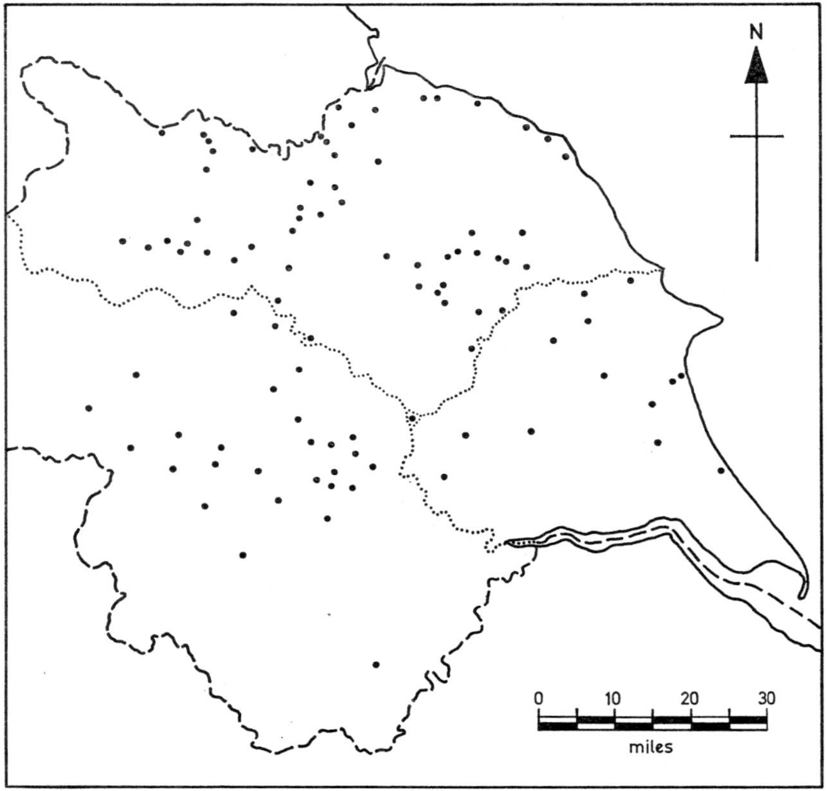

Figure 13 (right) A sketch map of Yorkshire showing the distribution of stone carvings decorated in Scandinavian style, based on a list prepared by David Wilson.

few may even have been carved before the end of the ninth century. The fact that many of these stones are found well away from the areas in which Scandinavian place-names are common, formerly led some scholars to doubt their Scandinavian character[41] but recent studies have removed those doubts and we should now recognise these monuments as evidence of an early stage in the Scandinavian colonisation of northern England. Many of the villages in which these carvings occur are on good settlement sites that must already have been occupied, and named, by the English when the Scandinavians came and in a few there are earlier stone carvings to confirm that these were indeed earlier settlement sites.[42]

The evidence of these crosses and of the Grimston hybrids suggests that the Scandinavian conquerors first seized the best land, the already existing villages, but without greatly affecting the names of these places. Most of the Grimston hybrids are new names for old places but relatively few of the estates taken over by the first generation of Scandinavian colonists seem to have been renamed, although strong Scandinavian influence is sometimes shown in the later forms of these names and, in some villages, in the names of fields and minor features of the landscape. A map of Scandinavian settlement names can therefore be a misleading guide to the first stages of the Scandinavian conquest. It is indeed remarkable how few Scandinavian settlement names are to be found in the vicinity of such important early centres of Scandinavian power as Derby, Nottingham, Leicester or even Lincoln. Another area in which demonstrably early Scandinavian settlements have left little or no trace is in Cambridgeshire where, according to the Anglo-Saxon Chronicle for 903, Edward the Elder 'harried all the land of the Scandinavians between the dykes and the Ouse, all as far north as the Fens'. This precise definition of the location of land held by Scandinavians is unique and it is noteworthy that the area lacks Scandinavian place-names.[43]

The survival of English place-names in the areas that were first colonised by the Scandinavians, together with the English element in the hybrid names, show that a substantial native population survived in those areas, a population that was in time to be deeply influenced by their Scandinavian masters. In contrast, the place-names in *by*, which are generally not found on the best settlement sites, seem to represent an early extension of the Scandinavian settlement in areas in which there were only slight English influences.] This would account for the absence of hybrid names in the areas in which *by* names are concentrated, and for the rarity of *by* names incorporating an English personal-name. The *thorp* names, which are even more markedly on secondary land and incorporate more English personal-names than the place-names in *by*, seem to represent an even later extension of the settlement at a time when there had been more assimilation between English and Scandinavians.[44] The concentration of these names in the East Riding of Yorkshire, particularly in the northern part of the Wolds, suggests that a great extension of settlement occurred in that area, probably in the last century before the Norman Conquest.

Place-names and stone crosses make possible at least the outlines of a chronology of the Scandinavian settlement but they cannot alone determine how many settlers there were. It is commonly accepted that the scale of Scandinavian influence was so great that there must have been a very numerous Scandinavian population, that there was a veritable folk migration from Denmark to England in the last years of the ninth century and, perhaps, in the early years of the tenth.[45] It is, however, also accepted that the Viking armies were not very large and it has therefore become necessary for those who believe the Scandinavian colonisation to have been on a massive scale, to assume that there was a secondary migration from Denmark under the shelter of the Viking armies that had established themselves in England.[46] There have even been attempts to reconstruct the routes by which these migrating peasants came. Professor Cameron has, for example, pointed out that Scandinavian place-names are very frequent at the south end of the Lincolnshire Wolds 'where penetrations could have been made from the coast along the numerous rivers and streams which flow from the Wolds. . . . The Danish-named villages near the Bain, itself a Scandinavian river-name, and on the south of the Wolds, could well have been established by settlers entering the country by the Wash, then following the Witham as far as the Bain. It cannot surely be coincidence that Danish settlement is

M

thickest on the lower Bain and along its tributaries to the east, as well as, still further east, along the Lymn and its feeders.'[47] This reconstruction is possibly correct, but the names could as well represent an extension of settlement from other parts of Lincolnshire. Settlements along a river do not prove that the settlers came up that river.

The fact that no such secondary migration is reported in contemporary sources does not necessarily rule out the possibility, for the Anglo-Saxon Chronicle is principally concerned with the efforts of the West Saxons and their allies against the Danish threat to Wessex; it contains little information about the internal affairs of Scandinavian Britain. It would, however, not be unreasonable to expect a migration on such a massive scale to have left some trace in later traditions, but apparently there is none. The description of the Danes in tenth-century English sources as 'armies'[48] and the absence of any later indications that the areas of supposed 'secondary migration' were in any special sense tributary or subordinate to the centres of Danish power, under whose shelter they are supposed to have been settled, strongly suggests that no such secondary, peasant migration ever took place. What is more, the apparent difficulty experienced by the 'army' of 892 in finding somewhere to settle suggests that newcomers were not always welcome. That there was some foreign immigration into England in the tenth century is shown by the Chronicle's complaint that King Edgar 'attracted hither foreigners and enticed harmful people to this country'.[49] William of Malmesbury is more specific in complaining that Edgar was intimate with foreigners, Saxons, Flemings and even Danes, from whom the English acquired drunken habits.[50] At the beginning of the eleventh century Danes were living in many parts of England, as is shown by their massacre in 1002, but they do not seem to have left much trace.[51] Some of the Danes feared by Ethelred may even have been settled by him to help the defence of England but others were probably earlier immigrants. There is, however, nothing to suggest that this Danish immigration, however widespread, was on a large scale or included many peasants. The Danish colonisation of England was not achieved by Edgar's friends and the like, or by a silent stream of peasants sheltered by the

Danish 'armies' whose course the Chronicler so carefully describes. It was, in fact, the work of the 'armies' themselves.

The belief in very large numbers rests not only on the number of place-names, but on the scale of general Scandinavian linguistic influence. The case is well stated by Professor Henry Loyn.[52]

'The language gives clearest proof of all that these Scandinavian settlements were migrations. Even the pronoun structure, notoriously conservative, was modified. Legal terms abound, but much more impressive are the common words in modern English that have a Scandinavian origin. *Take, call, window, husband, sky, anger, low, scant, loose, ugly, wrong, happy,* even grammatical words like *hence* and *thence, though* and *till,* are Scandinavian. As Jespersen says, an Englishman cannot *thrive* or be *ill* or *die* without Scandinavian words: they are to the language what *bread* and *eggs* are to the daily fare. This influence is much more marked in modern English than in classical Anglo-Saxon, not because of later accretions of Scandinavian peoples in the post-1066 period, but simply because the basis of modern English is the East Midland dialect where the mingling of English and Danish was so complete. It seems evident that we had in that area the unusual co-habitation of two languages, similar enough to be mutually intelligible with some patience and forbearance, different enough to have a contribution to make one to the other. Questions of social prestige seem not to have arisen; questions of political mastery were not important save in the legal sphere; the two languages grew together to the great enrichment of the dominant partner.'

When Professor Whitelock writes that it is difficult 'to see why a preponderant English population should adopt Scandinavian pronouns, auxiliary verbs and other everyday words because they were spoken by a minority of their neighbours'[53] the implication is clearly that the Scandinavian influence on English can only be explained by an immigration of Scandinavians on a scale large enough to constitute, in some extensive areas, a majority. The argument is seductive and the conclusion is widely accepted; but there is much room for doubt. Recent studies of linguistic change and, in particular, of bilingualism have shown how very complex and unpredictable the effect of one language on another can be.] Uriel Weinreich, in his important general work, *Languages in Contact: Findings and Problems*[54] shows how misleading it can be to draw conclusions about the number of people involved in linguistic changes from the changes themselves. In that book he set out to describe and analyse the ways in which languages affect each other when they come into contact in a person, or population, that is bilingual. This study is relevant because the Scandinavian influence on English must have been through a bilingual population.] Although English and Danish are closely related languages it would hardly have been possible for the Scandinavian colonists to communicate with the native English, unless each group had learnt at least something of each other's language. It is sometimes assumed that these languages were, in the ninth century, so similar that they were mutually comprehensible, but differences of pronunciation would alone have been a barrier to immediate understanding. The bilingualism needed for communication would doubtless have been facilitated by the similarity of the languages.[56] Weinreich shows that where languages come into contact in bilingual speakers, each language affects the other, but there is no ready formula for the ways in which this happens. Both phonetics and grammar, including inflexions, can be affected but the vocabulary of a language, being 'considerably more loosely structured than its phonemics and its grammar, is beyond question the domain of borrowing *par excellence*. . . . The need to designate new things, persons, places, and concepts is, obviously, a universal cause of lexical innovation.'[57] But there are also such internal linguistic factors as the low frequency of words, for words that are rarely used tend to be replaced more readily than words in common use. Another internal linguistic factor is pernicious homonymy, where words that mean different things are hard to distinguish because they sound alike, and a third is the need, apparently common to many languages, for synonyms for certain concepts such as 'talking', 'beating', 'sleeping', 'tallness' or 'ugliness'.[58] All these factors affect the the unilingual as well as the bilingual but 'whereas the unilingual depends, in replenishing his vocabulary, on indigenous lexical material and whatever loan words may happen to be

transmitted to him, the bilingual has the other language as a
constantly available source of lexical innovations'.[59] Weinrich's
conclusion that 'even for extensive word transferring, large
numbers of bilingual speakers need not be involved and the
relative size of the groups is not necessarily a factor'[60] is
clearly of the greatest importance in interpreting the impact of
Scandinavian speech on English. Linguistic arguments, on their
own, are insufficient to prove the scale of the Scandinavian
settlement.

Attempts have been made to find support for the theory of
massive Scandinavian immigration in other features of the
Danelaw. Sir Frank Stenton claimed that 'the sokemen of the
Danelaw represent, as a class, the rank and file of the Scandinavian armies which had settled this district in the ninth century',[61] and Professor Ekwall has accepted the proportion of
sokemen in the Danelaw as a criterion for the relative number of
Danish settlers.[62] Sokemen formed about half the population
as recorded by the Lincolnshire Domesday, and if they really
may be considered the descendants of the Danish settlers the
settlements must have been on a truly massive scale. Unfortunately there is no evidence for the association of sokemen
and Danes apart from the coincidence of their distribution,
and it must be emphasised that this coincidence is not very
close. In Yorkshire there are very few sokemen.[63] This has
been explained by the assumption that William the Conqueror's devastation in the north destroyed the class, but this
is to pile hypothesis on hypothesis. Even if the coincidence
between the areas in which Scandinavians seem to have settled
and the sokemen were exact, it would still not prove that the
sokemen were Danes; at the most it would suggest that
the sokemen were in some way the result of the Scandinavian
settlements and conquest. It is indeed more likely that the
sokemen were English peasants whose social, legal and economic status had been altered as a result of the Danish conquests.[64]
In any case, unless the connection between Danes and sokemen can be proved it is improper to use the number of Domesday sokemen as a guide to the number of Scandinavian settlers.
The argument is circular.

Another distinctive feature of the Danelaw has been seen in

the use of the ploughland as the unit of assessment for taxation and the imposition of public burdens. It has been argued that the ploughland, or carucate as it was called after the Norman Conquest, was imported from Scandinavia.[65] One important objection to this theory is that there is no evidence for the ploughland as a unit of assessment in Scandinavia until the thirteenth century.[66] Even more significant is the fact that the hide, the Old English unit of assessment, continued in use in the Danelaw until the beginning of the eleventh century.[67] The change from hides to ploughlands may well have been part of a general reorganisation undertaken in the last years of Ethelred's reign, in the course of which the Midland shires were also created,[68] but it can hardly be claimed that a unit of assessment that was first used early in the eleventh century can be of much value as a guide to the density or even character of the Danish settlement in the ninth. Another supposed sign of Scandinavian influence is the duodecimal system of assessment found in the 'Danish' parts of England. While in the south and west of England assessments for public burdens were generally in units of 5 and 10, in the Danelaw the units were 6 and 12. J. H. Round claimed that 'the district in which men measured by carucates and counted by twelves and sixes was not the district which the Danes *conquered* but the district which the Danes *settled*.'[69] There are, however, traces of duodecimal assessments in other, non-Scandinavian parts of England. The county of Worcester, for example, was assessed in the eleventh century at 1200 hides.[70] This is, it is true, a total and the individual estates in Worcestershire were often assessed in decimal units but as late as the thirteenth century new assessments for a tax based on ploughs were being made in both decimal and duodecimal units in such a non-Scandinavian county as Oxfordshire.[71] It is perhaps even more significant that both decimal and duodecimal patterns are also found in Normandy where, it has been argued, the duodecimal were Frankish and the decimal due to Scandinavian influence.[72] Neither ploughlands nor duodecimal units can be used as a guide to the density or character of the ninth-century Danish colonisation of England.

In short, apart from their settlements and their influence on the language and consequently on names and on some of the terminology of law and administration, the Scandinavians do not seem to have made a distinctive mark on England. Most of the so-called signs of Scandinavian influence are either dubious or demonstrably false and the linguistic influence cannot alone prove that there was a mass migration of Danes in the ninth century. It is, in fact, contended here that the Scandinavian character of the Danelaw is sufficiently explained by the conquests and settlement of the Danish armies of the ninth century and that there is no need to postulate a secondary migration of Danish peasants under the shelter of those armies.

The most satisfactory reconstruction of the Danish colonisation of England would therefore seem to be that the Danes who settled between 876 and 880 made such places as Lincoln, York, Nottingham, Derby and Cambridge the main centres of their power and took over the lordship of villages that had long been settled by the English. They were almost certainly a minority in these areas, but they were a dominant minority. They were soon converted to Christianity[73] and are remembered by the stone crosses and gravestones that were carved by English craftsmen to suit the taste of their new masters. The first settlers were joined by others in 896, and this second group may have brought much treasure with them; apart from the Chronicler's implication that only those with wealth could settle in England, it was at this time that the Viking rulers of York began to issue a silver coinage of their own.[74] The language these invaders spoke was closely related to English but for communication there had to be bilingualism. The similarity of the languages would, however, have facilitated the linguistic interference which resulted in local forms of English in which Scandinavian influence was very marked, an influence that was to pervade all parts of England before the end of the fifteenth century.

The expansion of settlement marked by the names in *by* was undertaken at an early stage before there had been much assimilation between the colonists and their English neighbours. The personal names used in the place-names are almost exclusively Scandinavian and in at least some areas the speech in the new settlements may well have been more purely Scandinavian than in the first settlements, where the majority of the population remained English. In the areas of new settlement the population could well have been almost exclusively of Scandinavian descent but not many Scandinavians would have been needed to make such a majority, for they were settling land that had not hitherto been occupied.

In the unconquered parts of England there were many interests opposed to the extension of the settled area. Both ecclesiastical and lay lords had claims on the unsettled land which were a significant restraint on new colonisation. In the Danelaw the destruction of the established church and the replacement of the power of the English kings and lay lords by the Scandinavian invaders meant that new land could be more freely occupied. What is more, men who had broken their home ties to find new homes overseas would have been less willing to accept such restraint, whether voluntary or imposed, than men in relatively undisturbed societies and it is likely that there was another powerful motive for expansion in the natural desire of the leaders of the Scandinavian colonists to reward and provide for the sons of the first generation warriors. All this combined with the economic stimulus afforded by invaders who brought with them the accumulated loot of years spent plundering Christendom encouraged the extension of the settlement and with it of Scandinavian influence in England. The extension of Scandinavian settlements in the *by* areas of England is, therefore, in large measure a continuation of that movement of expansion that began in Scandinavia and itself led to the migration overseas,[75] and this expanding Scandinavian settlement in England was the beginning of that process of internal colonisation that was to reach its greatest extent in the thirteenth century.[76]

The main driving force behind that internal colonisation was, however, economic. The strength or weakness of kings and other lords, and the attitude of the Scandinavian colonists towards renewed migration were no doubt important factors, but far more important was the economic pressure on peasants and lords alike to extend the area of cultivation and settlement. It was this that ensured the success of the precocious internal colonisation begun by the first or second generation of Danish settlers north of the Welland. In the eleventh century the

demand seems to have been above all for an extension of sheep
farming to satisfy the looms of Flanders and those parts of the
Danelaw that were well suited to sheep farming prospered
greatly, as did other good sheep country elsewhere in England.[77]
The extension of settlement in the Yorkshire Wolds, marked in
part by place-names in *thorp*, was a response to this demand as
were the expanding settlements in the Lincolnshire Wolds.
Both areas had more in common, economically, with the chalk
hills of southern England than they had with the 'Scandinavian'
areas of Northamptonshire or East Anglia.

It is likely that the initial Danish conquest and colonisation
affected the southern parts of the Danelaw, including Northamptonshire and East Anglia, as much as it did Lincolnshire
and Yorkshire. The differences in the apparent degree of
Scandinavian influence may be explained in part, as has been
suggested in this chapter, by the earlier and more effective sub-
mission of the southern Danelaw to the English kings, but it
probably owes more to the fact that Lincolnshire and Yorkshire
offered great opportunities for an expansion which soon proved
prosperous. Neither the expansion nor the prosperity was
peculiar to the Danelaw. Domesday Book shows that the
estates of Kent were more valuable than those of Lincolnshire[78]
and there are clear indications of expanding settlement at this
time elsewhere in England. The expansion in the Danelaw is
distinctive not because it is unique, but because it reveals itself
in distinctive, Scandinavian names. Where the opportunities for
expansion were slight, as in the long settled areas first taken by
the Danes, or where the growth was later, in response to the
demand of a growing population for food, the Danish colonisation has left fewer traces on the map.[79]

The Danish settlements in England were part of a wider
movement that also resulted in settlements on the other side
of the Channel, in particular in what became Normandy.
The evidence for this settlement of Normandy is, unfortunately,
even less satisfactory than for the settlement of the English
Danelaw, but it seems well established that early in the tenth
century Scandinavians were in control of the Lower Seine,
and that their influence was later extended to the Cotentin.[80]
The Scandinavian personal-names used in Normandy suggest

that the settlement was primarily the work of Danes, and there are also indications that at least some of the settlers in Normandy came from Britain[81] and it may be that a prominent part was played by those Danes who left England in 896 moneyless and went across the sea to the Seine.

There is no reason to suppose that the Scandinavian conquest and colonisation of Normandy was significantly different from that in England.[82] It is true that the colonists did not influence the language of Normandy as they did English, but the danger of drawing conclusions about the scale of settlement from such evidence has been sufficiently emphasised. The difference in linguistic influence cannot be explained by a smaller scale of settlement; it probably owes more to the dissimilarity of the languages offering fewer opportunities for linguistic interference, but it may also be, in part, because in Normandy there was no early extension of settlement of the type revealed in England by the place names in *by*, and there were therefore no areas in which Scandinavian was spoken by a local majority. The lack of such *by* areas in Normandy, was, in its turn, due not to any difference in the scale of colonisation but rather to the early authority of the Norman dukes. Under them, and the church they soon favoured, there were fewer opportunities for colonising unsettled land than in the north of England. What is more, Normandy is not very suitable for sheep farming and the situation there in the tenth and eleventh centuries must have been much closer to that in the southern parts of the Danelaw than to Yorkshire or Lincolnshire. In Normandy, as in Northamptonshire, it is in the names given to minor features of the landscape that the Scandinavian influence is most clearly marked.[83]

8. Towns and Trade

WESTERN European sources of the ninth century mention several places in Scandinavia and the Baltic that were then centres of trade. The *Vita Anskarii* shows that by the middle of the century merchants regularly gathered at both Hedeby and Birka, and Hedeby is also mentioned by Ohthere and Wulfstan in their contributions to the Old English translation of Orosius.[1] Ohthere describes how he sailed from his home in the north to *Sciringesheal* a '*port* in the south of that land', and thence to 'the *port* that men call *æt Hæthum*', which must mean Hedeby. That both places had some commercial importance is indicated by the use of the word *port* which generally meant a town with a market.[2] Wulfstan, who seems to have been an Englishman, described a journey of seven days and nights from *Hæthum* to *Truso* which may similarly have had a market. There has been much speculation about the location of *Truso* which, according to Wulfstan stood on the shore of a lake near the mouth of the Vistula. It is possible that its name survives in that of Lake Drausen and that on its site the town of Elbing now stands. Ohthere did not describe the position of *Sciringesheal* very precisely but other evidence suggested that it lay in the neighbourhood of Tjølling near Larvik on the western side of Oslo Fjord. This has now been confirmed archaeologically and the site of this Viking period market-place has been found at Kaupang, itself a suggestive name of the same kind as English Chipping, meaning a market. The sites of Birka and Hedeby have similarly been determined by excavation.

The first of these Viking towns to be thoroughly studied was Birka where Hjalmar Stolpe excavated about 1,100 graves between 1871 and 1895.[3] It stands at the north-west of the island of Björkö in Lake Mälar, about 18 miles (30 km.) west of Stockholm. The graves, of which there are over 2,000, are grouped around an area of about 22 acres (9 hectares) called the Black Earth because of its dark colour, which is especially noticeable when it is wet. No trace of a well-defined charcoal layer has been found and the colour is probably due to intensive occupation, not to burning. Stolpe excavated about a thirtieth of the Black Earth and found many objects of great interest and traces of both wattle and daub as well as timber buildings, but little is yet known about the form and layout of the structures, and the finds from this occupation layer, which was about 8 ft. (2·5 m.) thick have not yet been published. To the south-west of this town area is a hill about 100 ft. (30 m.) high on which stood a fort. From this commanding position it is possible to see the whole town area and far beyond over the lake. The town area, which seems to have been rather larger than the Black Earth, was probably enclosed by a wall, but only 550 yds. (500 m.) of it survive, the rest having been disturbed, probably by farmers and men in search of stone. This wall was constructed over a number of graves, and as one of these contained a coin of 925, the date of this structure is fairly well determined, although there may well have been earlier defences that have not yet been discovered. This tenth-century wall has been partly excavated and found to consist of a low stone base in which a palisade was set. In the surviving section of the wall there are no fewer than six openings which cannot have been for gates; a gate every 100 yards would hardly have been necessary, and Professor Arbman's suggestion that timber towers stood in these gaps seems very likely to be correct.

The graves of Birka have been more carefully investigated than anything else and it is their contents that have provided the main information about the history of the site. Many were cremations but, fortunately for the archaeologist, there were more inhumations than was then common in the area. Some of the graves were presumably of warriors, like that illustrated in Figure 3, but others were probably the graves of merchants. Certainly the three graves containing small balances of the kind used for weighing precious metal were probably of merchants and there were also about 130 graves containing one or more weights of the kind used with such balances. The objects found in the graves show such a diversity of contacts,

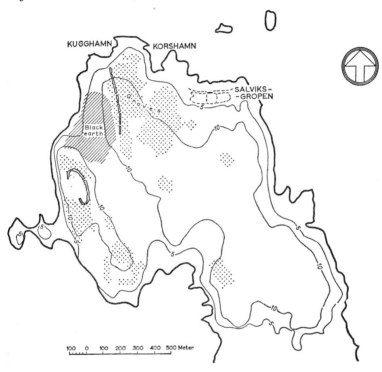

Figure 14a   Birka in Lake Mälar. See p. 183.

whether or not these contacts were direct, that there can be no doubt Rimbert was right when he described part of Birka's population as merchants (*negotiatores*).[4]

Anskar set out for Birka in company with some merchants from the West and when he reached the town he found many signs of contact with western Europe and with Dorestad in particular.[5] There are several objects from the graves that

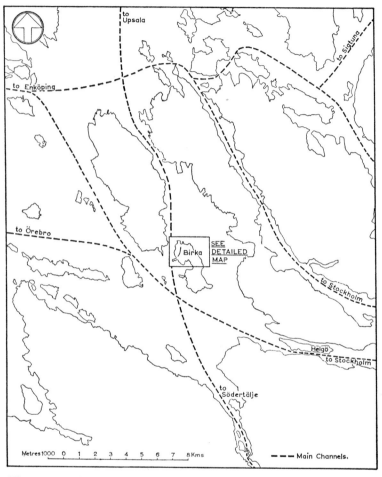

Figure 14b Showing Birka's situation in the lake and the main routes. See pp. 182–3.

confirm this connection, such as pottery and glass from the Rhineland[6] and, particularly important, because their provenance is not doubted, some twenty coins from western Europe, all of which had been adapted to serve as ornaments.[7] The most recent of these European coins were from the Kingdom of York in the early tenth century. There were also some so-called Birka coins which were modelled on Frankish types and which were probably being produced in Denmark during the ninth century.[8] Rimbert naturally emphasised the western connections that Anskar found at Birka, but the objects discovered there show that these can have played only a small part in the life of the town. The thirteen graves with coins from western Europe may be compared with the ninety-two in which coins or coin fragments from the Islamic East were found, and other finds confirm that Birka's main interests outside Scandinavia were in the East. Forty-five of the graves contained traces of silk and although much of this does not seem to have been of very high quality and its provenance is unknown, there were remains of some very fine silk, with a gold pattern, that is likely to have come from China.[9] Nothing else at Birka seems to have come from so far afield but there are ornaments of various kinds, glass objects and rings, including one set with an amethyst bearing an Arabic inscription, that came from the Islamic lands south and east of the Caspian Sea. Most of these imports seem to have come from the eastern parts of the Caliphate and confirm the impression given by the coins that Birka's contacts, like those of the eastern Baltic as a whole, were with the Volga rather than the Dnieper. Birka seems to have had hardly any contact with Byzantium. The graves have only yielded three Byzantine coins, two of silver and one of copper, and there is one Roman denarius. The scarcity of Byzantine coins in Scandinavia as a whole might be explained by the assumption that trade was balanced and that goods, not coins, reached the north, but there are few objects either at Birka or elsewhere in Sweden that seem to have come from the workshops of the Byzantine Empire. It is only in the second half of the tenth century, when Birka ceased to exist as a centre of trade, that the number of Byzantine coins found in Scandinavia increased.

Birka was very well placed as the starting-point for a trade route to the East, particularly to those parts of the East that were richest in silver in the ninth and tenth centuries. The map (Fig. 1) shows how direct the route was to the Volga, and it was on the Volga, among the Bulghars, that merchants from Scandinavia met the Muslims with whom they dealt. From

Birka to Bulghar was a shorter and easier journey than to
Byzantium and the way lay, for the most part, through easily
navigable waters. What is more, the whole route from the
western entrance of the Gulf of Finland was through country
inhabited by Finnish-speaking peoples. Any traveller who
could make himself understood in Finnish would have had
few language difficulties on the route to the Volga. As Middle
Sweden lay very close to Finnish-speaking areas it would not
have been difficult for the men of Birka to have found opportunities to learn the language, if only from Finns who had
been captured, married or enslaved.

In the Viking period Lake Mälar had many more outlets
than nowadays and one of these may have been almost directly
south of Birka through Södertälje. This was in fact the lake's
last southern opening to the sea and Birka was very conveniently situated in relation to it.[10] Unfortunately the date
at which this entrance ceased to be navigable is uncertain,[11]
but if it was still open in the ninth and tenth centuries one of
Birka's greatest assets must have been its position at the junc-
tion of the two routes, one south to Gotland, the southern
Baltic, Hedeby and beyond, the other through the Gulf of
Finland to the Volga. Birka also had easy communications
with many parts of Middle Sweden by the lake and rivers
and, what may possibly have been even more important, with
the north of Sweden which could be reached by sea, or by a
succession of lakes, rivers and glacial moraines. In summer this
inland route might not have been very convenient but in
winter, when the rivers and lakes were frozen, they could serve
as highways through the forest and there would then have
been few obstacles between Birka and the north. In winter
furs are at their best and during the Middle Ages winter
markets called *Distingen* were held near Uppsala and it is very
likely that a similar winter market was held at Birka.[12] The
discovery of bones that were used as skates, ice-axes and, in
some graves, of shoes furnished with spikes to grip the ice,
shows that life went on in Birka during the winter and supports
the hypothesis of winter market trading there.

The island of Björkö is, therefore, very conveniently placed
for communication by water or ice with many parts, and the

market was probably established there because of these advantages. The site of the town itself on the island seems to have
been well chosen. There is the protection of the hill fort, which
could also be used as a look-out from which it is possible to
see great distances along the waterways that led to the island,
including that through Södertälje. The town itself faced a
gently sloping beach and the timber piles that have been reported here were probably the remains of piers and moorings
which would have been suitable for ships of shallow draught.
For bigger vessels there were two coves close by the town in
the northern tip of the island. Sailing vessels that used these
could very easily be moved out in order to catch the wind,
which in the summer is prevailingly from the south-west.[13]

The outline of the island has been transformed since the time
Birka flourished by the changed level of the lake. The land in
eastern Sweden has been rising out of the water since long
before the Viking period. It is very difficult to establish the
level of the water in earlier times but at Birka a tenth-century
grave that now stands about 18 ft. (5·5 m.) above the present
water-level shows clear signs of having been eroded by the
action of the lake.[14] This erosion must have been in a storm
that lashed water well above its normal level. Observation
elsewhere indicates that such erosion could occur in a storm
up to about 3 ft. above the normal water-level. On this basis
the water-level at Birka would have been about 15 ft. (4·5 m.)
above the present level, with the mound about 3 ft. above the
normal surface at that time. The possibility that the water
had already receded when the damage occurred and that the
damage was caused by a water rise of less than 1 m. means that
this figure of 15 ft. should be taken as a minimum change since
the Viking period.[15] In the map of Björkö given here the 5 m.-
contour is indicated, and this gives some idea of the remarkable
changes that have taken place since the Viking period. The
most interesting if not the most dramatic change is the disappearance of a small lagoon about 275 yds. long and 65 yds.
across (250 m. × 60 m.) east of the town area. The natural
opening of about 33 yds. (30 m.) is closed by a stone wall in
which a narrow passage has been left. In the centre of this
lagoon is a square basin that was probably artificial called

Salviksgropen. The floor of this now stands about 5 ft. (1·5 m.) above the lake level and in the Viking period it would therefore have been filled with water to a depth of about at least 10 ft. (3 m.) without any allowance for silting. Only excavation can show if this curious arrangement dates back to the Viking period, but a sheltered basin of this kind would have been a very remarkable asset for the town. Birka was in existence in about 829 when Anskar first visited it, but there is no means of telling how old it then was or how large. The material that has been excavated includes very few objects of the kind associated in the area with the pre-Viking period. Unfortunately this archaeological transition from the Vendel to the Viking period cannot be dated historically and attempts to do so have, in large measure, depended on the assumption that Birka's history began in about 800.[16] It is possible that when more of the site has been excavated, and the material more critically examined, the date of Birka's foundation may be determined more closely, but for the present it would be as well to accept that it was established sometime between about 780 and 830. Its end can be dated rather more closely. The complete absence of the late tenth-century German and English coins which are so common in Sweden indicates that it had been deserted before the year 1000 at the latest, and probably before 980. The most recent coin found there was struck in either 963 or 967 and the end may well have been very soon after that.[17]

The causes for the disappearance have been discussed by many scholars. The absence of a well-defined charcoal layer makes it unlikely that it was destroyed by some act of violence, which would, in any case hardly be a satisfactory explanation on its own, for had the sources of Birka's prosperity remained unchanged there would obviously have been some incentive to rebuild. The changing water-level has been suggested, but this could not have made the island useless in the late tenth century. Less directly the lowering water-level has been blamed for closing the southern inlet through Södertälje.[18] The argument is that when ships could no longer pass direct to Birka, and had to use one of the eastern entrances to the lake, Birka's place was taken by Sigtuna on the direct route from

Stockholm to Uppsala and the north. This explanation is not satisfactory because the evidence for a change in the character of the southern inlet to the lake in the late tenth century is by no means clear and there is also nothing to suggest that Sigtuna was founded much, if at all, earlier than 1000.[19] A far more satisfactory explanation for the decline of Birka is that some time between 965 and about 970 the direct connection between the Baltic and the Volga was broken. The coin evidence shows this very clearly.[20] The effect on Birka must have been catastrophic. Its main connections were with the Volga, and once this route was broken Birka was cut off from its principal, if not only, source of wealth. Its survival depended on the discovery of some alternative source of wealth but the merchants of Birka were not well equipped to exploit any other route: their advantages were in the Eastern trade. Birka therefore ceased to exist because it ceased to be profitable. New sources of wealth were found, but not by the merchants of Birka; the men who profited were the Gotlanders.

The dates of the Islamic coins found in the Birka graves are given in the following table. They suggest that its main period of prosperity only began towards the end of the ninth century and this agrees well with the general impression of the material found on the site.[21]

Date of Coins	Number found in Birka graves
700–750	12
750–800	14
800–850	17
850–890	4
890–950	42
950–	1

The presence of coins of the eighth century does not, of course, mean that the graves can be dated to that time, for these older coins remained in circulation for a long time in Scandinavia. Some of the older coins were in fact found in graves along with later ones; for example in one grave a coin of 818–19 was found together with four from 913–32. Many of the other early coins may similarly have been buried in the tenth century.

The grave finds of Birka give some idea of the objects, at least the durable ones, that were imported. Some imports may well have been of organic material that would have disappeared, like food, cloth, wooden objects, and even salt, but those that survive give some idea of the town's connections. Far less is known of its exports. The probability that coins were minted here as ornaments or currency suggests that metal may have been worked, and there are some finds of reindeer horn that were partially worked. There may very well have been other local handicrafts as there seem to have been somewhat earlier on the nearby island of Helgö, where traces of iron smelting have been found, and large quantities of broken glass suggest the making of glass beads, probably from broken waste.[22] The most valuable goods that merchants are likely to have brought to Birka and exported— furs and skins—are not likely to have left much trace, although remains of such animals as the marten and beaver have apparently been found. There are, however, good reasons that will be discussed below for doubting if Birka can ever have been very important as a collecting centre for furs.[23] It is more likely to have been a market at which merchants rich in Islamic silver were tempted to spend it.

The settlement area of Hedeby has been much more thoroughly excavated than that of Birka and such details as the construction of the houses and the local handicrafts are much better known.[24] There are unfortunately some uncertainties about its origin but the general opinion is now that its foundation is in fact described in the Frankish Royal Annals for 808 which report an attack by the Danish king Godfred on the Slav town of *Reric* and the forcible transfer of its merchants to *Sliastorp*, which is generally identified as Hedeby, although some still argue that it means Sleswig. The settlement of Hedeby lay on the shore of Haddeby Noor, a lake at the head of the River Schlei. Originally it seems to have been undefended but later in the ninth century it was surrounded by a semicircular wall which was rebuilt several times and remains a prominent feature of the landscape. Iron and glass were worked here and ornaments made of bronze and silver. Raw materials were brought from far afield, including stone from

Eifel for millstones and walrus tusks from Norway and there is
good evidence of cloth-making. Hedeby must, however, have
been far more important for its transit trade than for its handicrafts. It was ideally suited for through traffic. It lay at the
head of the long and navigable Schlei and there is from
Hedeby only a short land crossing of about $10\frac{1}{2}$ miles (17 km.)
to Hollingstedt on the River Treene which was similarly navigable and led to the North Sea. This short cut across the base
of the Jutland peninsula, a few miles north of the modern
Kiel Canal, made the dangerous circuit of the Jutland peninsula
unnecessary. The route was, however, only convenient for
relatively small vessels of shallow draught that could be
propelled by oars.[25] The Schlei is about 22 miles (35 km.)
long but in places it is no more than 220 yds. (200 m.) wide,
and the Treene is both longer and very much narrower, in
places no more than 17 yds. (15 m.) As it would have been
impossible to rely on sailing in such narrow channels, oars
must have been used. Moreover, the entrance to the lake on
which Hedeby stands is very shallow and the town can only
have been reached by ships of shallow draught. These limitations, and the need to transport goods by land between
Hedeby and Hollingstedt, meant that the route could not be
used for heavy bulk traffic, but only for relatively light and
valuable goods. Hedeby was destroyed in the middle of the
eleventh century but the excavations have indicated that it
had long before then ceased to be very important, its place
having been taken by Sleswig, which could be reached by
deeper vessels. The passage from the Baltic was still long and
difficult and Sleswig was soon overshadowed by Lübeck, just
as Hollingstedt was overshadowed by Hamburg, both with
harbours that were far more accessible to the heavier sailing
vessels of later times when bulk traffic became so much more
important. There is evidence for this through traffic in the
contributions of Wulfstan and Ohthere to the Old English
Orosius; Wulfstan sailed from Hedeby to *Truso* and Ohthere
travelled to Hedeby from *Sciringesheal*, presumably on his way
to England, just as in Anskar's time men passed through Hedeby
on their way to Birka. It is indeed likely that many of the
objects of western European origin that have been found in

Figure 15   Map of Scandinavia and the Baltic

different parts of Scandinavia entered the Baltic by way of Hedeby.[26]

The material found on the site and the stratification of the bed of a stream that flowed through the middle of the town both suggest that Hedeby was most prosperous and active as a trading centre in the middle Viking period. It is of course difficult to determine dates with any precision but there are good reasons for believing that Hedeby flourished most at the end of the ninth century and in the first half of the tenth. Its prosperity seems therefore to have begun at the time Kufic silver was apparently being exported from the Baltic, and it was at the

same time, at the end of the ninth century, that the town was
occupied by a Swedish dynasty.[27] This dynasty was overthrown
in 934 by the German king, Henry I, and for the middle years
of the tenth century Hedeby seems to have been under German
control. This German conquest does not seem to have brought
Hedeby's prosperity to an end, although it may have led to a
cessation or reduction of silver exports from the Baltic, but in
the second half of the tenth century its contacts seem to have
been more with the Slav lands east of the Elbe than with
the eastern Baltic. This is certainly the impression given by the
distribution of the coins minted at Hedeby at this time, the
Hedeby half-bracteates.[28]

The third of these Scandinavian trading centres to have
been excavated is the market-place of Kaupang in Vestfold,
the *Sciringesheal* of Ohthere.[29] At Kaupang many graves have
been investigated and work has begun on the settlement area,
the Black Earth. The bay on which this settlement stood was
sheltered from the open sea by many small islands, some of
which were, in the Viking period, beneath the surface of the
water which has dropped some $6\frac{1}{2}$ ft. (2 m.). The channels
into the bay must have been complicated and the underwater
obstacles would have been an effective defence against un-
wanted intruders. Unlike Birka and Hedeby there is no sign of
any fortification.

It has been claimed that the finds from Kaupang show
that it flourished from the beginning of the ninth century
until the early years of the tenth, but as with all these sites it is
difficult to determine the date and character of the early
stages. Ohthere shows that the port existed at the end of the
ninth century and nothing in the finds seems to be incon-
sistent with the hypothesis that this market, like the others,
first became important at about that time. There seems to be
no evidence that requires the assumption that it was an important trading centre much earlier than either Hedeby or
Birka. It certainly seems to have been abandoned rather
earlier than either of these other sites, possibly because of the
lowering water-level.

The material found at Kaupang comes from many parts of
Scandinavia and the outside world. There are ornaments from

the British Isles, pottery from the Rhineland, glass from western Europe, and some objects indicate connections with the eastern Baltic. The range of finds is, in fact, well represented by the six coins that have so far been found.[30] There is one English coin, a penny of Cenwulf of Mercia (796–822), and the others were all fragmentary: one was a Frankish denarius of Louis the Pious (814–40), two were Kufic dirhems of which one seems to have been an Abbasid of about 780–830, one was a coin that was probably minted at Birka in the second half of the ninth century and the sixth cannot be identified. One of the most interesting features of Kaupang is that its hinterland is extraordinarily rich in graves of the Viking period and this suggests that the wealth of Kaupang was dispersed among many of the families living along the southern reaches of the River Lågen.[31]

There has, naturally, been much speculation about the commodities that were dealt in at Kaupang. It does not at first sight seem to be well situated for traffic in furs or hides, and although iron and soap-stone may well have been exported these would hardly have justified Kaupang's existence. The excavator of the site, Mrs. Charlotte Blindheim, has recently suggested that fish and down were important exports. Fish would have had to be exported in bulk to make it worth while and Ohthere suggests that the route from Kaupang was to Hedeby which would have made bulk shipments of fish difficult. This and the fact that fish were not an exclusively northern product makes it a less likely item of export from Kaupang than down, which may well have been as useful then as in more recent times and was certainly light and not universally obtainable. Ohthere called at *Sciringesheal* on his way from the north to Hedeby and this suggests that merchants on their way from the rich fur and hide lands of the north may have called there regularly on their way south. The direct crossing of the North Sea would of course have been possible but the route through the sheltered waters east of Jutland would have been safer, at least from the elements. Kaupang would have been a very good starting-point for the last stage of the journey to Hedeby not only for northerners like Ohthere but also for men from the eastern and central parts of Norway. It is, moreover, not unlikely that travellers to Hedeby gathered at Kaupang so that they could combine against the threat of pirates. This would, at least, have been a sensible precaution.

That Birka, Hedeby and Kaupang were trading centres is clear, but in considering their significance it is important to recognise that there were other places of the same kind in the Baltic region and that more may yet be discovered in Scandinavia. There are several places in Norway called Kaupang and it is possible that some of these may be as old as the Kaupang in Vestfold. There are certainly some areas with concentrations of Viking period grave finds similar to that observed in Kaupang's hinterland.[32] One other place that may possibly prove to be a Viking period trading centre is Västergarn on the coast of Gotland, about 15 miles (25 km.) south of Visby.[33] There is at Västergarn a large semicircular earthwork and it has been suggested that this sheltered a trading centre rather like and contemporary with Hedeby. Small excavations have revealed nothing; but local farmers report that when they dig deep pits they find remains of timber under a layer of sand and it is possible that there was a Viking period settlement here that has been covered by blown sand, like the Danish village of Lindholm. Only excavation can settle this, but if it does prove to be like Birka and Hedeby there will be at least one significant difference. The other sites lie in sheltered waters that are relatively difficult to reach; Västergarn is open to the sea and would have been very hard to defend against raiders. South and east of the Baltic there were also several Viking period trading centres. The most important of these were probably Wollin, on the estuary of the River Oder, described by Adam of Bremen as a most noble city, a trading centre that was rich in all the wares of the northern lands,[34] and Novgorod, whose early history is now better known because of large-scale excavations that have been undertaken in recent years.[35] Both Wollin and Novgorod seem to have first become important in the tenth century.

Some of the reasons for thinking of Birka, Hedeby and Kaupang as trading centres have already been mentioned, but before considering the nature and direction of the trade conducted from these places, it would be as well to consider the evidence for trading activity in the Viking period in general. All too often archaeologists and historians assume that the evidence proves the existence of trade when all it really does is to prove that objects were moved from one place to another. Such removals may have been by war, piracy or even gift, and the fact of trade should not be too readily assumed.[36] The Kufic coins that reached Scandinavia in such large quantities in the ninth and tenth centuries may have been the profit of trading ventures but they could equally well have been the profit of war, or the pay of mercenaries like the English coins that reached the north later. Similarly, the discovery of objects of western European origin in Sweden or in Norway cannot alone prove that they were transported by traders; they may have come as plunder or even as gifts. It is therefore desirable in the first place to consider whether trade is an explanation for these material contacts that can reasonably be preferred to other, non-commercial explanations.

Some objects undoubtedly reached their ultimate destinations by a combination of trade and piracy. The ship in which Anskar first set out for Birka was attacked by pirates who took his belongings, and according to Rimbert piracy was making contact between Birka and the West difficult in the middle of the ninth century.[37] In the eleventh century the Baltic was still infested with pirates and Adam of Bremen explains what a serious menace they were.[38] Many of the coin hoards that have been found in the north were probably buried for fear of pirates and the large number of Gotlandic hoards that have been discovered from the middle years of the tenth century and the early years of the eleventh century suggests that pirates were then particularly active.[39] Piracy is, however, only profitable if there is loot to be taken. Pirates must have someone to plunder. Moreover, they had to be able to exchange their loot. Silver may have been valued for ornaments but pirates who won nothing but silver and could not use it to buy other things would have been in danger of starving. The existence of piracy therefore implies that there was wealth to loot and that it could be converted into other useful things.

The existence in the Baltic area of hacksilver, that is silver that has been hacked about presumably to obtain some definite weight, itself suggests that silver was used as a means of exchange. Some hacksilver may well have been used to pay blood money or other primitive compensations, but there is too much for this to be its only use. The existence of very large numbers of coin fragments also suggests that silver was used for trade. The cutting of silver dirhems or pennies into halves, thirds or other fractions indicates the need for the small quantities of silver that would have been required in trading exchanges. That there were exchanges by way of trade inside Scandinavia and the Baltic is also indicated by the remarkably uniform character of coin hoards in the area at any one time.[40] The slow but steady change in the composition of these coin hoards and the dispersal in them of the available coins, for example the Byzantine coins,[41] implies circulation of a kind that is unlikely to have been the result simply of piracy or the payment of warriors. There was certainly war and piracy in the Baltic and Scandinavia during the Viking period, but there was also trade.

In Russia there seems to have been a similar blending of trade and violence. Constantine Porphyrogenitus describes how the chieftains of the Kiev *Rus* with their followers traded at Constantinople with goods that they had spent the winter gathering from the surrounding Slavonic tribes,[42] and the goods sold by other *Rus* to Muslim merchants in Bulghar were apparently gathered in much the same way. These operations were not simply commercial, it was tribute that was traded. The process was, however, partially commercial. The *Rus*, whether of Kiev or elsewhere, extorted tribute from the Slavs and Finns in order to trade in Bulghar or Byzantium.

The activities of the Kiev *Rus* had little or no significance for Scandinavia until late in the Viking period; for Scandinavia the important market was the Islamic East.[43] Muslim merchants came from lands that were extraordinarily rich in silver and they bought a great variety of northern produce in the markets of Bulghar. Furs and slaves were among the most valuable but these were not the only goods they sought. According to the late tenth-century Persian geographer al-Mukaddisi the exports from Bulghar included such things as horse and goat skins, arrows, swords, armour, sheep, cattle, falcons, fish teeth, birch wood, walnuts, wax and honey as well as many kinds of fur and Slavonic slaves.[44] The Scandinavians were not the only merchant people prepared to take advantage of this demand, for the Bulghars themselves exacted tribute from their neighbours, and there were other markets further south in Khazaria where the Kiev *Rus* may have traded, but there is good evidence to show that the Scandinavians did at least take some part in this trade. Ibn Rustah[45] describes how the *Rus,* who lived on an island (or peninsula) in an inland lake, an island that was wooded and with a circumference of three days' journey, were ruled by a Khaqan, and how they raided among the Slavs by ship. They did not cultivate the soil but lived off the Slavs; their only work was trade, and they traded with sable and other kinds of fur and slaves for coin. It is probable that Ibn Rustah used *Rus* for Scandinavians, not the *Rus* of Kiev, but there can be no doubt in the case of Ibn Fadlan whose evidence has great weight because he was an eyewitness and the original manuscript of his *Risala* has been found.[46] Ibn Fadlan describes the ship-burial of one of the leaders of the *Rus* and so makes plain that these men he encountered in Bulghar were Scandinavians. According to his account, when the *Rus* merchants arrived at Bulghar in their ships they made offerings to their gods and prayed for a merchant rich in dinars and dirhems. He also says that the *Rus* men gave their wives a necklace for each 10,000 dirhems that they gained and that some women wore several of these necklaces. This evidence shows that the silver wealth of Scandinavia at this time, which in any case seems to have come from Bulghar, was acquired there by Scandinavian traders who had such wares as furs and slaves to offer. It is of course very improbable that these traders brought their furs and slaves all the way from Scandinavia: these goods could be better gathered in North Russia, but there is no doubt that much of the silver was taken back to Scandinavia, probably by the traders themselves.

It is of course also possible that some of the silver wealth of the north was in the first place acquired as loot plundered from Muslims or from Slavs who had traded with the Muslims but the

evidence is against the assumption that much silver can have
been won in this way. Muslim chronicles do report a few raids
by the *Rus*, but these do not seem to have been very successful
or very frequent and at least some of these raids were the work
of Kiev *Rus* not of Scandinavians.[47] That the coins hoarded in
Scandinavia in the ninth century were identical with the coins
hoarded in Russia might be taken to show that some of the
Scandinavian silver was gathered in Russia rather than
Bulghar, but the provenance of the most recent coins in the
hoards tends to be different in the two areas, at least in the
third quarter of the ninth century, and this suggests that
the Scandinavian silver came direct from Bulghar rather than
from the coins available for hoarding inside Russia.[48] No such
differences can be observed in the tenth century and it is
possible that raids in Russia were then responsible for some of
the Scandinavian silver; but there is nothing in Russian
tradition to confirm this nor are there sufficient concentrations
of hoards, such as that to be found in Gotland in the tenth
century, indicating violence and raiding on a sufficiently large
scale to explain the silver wealth of the north. Most if not all
of the Kufic silver in Scandinavia was acquired by way of
trade. The goods that were sold were probably gathered by
violence, and the silver that reached the Baltic was at least
partly distributed by piracy, but there was also commerce.
In the north as well as in Russia, Scandinavians were undoubtedly active as traders.

Objects found in ninth-century Scandinavia show that there
were material contacts between Scandinavia and the West,
and the evidence of the *Vita Anskarii* suggests that these contacts
may have been partly by way of trade. The material finds at
Birka and elsewhere in eastern Scandinavia show that these
western contacts were very much less important than the
eastern, and the finds at Birka would be consistent with the
assumption that its western contacts were more important
early in the ninth century than later. The discovery of two
English coins from the middle of the century and of Frankish
coins from the first half of the century does not of course prove
that these reached Birka before 860, but the probability that
coins modelled on Frankish types were being produced in

Denmark fairly early in the century[49] confirms Rimbert's
evidence for these western contacts, and the absence of
Frankish coins after the reign of Charles the Bald (840–75)
agrees with Rimbert's claim that communications between
Birka and the West were being made very difficult by pirates
in the middle years of the century.

It has been suggested that these early trading contacts
between Scandinavia and the West were developed in response
to a Muslim demand for northern goods, and that when
alternative routes were exploited across Russia this demand
declined.[50] It is not unlikely that some of Dorestad's trade was
indirectly with Muslims,[51] for they at least were the market
for slaves, but the collapse of this trade is more reasonably
explained by the increasing insecurity of the sea passage. It
has also been suggested that Hedeby and Birka were not
really Scandinavian phenomena at all but were established by
western merchants. Birka has in fact been described as a Frisian
trading station.[52] This hypothesis has nothing to commend it.
It is not supported by the archaeological evidence, for there are
no graves of Frisian type at Birka nor are there enough material
finds from the West to prove such a western foundation. It is
entirely unsatisfactory to postulate that this western trade
was in such goods as cloth, food, salt and wine that would
have left little or no trace. It is as inconceivable that such a
trade could have been exclusively in objects that disappear, as
it is that any trade would have been so carefully balanced that
western coins were not taken north or Kufic coins west. The
almost exclusive concentration of Kufic coins before 890 in
the eastern Baltic and the eastern parts of Scandinavia is a
powerful argument against lively contacts between western
Europe and the north.[53] When this Kufic silver is more widely
dispersed in Scandinavia and is also exported to the British
Isles the initiative seems to have been Scandinavian, indeed
Swedish. The coin hoards of Scandinavia show that at the end
of the ninth century and the beginning of the tenth large
quantities of silver must have been exported from the Baltic.
This is the very period in which Kufic coins are found in hoards
in the British Isles.[54] It cannot be a coincidence that this was
also the period of a Swedish conquest of Hedeby and of

Hedeby's greatest prosperity.[55] Nor can it be simply a coincidence that this export of silver from the Baltic seems to stop at
just the period when control of Hedeby was taken from the
Swedes by the German king.[56] There was therefore a short
period of about four decades from the end of the ninth century
when some of the abundant wealth of Scandinavia was used
to buy goods in western Europe. After the German conquest
of Hedeby this outflow of silver seems to have been severely
restricted if not altogether stopped, but silver continued to
reach the north. Birka remained in close contact with the East,
and this was indeed its most prosperous time. The silver that
the Scandinavian traders continued to earn in Bulghar was
now more or less confined to Scandinavia but it was there
widely dispersed by both piracy and trade. At this time the
eastern Baltic seems to have been almost entirely cut off from
western Europe, but western Scandinavia, especially Norway,
maintained contacts with the British Isles. A large number of
objects from the British Isles has been discovered in Norway
and although some of these may have been loot, trading
contacts cannot be excluded.[57] Ohthere's visit to Alfred's
court seems to show that even at that time Norwegians could
bring their wares to England, and in the early tenth century,
when a large part of England was under Scandinavian control,
such contacts were probably strengthened. York was until
954 the centre of a Scandinavian kingdom and for long after-
wards a centre of Scandinavian influence. A recent survey of
the Viking finds from the city has shown that contacts
between York and Scandinavia were as lively after 954 as
they were before.[58] In Ireland Scandinavians established themselves in towns as the Ostmen, the men from the east, and
Dublin became an important trading centre for the western
parts of the British Isles, but this development belongs to the
eleventh century rather than the tenth.[59]

The almost exclusively oriental character of Birka's trade
in the middle of the tenth century is proved by its sudden
disappearance when the silver supply from Bulghar was
interrupted. There are very few Kufic coins in Scandinavia
that were minted between 965 and 983 and when they again
reached the north it was by a different route and from the

central, not the eastern parts of Islam.[60] The cause for this
break in silver imports into Scandinavia from Bulghar is not
known, though it may have been the result of Kiev's growing
power; but its effect on Birka is most revealing. It shows, in the
first place, how dependent Birka was on this Eastern traffic.
Had Birka had much trading contact with the southern and
western Baltic or with western Europe it might have survived,
at least in an attenuated form. More important, the close
association between the end of Birka and the end of the silver
imports from Bulghar shows that Birka was less a collecting
centre for the goods sold for Muslim silver in Bulghar, than a
market at which the silver acquired in Bulghar was spent.
If furs and other goods had been gathered at Birka to be taken
to Bulghar the breaking of the route to Bulghar would have
simply meant that the merchants would have had to find some
new customers. There were certainly potential customers as the
Gotlanders were soon to prove. Birka did not find new customers for its exports because its exports had never been very
important. Traders brought silver to Birka, and used it to buy
luxuries and necessities, ornaments, food, weapons. Birka was
perhaps the most important Scandinavian centre for the
dispersal of this Kufic silver. The men who made it important
were the silver rich traders from Bulghar. When they no
longer came to Birka, Birka disappeared.

This interruption of the flow of silver had even more serious
consequences for western Europe, for the pirates who had
flourished on this Baltic wealth were forced to turn elsewhere
in search of alternative sources of loot. They found it in the
West which was becoming rich in silver, largely because of the
exploitation of the silver mines in the Harz mountains which
seem to have become important in the middle of the tenth
century. That England was also rich in silver at the end of the
century is indicated by the elaborate currency arrangements
made at the end of Edgar's reign.[61] The Scandinavian raiders
certainly found great wealth there, as both the Anglo-Saxon
Chronicle and the coin hoards of Scandinavia testify. The source
of this English silver is not certainly known, but at least some
of it is likely to have come from the Harz mountains. London
seems to have had an active trade with the Rhineland early

in the eleventh century, and the location of the largest towns in the middle of the eleventh century also shows how important trading relations must then have been with Germany and Flanders.[62] Much of this English wealth must have depended on the export of wool to the cloth towns of Flanders that were already becoming important. Whatever its ultimate source, this English silver as well as the German was looted ruthlessly by the Viking bands of the late tenth and early eleventh centuries, and after England was conquered its wealth continued to be drained to pay for Danish mercenaries.

Not all the silver that reached Scandinavia after about 980 was loot or soldiers' pay. The German silver which has been found in such large quantities and continued to be abundant especially in Gotland late in the eleventh century was in part the profit of trade, a trade that was skilfully exploited by the Gotlanders. The clue is given by Adam of Bremen who describes the *Sembi* or *Pruzzi* who lived on the island of *Samland* as 'a most humane people who go out to help those who are in peril at sea or who are attacked by pirates'.[63] He continues, 'Gold and silver they hold in very slight esteem. They have an abundance of strange furs, the odour of which has inoculated our world with the deadly poison of pride. But these furs they regard, indeed, as dung, to our shame, I believe, for right or wrong we hanker after a martenskin robe as much as for supreme happiness. Therefore they offer their very precious marten furs for the woollen garments called *faldones*.' Whether or not Adam was correct in describing the *Sembi* in this way there can be no doubt that his words apply extraordinarily well to the situation of the Gotlanders. They certainly had an abundance of silver and gold. They had no native furs but they were in close contact with the very rich fur-producing region of Karelia where many Gotlandic ornaments are found from the eleventh century.[64] This was archaeologically an extremely rich time in Karelia and the Gotlanders who were later active in the Novgorod trade seem to have begun their visits to that city by the eleventh century. It was from this area, where furs would have undoubtedly been cheap, that Gotlanders were able to ship them to the West where they could be sold at a great

o

profit, which would have been taken partly in cloth to be sold in Karelia and elsewhere. The Gotlanders certainly had the ships, for their picture stones show how well developed their vessels were,[65] and these had to be of shallow draught because Gotland has no harbours. Gotlanders had to use ships that could easily be beached and their light and shallow craft gave them great advantages in the luxury traffic. They could penetrate further up the Russian rivers, possibly even to Novgorod, without having to tranship their cargoes, and their speed was probably their best defence against pirates.[66] The German coins that are so abundant in Gotland and are also found in North Russia must be the profit from this rewarding trade.

In the eleventh century, as in the earlier parts of the period, long distance trade was in luxury goods,[67] and it was for this kind of trade that the Scandinavian ships were so remarkably suitable. With the development of bulk traffic these advantages counted for less. The long distance luxury trade tends to attract most attention but it should not be forgotten that there was at the same time, inside Scandinavia and the Baltic, a more localised trade, perhaps even in necessities, that had been stimulated by the wealth accumulated by the men whose commerce was with Bulghar. It was this local trade inside Scandinavia that produced such concentrations as that in Kaupang's hinterland and was also responsible for the even dispersal of coins throughout wide areas of the north.

When Professor Grierson commented recently that the Vikings were important in European commerce because 'by their accumulation of treasure they naturally encouraged enterprising merchants to attempt to relieve them of it by offering goods in exchange', he seems to have been thinking particularly of the wealth gathered by the Vikings at the expense of western Christendom.[68] His comment is, however, no less appropriate to the situation inside Scandinavia where great wealth in silver was accumulated, but where the merchants who offered goods in exchange were not westerners but Scandinavians. That this development of local traffic was not irrelevant to the later economic history of Scandinavia is shown by the fact that one of the most widespread types of urban law in medieval Scandinavia was known as the law of Björkö, and there can be little doubt that it takes its name from Björkö in Lake Mälar where one of the most important, if not the most important, of all such local Scandinavian markets had once flourished.[69]

9. Causes and Consequences: A Survey of the Viking Period

DESPITE the many attempts that have been made to explain the outburst of Scandinavian activity in the Viking period and the rich variety of interpretations that have been suggested, there remains, in the minds of at least some scholars, a feeling that these are inadequate. Many years ago Sir Thomas Kendrick argued that it 'was impossible to explain in final and satisfactory terms the huge outpouring of the northern peoples that is known as the Viking expansion',[1] a sense of inadequacy that has at its root the belief that the raids and migrations were on such an extraordinarily large scale that some extraordinary explanation is called for. This point is made explicit by Kendrick: 'It may well be that over-population, lack of land, and political grievances were the most urgent motives, yet . . . it must be conceded that neither severally nor together do they seem sufficient to explain migrations so considerable and so long-sustained.'[2] It has, however, been one of the main purposes of this book to demonstrate that, at least as far as western Europe is concerned, the scale of the raids and the density of the settlements have been greatly exaggerated as a result of accepting too readily the judgements and estimates of contemporary writers and of allowing these to influence unduly the interpretation of the unwritten evidence. If this argument is accepted, the main obstacle to explaining the 'Viking outburst' is removed; once the prejudices and exaggerations of the primary sources are recognised the raids can be seen, not as an unprecedented and inexplicable cataclysm, but as an extension of normal Dark Age activity made possible and profitable by special circumstances.

Neither Scandinavians nor the peoples of western Europe were strangers to war and bloodshed. The chronicles of the Christian world, long before the Vikings irrupted into it, are full of wars and campaigns. Fighting, whether among families or between kingdoms, must have been a common experience. Men fought for many reasons, to defend their rights, to steal the rights of others, to avenge wrongs, to punish disloyalty, to gain glory, to win rewards, to prosecute old quarrels, to extend kingdoms. Franks fought each other, and in the sixth century Gregory of Tours describes their civil wars with horror and incomprehension. Strife was the major theme of poetry, and the virtues most highly praised and greatly prized were those of the warrior: loyalty to his lord, bravery, skill in arms. Warriors were the backbone of society; to Bede[3] they were the defenders of his native land against the barbarians (the barbarians were Christian), for kings and chieftains warriors were the basis of authority. In the eighth century, as in the time of Tacitus, 'the Germans had no taste for peace; renown is easier won among perils, and you cannot maintain a large body of companions except by violence and war'.[4] There is nothing to suggest that Scandinavian society was very different in this respect from the Christian world we know through written evidence. Graves richly furnished with weapons confirm the impression, if confirmation is needed, that the Scandinavians who attacked the coasts of western Europe, were not unused to war.

The Chronicles and other writings of the Christian West are generally content to record the outcome of battles or wars by noting the success or failure of a king. Only rarely in the writing of such men as Gregory of Tours or Bede is there a chance of glimpsing the destruction, the suffering and the misery such conflicts entailed. Much remains concealed and we can never know what bloodshed lay behind such brief annals as 'And that year (776) the Mercians and the people of Kent fought at Otford'.[5] This ignorance does not, however, entitle us to assume that internal strife before the Vikings came was little more than cattle rustling. We are, of course, very

thoroughly informed about much of the destruction wrought
by the Vikings but this was not because the Vikings did
more damage. The simple reason is that the Vikings were not
Christians but pagans, who attacked the churches which their
Christian counterparts, in general, treated with respect.

It would be absurd to claim that the conflicts of the seventh
and eighth centuries did not affect the annalists who recorded
them, but they were certainly not affected so directly and
violently as they were by Viking assaults. Before the Vikings
came, the treasures of the churches and monasteries of the
Christian world were more or less safe from the covetousness
of lay society. Laymen recognised the force of the spiritual
sanctions protecting these places and, in some senses, the
wealth was their own. To rob the churches was to rob themselves. In any case, the Christian laity had no need to resort
to force to have their way, if need arose. Charles Martel and
Æthelbald of Mercia earned the enmity of the Church by
taking land and privileges away. Displays of force were not
required. The chroniclers, hagiographers and other clerical
writers on whom we must very largely depend for our knowledge of this period, were rarely affected so directly or violently
by the strife of the world in which they lived as they were to
be by the Viking raiders. In the seventh and eighth centuries
our records are baldly of victories and defeats, of changing
overlordships. Kingdoms grow and disappear as in a kaleide-
scope; we rarely see the cruel realities of power behind the
transformations.

When the Vikings came the churches were, for the first
time, exposed to the general plundering of armed bands.
Against these pagans, the spiritual sanctions that protected
the shrines and treasures of the Church were powerless. The
only deterrents these men recognised were well-manned
defences or an army prepared to fight. In their absence,
tribute was demanded and if it was not paid churches were
ransacked, and the churchmen complained. It is hardly
surprising that the victims should have shown such a lively
hostility to these heathens but we must not assume that all men
thought the same way, for the response of the lay aristocracy
and of the peasantry is unknown. There are, however, indica-

tions that the reaction of some people was not entirely hostile and that some even welcomed them. In England, as in Frankia, there were men who were prepared to join the Viking raiders, to help them, to call for their aid, and make alliances with them.[6] At least for some the Vikings were little more than a complication, an additional factor in the already confused world of their quarrels and disputes. The wars between the sons of Louis the Pious may seem strange to our eyes, but they would not have surprised Gregory of Tours or, for that matter, Charlemagne. Such disputes were the stuff of Frankish life, a life in which the Vikings were a complication, possibly even a welcome one. When Charles the Bald was making great efforts against the raiders in 858 his brother invaded his lands and claimed the loyalty of his followers.[7] In the eyes of many churchmen this was regarded as nothing but the basest treachery, but that it happened at all, and that many of Charles' men did desert, suggests that the defeat of the invaders was not the first preoccupation of the Franks. They had other, more familiar business at hand.

The Vikings then, a scourge to the Christian, were in the eyes of many laymen only intruders of a recognisable type with whom it might be profitable or convenient to come to terms. The Viking raids were not so very different from the raids of Saxons on the Franks or the Frankish attacks on the Saxons and on the Avars. Charlemagne was certainly filled with a sense of Christian mission, but he too was compelled by the need to reward his followers with land and treasure.

For the Scandinavians the Viking raids in the West were simply an extension of the activity that was normal in their own society, an extension made possible and profitable by special circumstances. The profit came, in the first place, from the rich accumulations of treasure in the churches and monasteries of the West. Often undefended, exposed on lonely islands or near the coast, these were easy prey and the early raiders must have been as almost surprised as their victims by the ease with which they were able to accumulate rich loot. Once the possibility was known, the news must have spread fast and it is not surprising that the number of raids increased. The raiders were fortunate not only in the accessibility of treasure, but in the tactical advantages they had in their crossing of the sea. Land-based raiders, like the Saxons penetrating the Rhineland, might move fast but news of their approach would precede them. When the Vikings came, there was little chance of any warning, and this meant that there was little time to assemble opposition. Equally, their way of retreat was often safe, certainly from pursuit. The main dangers came from the sea.

At least some of the raiders wanted more than booty: they wanted land on which to settle. The first raids on Britain were, in fact a by-product of the Norse colonisation of Orkney and Shetland which began in the second half of the eighth century.[8] After the attacks on Lindisfarne and Portland the English were, apparently, not much troubled by Vikings until the Danish attacks began in 835, a neglect that suggests that the Norwegians were more interested in settlement than in plunder. They were, of course, ready to exploit what opportunities came their way, but that lay among the islands of the north and west of Britain, where they found a familiar environment in which the techniques of farming, fishing and bird catching that had been developed in western Norway could be used with little or no adaptation. Lowland Britain was not particularly attractive to these colonists and they generally left it alone.

Ireland was a different matter. The chain of Norse settlements led naturally to Ireland which, with its indented coastline and navigable rivers, was easily accessible to seaborne raiders, and from the beginning of the ninth century Ireland was often attacked by Viking bands. These newcomers did not settle very extensively there but were for the most part content to establish coastal bases, like Dublin, from which raids were directed against the Irish or against such centres as Dumbarton, the 'capital' of Strathclyde, across the Irish Sea.[9] Church treasures were certainly stolen in these raids but the Vikings seem to have been as interested in cattle rustling as in the plunder of gold and silver.[10] The close connection between Viking activity in Ireland and the Norwegian emigration is clearly demonstrated by what is known in Irish history as 'the forty years' rest', from 873 to 913, when far fewer raids are reported in Irish sources than before or after.[11] The start of the 'rest' is apparently marked by the death of Ivar, a prominent leader of the Dublin Vikings, who is called by a contemporary Irish chronicler, 'king of the Northmen of all Ireland and Britain'.[12] The relative quiet may have been due in part to Irish resistance, culminating in the expulsion of the Dublin Vikings in 902, and this resistance was doubtless facilitated by the divisions among the Norsemen which appear to have become particularly acute in the last years of the century, but a far more important cause was the discovery and colonisation of Iceland. The movement to Iceland began in about 870 and although many of the settlers went directly from Norway, a large number were Norsemen who had earlier settled in Britain and some of these had Irish wives and slaves.[13] The importance of the Irish element in the personal nomenclature of Iceland has often been remarked. It is possible that this movement from Ireland to Iceland was stimulated by Irish resistance, but there is more to be said for the alternative view that this migration of Norsemen from the west of Britain does much to explain the success of the Irish at that time. The discovery of new opportunities for colonisation in an unpopulated land led to a diversion of effort and a movement of people that reduced the pressure in Ireland and allowed the Irish their 'forty years' rest'. The rest lasted no more than forty years because by then the opportunities in Iceland must have appeared much less attractive than at first. Traditionally the settlement of Iceland took fifty or sixty years, and by the early tenth century much of the best land had been taken. We should therefore not be surprised that ten years after the Dublin Vikings had been expelled, Norsemen returned to exploit Ireland once again, and to fight among each other for a share of the spoils. In 914 fleets reappeared in Ireland and bases were soon re-established: on the coast, at such places as Dublin and Limerick, and inland on Lough Ree, Lough Erne and Lough Neagh. The annals are once again filled with reports of plundering, burning, killing and devastation.

There has been much discussion about the motives for this emigration from Norway to the islands of the North Atlantic. The descendants of the emigrants believed that their ancestors were fleeing from the tyrannical growth of royal power in Norway, and there is probably an element of truth in that tradition.[14] Certainly the colonists who eventually reached Iceland avoided creating any central executive authority and in doing this seem to have attempted to preserve an old form of society that was, in Norway as elsewhere in Europe, succumbing to the growth of royal power.[15] Another cause of the emigration seems to have been a dramatic growth of population attested by place-names and archaeological evidence.[16] This increase of population may well have been stimulated by the massively increased exploitation of Norway's abundant resources of iron, which, by making iron tools and weapons both cheap and plentiful, facilitated the extension of settlement into the virgin forest and led to the breakdown of long-established habits.[17] In the eastern parts of Norway, the early Viking period is marked by a significant growth of the settled area, but in the west, where the reserves of exploitable land were more limited, the path across the sea to new and often underpopulated lands must have seemed attractive. What is more, this migration to the islands of Britain and beyond could be undertaken with confidence in the eighth century, for by then the Norwegians had developed excellent sailing ships.[18]

The Danish attacks began some forty years after the Norwegian but at first their motive was not settlement but the search for plunder. It has been suggested, on the basis of place-name evidence, that Denmark, like Norway, experienced a remarkable growth of population in the early Viking period, but doubt has recently been cast on this interpretation of the evidence.[19] It can, however, be said that if such an expansion had occurred, the Danes would not have needed to journey to England in search of new homes, there was ample scope for expansion in Denmark itself and in Skåne. If, on the other hand, there was no population growth, there would have been even less need for the Danes to look for land overseas. The Danish Vikings were, therefore, not colonists, in the same sense as the Norwegians, but pirates who extended the range of their activities into western Europe. The *Life of Saint Anskar* shows that before the Danish raids began, merchants who ventured into the Baltic were liable to be attacked by pirates.[20] The fact that the first raids in Frankia were directed against Dorestad, the port of embarkation for the Frankish trade with the north, suggests that it may well have been the prospect of plundering these traders as they travelled between Hedeby and Dorestad that first drew the Danish pirates to western Europe. Once there, they soon discovered other rich and ill-defended possibilities and the number of raids, and raiders, soon multiplied.

These Danish Vikings appear to have been exiles from their homeland and at least some of them established temporary bases in Frisia from which they extended their looting expeditions against both Frankia and Britain.[21] The plunder accumulated by these men, which is so conspicuously absent from Denmark, may be represented in the ninth century coin hoards of Frisia, just as the loot of a later generation of raiders based in Britain is found in such coin hoards as Cuerdale.[22] The Danes abandoned Frisia before the end of the century leaving no trace of their stay, apart, possibly, from some of the hoards. This lack of archaeological or linguistic evidence is unfortunate but hardly surprising. Even in England, where they settled permanently, extraordinarily few material remains have been discovered; the main traces are the crosses and their effect on the language and place-names, the first depending on a native tradition of stone carving and the conversion of the invaders, while the other is clearly the result of permanent colonisation. Nothing of the kind can be expected in Frisia which the Danes only occupied for 40 years. In the middle of the century the Danes began to operate from bases in England. At first these were temporary but by 880 they had settled permanently in the north and east of the country. The Danish colonisation of England was, therefore, not the result of a mass migration of land hungry peasants but was, in contrast, achieved by a relatively small group of warriors who had made themselves rich by plunder and hoped to continue in that way of life.

The first Danish settlers, or conquerors, of England were joined by a second group of Danes in 896 that had, for more than a decade, campaigned in Frankia and England, but there is no evidence of any later invasions by Vikings from Scandinavia until the end of the tenth century. The colonisation of Normandy, like the tenth century raids in Ireland, seems to have been the work of Vikings who came from bases in Britain, not direct from Scandinavia.[22a] This temporary cessation of Danish attacks at the end of the ninth century may have been partly due to the improved defences of the Christian West. The successful defence of Paris in the siege of 885–6 had shown that cities need not be vulnerable, and Arnulf's victory at the battle of the Dyle in 891, which led the defeated Danes to try their fortune in England, was followed by the successful defence of Wessex and English Mercia by Alfred and his children. These victories helped to stem the flood of Danish pirates, but a more important explanation is probably to be found in the increasing quantities of kufic silver that were by then reaching the Baltic.[23] By the year 900 the Baltic had become a pirates' paradise and men who sought wealth by plunder had no need to venture far from home. It was only when this supply of silver was interrupted in about 965 that the Scandinavian pirates turned again to the west and a second Viking age began. The stream of Norwegian emigration to the Islands of Britain and the north Atlantic also dried up in the tenth century: by then most of the best land had been taken and would-be emigrants had to compete with the original settlers or their descendants.

The Danish and Norwegian conquerors of Britain had little contact with Scandinavia in the tenth century. The Vikings who broke the Irish 'forty years' rest' and who went on to take for themselves the Scandinavian kingdom of York did not come fresh from Scandinavia, but were recruited from families already established in Britain. The indigenous nature of this tenth-century Viking activity in Britain is confirmed by archaeological and numismatic evidence. Relatively little tenth-century Irish material has been found in Scandinavia and Mr. Dolley has pointed out that the 'paucity of hoards from Scandinavia with pre-Æthelred coins of the Chester area not only contrasts with a picture of such pieces in hoards from Ireland and the Isles, but suggests very strongly that already by the tenth century the Vikings in Ireland could not look further than the Scottish settlements for recruits for their campaigns of conquest.[24] In 918 Ragnald, after some campaigns in Ireland, followed the example of his grandfather, Ivar of Dublin, in crossing the Irish Sea to fight the Scots but he went to make himself king in York.[25] He was followed by a confusing succession of Scandinavian kings, almost all of whom came from, and maintained close links with, Dublin. The fact that the last Scandinavian king of York was Erik Blood-Axe, an exile from Norway, should not be allowed to obscure the essential Hiberno-Norse character of this Scandinavian kingdom.

It is sometimes suggested that even in the ninth century the king of Norway had a close interest in and some control over Norse activity in Britain. The main contemporary support for this anachronistic notion seems to be the description in the Annals of Ulster of the Olaf who arrived in Dublin in 853 as 'son of the king of Lochlann'. Lochlann is normally taken to mean Norway and Mrs. Chadwick has written: 'It would seem likely on the whole that the arrival of Olaf from Lochlann . . . was due to a determination on the part of his father, the ruler of Lochlann, to quell the incipient Danish power and consolidate the Norwegian settlements which had sprung up under Turges and other Norwegian leaders earlier in the century. This view, if accepted, would suggest that the Norwegian activities in Ireland were the expression and implementation of a fully thought out scheme of expansion and conquest from a given district in south-western Norway. The Danish threat was met by a stunning blow from Norwegian headquarters.'[26] As Mr. Dolley has recently pointed out, Lochlann could as well describe the western parts of Scotland as of Norway,[27] and a connection between the Vikings of Ireland and the colonists in the Hebrides seems far more probable than the connection suggested by Mrs. Chadwick. The Irish and Icelandic sources that appear to prove a close ninth-century connection between Norway and the Vikings of Britain are all late and contain a great deal of demonstrable confusion.[28] It is true that the Norse emigration in the eighth and ninth centuries had created a sort of extension in Norway in the Atlantic Islands, but the Norwegian kings did not attempt to extend their authority over the Hebridean colonists until the last years of the eleventh century, and it was only in the thirteenth century that Iceland was brought under the Norwegian crown.

The Scandinavian colonists of western Europe were soon assimilated. Only those who found homes in the virtually uninhabited islands of the north Atlantic preserved their native speech, the others soon adopted the language of their neighbours. They also adopted the religion of their neighbours and such evidence as the crosses at Middleton in Yorkshire shows that some did so early.[29] The conversion of Iceland in the year 1000 may possibly have been facilitated by the experience of those settlers who reached Iceland by way of Ireland and the Western Isles. There was also political assimilation. The Vikings may have attempted, by their migration, to escape the growing authority of the Scandinavian kings but before the end of the tenth century few had been able to escape the authority of some other king. Normandy was in fact created by the royal recognition of Rollo as Count of Rouen. The situation in England was more complicated, but by 925 the settlers south of the Humber had accepted the kingship of the West Saxons and thirty years later the Scandinavian kingdom of York was finally incorporated into the kingdom of England. The contrast between the hazardous situation in the ninth century, when it appeared to some contemporaries that the Vikings would overcome England, and the rapid and confident recovery of the Scandinavian conquests, was not due to any sudden degeneration of the Scandinavian settlers or to an equally sudden improvement in English military capacity. The explanation for the change is, quite simply, that in the tenth century the English had the advantage of dealing with a settled enemy instead of a mobile one. As long as the Viking bands were on the move they were extraordinarily difficult to combat, but once these warriors settled in farms and villages they were as vulnerable to military pressure as their victims had earlier been and were soon brought to acknowledge the English kings.

The Irish faced more difficult problems than their English neighbours. In the first place there were many Irish kings who did not always work together and were at times prepared to ally with the Norsemen to further their separate interests. Even more important, the Vikings never settled widely in Ireland as farmers; they were content to establish themselves in strongholds from which they could launch plundering raids on the Irish countryside. The Irish had, therefore, to deal with a mobile enemy operating from defensible bases. What is more, the Norse were sometimes able to call for help from their friends across the sea, from the Isle of Man, Wales, the Hebrides and beyond. Even with these advantages the Norse invaders of Ireland suffered many defeats at the hands of the Irish and by the end of the tenth century the Dublin Norse had been forced to submit to King Brian.

While the Danes and Norwegians were busy in the west, the Swedes were active in Russia. This Swedish penetration of Russia seems to have begun at the end of the eighth century, at about the same time as the early Norwegian raids on Britain. The Kiev Chronicle with its artificial chronology is no help in determining the date of this activity in Russia but the Annals of St. Bertin provide one sure limiting date when they show that already by 839 a group of Swedes called *Rhos* had reached Byzantium. The sudden appearance of a number of Kufic hoards in various parts of Russia in the period 800–825 shows that not only that Muslim silver was already then reaching Russia, but that this was probably a very disturbed time there. It is likely that the disturbers came from the North, where, at about the same time hoards of the same kind were being deposited.

The nature of this ninth-century Swedish activity in Russia has been vigorously debated although there is little evidence.[30] The Annals of St. Bertin state that the king of the *Rhos* was called *Chacanus*, Khaqan, and early in the tenth century Ibn Rustah says that the Rus had a Khaqan, a term also used for the ruler of the Khazars who lived on the lower reaches of the Don and Volga. By the end of the ninth century Scandinavian warriors had certainly established themselves in control of Kiev and it is not unlikely that similar bands of adventurers had earlier achieved more or less temporary local ascendancies in the north of Russia under leaders who could easily have been given such a title as Khaqan, at least by Byzantines or Muslims. These invaders from the north seem to have extorted tribute from the native inhabitants and used this to trade in Byzantium, Khazaria and Bulghar. Such contacts are mentioned by Ibn Khurdadhbih in a passage that is full of difficulties, but which probably means that some *Rus*, whom Ibn Khurdadhbih thought of as a sort of Slav, were trading directly on the Volga as well as with Byzantium and Khazaria.[31]

However this Scandinavian activity is understood, one thing is clear; the Swedes can never have been very important in Russia as settlers. Their influence on place-names is confined to the river routes[32] and there is nowhere archaeological evidence sufficient to justify the assumption of extensive, dense Scandinavian settlement. The Finnish graves south-east of Lake Ladoga, of which some 400 have been excavated, certainly contained many objects, especially ornaments, that probably came from Sweden,[33] but this would not be surprising if Scandinavians had been active in the area in the tenth century acquiring furs by force or barter. A far closer study of the burial customs here and elsewhere will be needed before the apparent similarity between these graves and those of the Mälar region can be taken to prove Scandinavian settlement. Further south the great cemetery at Gnezdovo near Smolensk has been claimed to be of a Swedish colony but very few graves can clearly be identified as the burial of Scandinavians.[34] The evidence of this cemetery gives much the same impression as the literary evidence for Kiev; namely that these communities were, at the end of the ninth century and beginning of the tenth, dominated by Scandinavian warriors, but that this dominant class, which was never very numerous, was soon Slavicised although still called *Rus*. The early princes in Kiev had undoubtedly Scandinavian names, such as Oleg (*Helgi*) or Igor (*Ingvar*), but in 942 a son of the ruling dynasty was given the Slavonic name, Sviatoslav.

Kiev under its Scandinavian or *Rus* dynasty had little contact with the Baltic.[35] The chieftains lived by collecting tribute and trading it. Their contacts with Byzantium are well attested, and have perhaps been exaggerated, for the coin evidence suggests that the Kiev *Rus* like the Scandinavians gained most of their silver from the Muslims in Bulghar, although they may have traded in Khazaria as well.[36] To the Muslims, the Kiev *Rus* and the Scandinavians were both *Rus*, and their activities were not distinguished, in fact most of the references in Muslim writings were probably to these rapidly assimilated Scandinavians of the Dnieper.[37]

The Scandinavians from beyond the Baltic, also called *Rus*, were active in the north of Russia collecting tribute to sell in Bulghar. This trade brought a great wealth of silver to Scandinavia and the Baltic, especially after about 890 when silver production under the Samanids seems to have increased, and it was then that Birka, Hedeby and other places in the north became most prosperous. This prosperity encouraged piracy and made Denmark, through which, for a short time, some of the silver overflowed to the West, a coveted prize that was disputed between rival dynasties, Swedish, German and Norwegian.

The flow of Kufic silver to the north from the Volga was stopped in or soon after 965 and the cause of the break may well have been Sviatoslav's campaign in Bulghar in 965.[38] If so, the Kiev *Rus* did, indirectly, have a critical influence on Viking Scandinavia, for not only did the flourishing market of Birka disappear and with it, no doubt, the local traffic which it had stimulated, but the Scandinavian pirates who had depended on this abundant supply of treasure now had to turn elsewhere. Before the end of the century some had found an alternative source in England. Scandinavian leaders whose early careers had been spent in Baltic adventures were able to recruit and organise large armies for the assault on the English, from whom they were able to extort large sums as tribute. There are many differences between these renewed attacks and those of the ninth century. The earlier raiders had generally kept together in groups that were recognisably Danish or Norwegian, but at the end of the tenth century the armies were recruited from all parts of Scandinavia.[39] In the ninth century the purpose of most of the Vikings was to win land or to establish a base in the west from which to continue the search for plunder, few of them returned home; when the attacks were resumed there was little new settlement, most of the warriors returned to Scandinavia with the wealth they had set out to win. The armies of the ninth century were small, a century later they could be very large indeed and some leaders, notably the Danish kings, commanded large and apparently well disciplined forces in which a normal unit could be 16 ships, with crews numbering about 1,000 men.[40] The ninth century Vikings were pagans; in the tenth

P

century the raiders came from lands in which the conversion had been well begun, and their leaders either were, or soon became, Christian.[41] Perhaps the most important difference of all between these two phases of Viking activity is that in the ninth century the Vikings ranged far afield in western Europe while at the end of the tenth they concentrated their attacks almost exclusively on England, for the good reason that England was by then a rich country and the English, as the Vikings soon discovered, were ready to pay large sums for peace. Among the rune stones of Sweden there are several that were erected as Christian memorials to men who joined the raids on England,[42] and the tens of thousand of Anglo-Saxon coins in the hoards of Scandinavia are rich testimony to the success of those raids.

The differences between these two phases of Viking activity and the significant concentration of the late tenth-century Vikings on England has been obscured by the contemporary conflicts between the Irish and their Norse neighbours. The battles of Tara and Clontarf appear, at first sight, to be part of the Viking movement that led to the collapse of Ethelred's England, but that would be a mistaken interpretation. The problems of Brian of Ireland and Ethelred of England were very different. The English had to face large, freshly recruited and highly mobile armies that came direct from Scandinavia, determined to extort treasure. The Irish on the other hand, were fighting against men who had long been settled in the British Isles, and the battle of Clontarf was but a stage in the long drawn-out dispute over the distribution of Ireland's limited wealth.

The raids on Ethelred's England, and its eventual conquest by the Danish kings, mark, in a violent and dramatic way, the re-orientation of Scandinavia from its temporary 'oriental' phase, back to its traditional association with western Europe. The resources of the north, whether in goods such as furs, hides and iron, or in the skills of the Northerners, in metal work, in ships and sailing, were turned to the West, at first in war and then in peace. In return the Scandinavians received not only treasure as the reward of military or commercial enterprise, but also many influences, artistic as well as administrative.[43] Most important of all they received a new religion, Christianity. With its conversion Scandinavia at last became effectively a part of Europe. It was not that Christianity had softened their martial vigour, for its pacifying effects have rarely been conspicuous, but now that the Scandinavians were no longer outsiders the north along with the rest of Europe was slowly civilised. Piracy continued in the waters of the British Isles as well as in the Baltic but it grew less significant as the trade in luxuries was increasingly replaced by bulkier commerce and as men came to prefer the more certain profits of trade. Scandinavians and others still embarked on military adventures in search of land and honour, in Crusades, in the Levant or beyond the Baltic; the Anglo-Normans invaded Ireland, the English fought the Scots and the French fought the English.[44] But this conflict was licensed, and took place within Christendom or was directed against the heathen.

Historical periods are the subjective creation of observers, whether or not they are contemporaries—observers who seize on some, to them, essential characteristic in terms of which the 'period' is defined. The Christian society of the West in the ninth and tenth centuries regarded the Scandinavians as strange and extraordinary because they were pagans and the Viking period begins with the first attacks of these pagans on the Christian churches of the west, The end is not so well defined. Outside the Baltic and Scandinavia it was only in Britain and the North Atlantic that the 'Age of the Vikings' was prolonged beyond the tenth century. The consequences of the ninth-century Norse colonisation of the Atlantic islands were still being worked out in the thirteenth century and Orkney and Shetland were not ceded to the Scottish crown until 1472.

In England the death of Harald Hardrada at Stamford Bridge could be taken to mark the end of the Viking age but a better end is the failure of the Danish invasion planned by St. Cnut in 1085. The Anglo-Saxon Chronicler describes William's reaction to this, the last but abortive, Scandinavian attempt to conquer England. 'When William, king of England, who was then in Normandy . . . found out about this, he went to England with a larger force of mounted men and infantry from France and Brittany than had ever come to this country, so that people wondered how this country could maintain all that army.' The brief reappearance of English coins at that time in the coin hoards of Scandinavia suggests that some of the men recruited by William were more interested in the wealth of England than in the claim of Cnut.[45] Scandinavian armies never again threatened the security of England, the wealth that had proved such a great temptation to generations of Viking raiders also provided the means of their ultimate defeat.

Analysis of Russian
Coin Hoards

The following tabular analysis is from Professor
Sture Bolin's work *Mynt och Myntfynd*, pp. 74–88,
147–8

Figure 16   Map of Russia showing the former provinces (in small capitals)

I. NINTH-CENTURY HOARDS

Percentage of Kufic coins per decade

Latest coin in hoard	Province in which hoard was found	-700	700	710	720	730	740	750	760	770	780	790	800	810	820	830	840	850	860	870	880	Number of determinable Kufic coins in each hoard
786	Petersburg	2·6					6·9	6·9	6·9	41·4	37·9											29
805	Don	16·9	5·2	1·3		1·3	1·3	2·6	5·1	23·1	33·3	26·9	2·6									78
808	Petersburg	3·2	3·2	3·9	1·3	5·2		1·3	5·2	23·4	18·2	10·4	9·1									77
809	Kursk	3·2	1·0		3·2		6·5	3·2	3·2	25·8	19·4	16·1	16·1									31
812	Yaroslavl'	5·9	0·9	1·0	2·4	2·9	2·0	2·9	3·9	15·7	22·5	27·5	11·8	2·9								102
820	Chernigov	12·3		3·3	2·5	0·9	2·4	0·9	3·3	18·5	23·7	17·5	8·1	5·2	0·5							211
828/32	Yaroslavl'	10·6	2·5	5·6		2·0	1·0	1·5	2·5	15·2	14·1	10·1	17·2	9·6	5·1							198
837 or 833/41	Estoniya		2·8	0·2	0·2		2·3	4·1	8·8	17·3	9·2	13·5	25·7	14·4	2·9	1·3	1·4					444
842	Vyatka	4·2		9·7	4·2	4·2		2·8		4·2	9·7	9·7	12·5	12·5	12·5	8·9						72
852	Vitebsk						4·2	4·2	4·2	8·3	4·2	8·3	37·5	16·7			8·3	4·2				24
861	Latviya				2·4				7·1	11·9	9·5	14·3	23·8	19·0	4·8		4·8		2·4			42
864	Novgorod					1·0	6·4	2·5	4·9	11·3	4·4	11·3	27·8	6·4	0·5	4·4	5·9	6·4	6·9			203
868	Kaluga						3·1		3·1	6·3		6·3	21·9	18·8			6·3	6·3	28·1			32
875	Kursk			0·5		0·5	2·9	2·4	6·3	10·7	6·3	7·6	22·3	13·6	4·4	1·5	1·0	5·8	13·1	1·0		206
882	Poltava							4·9	4·9	11·5	3·3	11·5	26·2	9·8	1·6	1·6	1·6	3·3	14·8	1·6	3·3	61

II. TENTH- AND ELEVENTH-CENTURY HOARDS

Latest coin in hoard	Province in which hoard was found	Percentage of Kufic coins per decade														Number of determinable Kufic coins in each hoard
		-889	890	900	910	920	930	940	950	960	970	980	990	1000	1010	
905	Pskov	11	45	44												84
911	Mogilev		18	65	17											76
913/42	Chernigov		15	73	12											26
916	Vyatka		4	47	49											394
935	Kiev		5	17	20	36	22									169
935/42	Kazan	2	2	4	18	42	31									45
943	Vilna		7	16	12	19	37	9								108
952/54	Estoniya	1	5	17	18	21	23	12	3							722
952	Latviya	2	13	21	27	19	10	4	4							48
954	Estoniya	1	11	16	26	16	8	14	8							97
955/60	Smolensk			6	2	6	20	25	41							64
969	Chernigov		3	4	11	18	12	14	15	23	14					114
976	Pskov		3			4	12	18	24	28	9					50
976	Ryazan						11	11	20	46	12					35
978	Mogilev	1	3	5	7	10	14	10	15	23	21					162
994	Kazan				3	3	7	3	3	3	23	46				37
996/1031	Minsk	5	3	4	5	5	18	15	17	24	3		19	3		75
1002	Latviya	7	4	10	15	8	11	20	5	8	3		3			39
1002/14	Estoniya		4	26	8	14	5	14	3	1	2	2	6	3		72
1008	Kazan			3	1	1	3	5	8	21	28		10			51
1008	Poltava			2	1	3	6	14	10	21	30	25	2	86		346
1011/61	Pskov				6	2	13	7	27	25	8	10	4	1		71
1013	Latviya	2	4		20	10	13	15	3	10	3	2	4	1	4	49
1014/24	Latviya		7	23	2	2	17	27	4	13	13		3	8		30
1016/35	Mogilev	4	2	4	10	12	3		17	2	5	10	11		6	52
1030/39	Petersburg	5	5	7	3	10				10		2	2	2		40
1039/56	Mogilev	5									21	7	7	14	7	29
1059/71	Pskov		1	1	1	2	11	13	14	23	21	5	3	4	2	148

Chronological Composition of Hoards

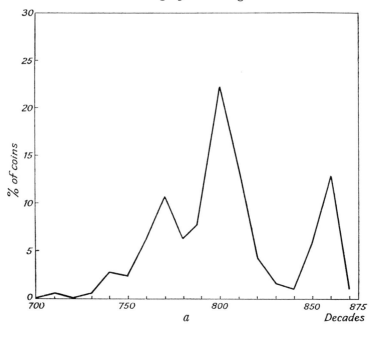

a

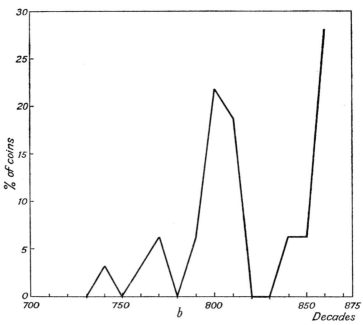

b

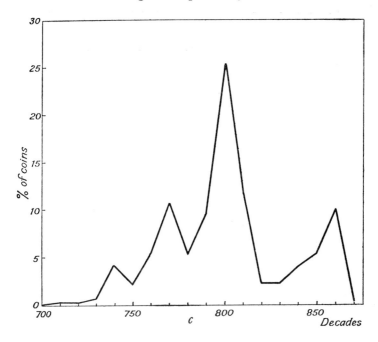

Figure 17 The Chronological Composition of ninth-century Russian hoards. (From Sture Bolin, *Mynt och Myntfynd*, pp. 86, 87, 92.)

a From Pogreben, Sudza, Kursk: 206 determinable coins, the most recent from Baghdad, A.D. 875.

b From Misnev, Lichvin, Kaluga: 32 determinable coins, the most recent from Armenia, A.D. 868.

c Five hoards in which the most recent coins were of the period A.D. 851–75: 507 determinable coins.

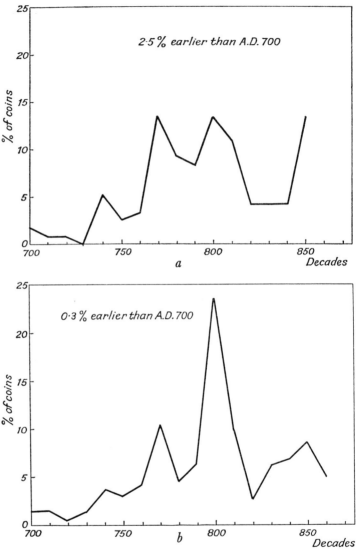

Figure 18 The Chronological Composition of ninth-century Swedish hoards of Kufic coins.

a From Fittja, Uppland: 120 determinable coins, the most recent from Tashkent, A.D. 864. (U. S. Linder, *NNÅ*, 1938, pp. 109–24.)

b Four hoards in which the most recent coins were of the period A.D. 857–68: 1,254 determinable coins. (Bolin, *Mynt och Myntfynd*, p. 217.)

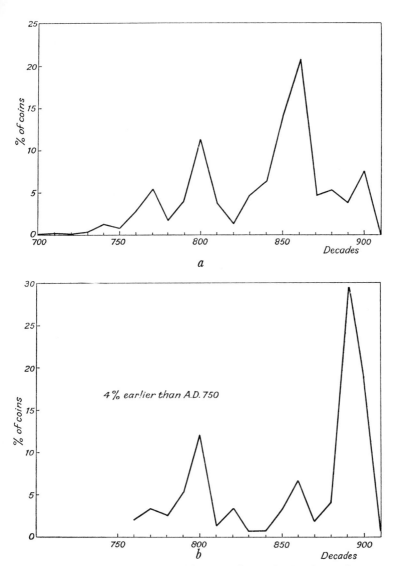

Figure 19 The Coin Hoard of Stora Velinge, Gotland and Over Randlev, Denmark.

a Chronological Composition of a hoard of Kufic coins from Stora Velinge, Gotland: 1,902 determinable coins, the most recent a Samanid, A.D. 910–11. (U. S. Linder, *NNÅ*, 1941, pp. 74–119.)

b Chronological Composition of the Kufic part of a coin hoard from Over Randlev, Denmark: 150 determinable Kufic coins, the most recent a Samanid, A.D. 910–11. (G. Galster, *Numismatisk Forenings Medlemsblad*, xiv (1934), pp. 18–22, 33–42.)

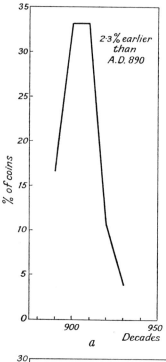

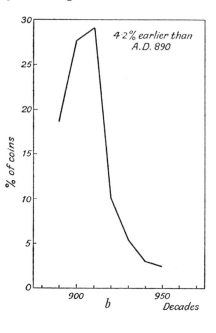

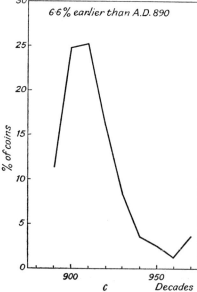

Figure 20 The Chronological Composition of the Kufic part of Gotlandic hoards. (Bolin, *Mynt och Myntfynd*, p. 247.)

a Five hoards in which the most recent coins were of the period A.D. 930–39: 1,079 determinable Kufic coins.

b Nine hoards in which the most recent coins were of the period A.D. 950–59: 2,040 determinable Kufic coins.

c Hoards in which the most recent coins were of the period A.D. 978–1016: 560 determinable Kufic coins.

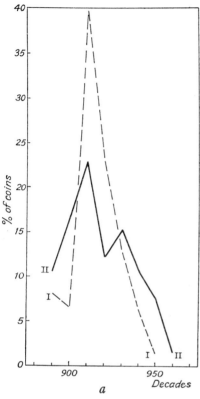

Figure 21 The Chronological Composition of the Kufic part of three tenth-century Scandinavian hoards

a I A Kufic hoard from Holte, Orkedalen, Norway: 61 determinable coins, the most recent from Bukhara, A.D. 950. (B. Hartmann and T. Petersen, *Det Kgl. Norske Videnskabers Selskabs Skrifter*, 1916, nr.9.)

II A Kufic hoard from Salem, Sweden: 65 determinable coins, the most recent from Hirat in Khorasan, A.D. 970. (U. S. Linder, 'Salemsfyndet', *Kultur historiska Studier, tillägnade Nils Åberg*, Stockholm, 1938, pp. 166–80.)

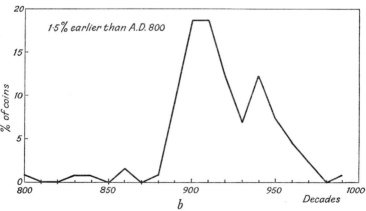

b A hoard from Vaalse, Falster, Denmark: 130 determinable Kufic coins, the most recent from Samarkand and Tashkent, A.D. 971–72. (C. J. Thomsen and J. C. Lindberg, 'Fund ved Vaalse paa Falster', *Annaler for Nordisk Oldkyndighed*, 1842–43, pp. 21–142.)

Abbreviations

AA	*Acta Archaeologica*
ANOH	*Aarbøger for Nordisk Oldkyndighed og Historie*
Birka I	Holger Arbman, *Birka Untersuchungen und Studien I, Die Gräber*, i Text, ii Plates (KVHAA, 1940, 1943)
EHD	Dorothy Whitelock, *English Historical Documents c. 500–1042* (London, 1955)
KHL	*Kulturhistorisk Leksikon for nordisk middelalder*, 15 vols. published, *Abbed-Skude* (København, 1956–70)
KVHAA	Kungl. Vitterhets Historie och Antikvitets Akademien
NNÅ	*Nordisk Numismatisk Årsskrift*
SG	Mårten Stenberger, *Die Schatzfunde Gotlands der Wikingerzeit*, 2 vols. (KVHAA, 1947, 1958)
Skovmand	R. Skovmand, *De danske Skattefund fra Vikingetiden og den ældste Middelalder indtil omkring 1150* (*ANOH*, 1942)
SS.R.G.	Scriptores rerum germanicarum in usum scholarum
UOÅ	*Universitetets Oldsaksamlings Årbok* (Oslo)
VA	*Viking Antiquities in Great Britain and Ireland*, ed. H. Shetelig, 6 vols. (Oslo, 1940–54)

Notes

1. INTRODUCTION: pp. 1–11

1. *EHD*, p. 776.
2. *EHD*, p. 166.
3. For general surveys of the Viking period giving references to these and other raids see pp. 265–8.
4. A. W. Brøgger, *Ancient Emigrants*, chapters iii and iv; C. Marstrander, *Bidrag til det norske sprogs historie i Irland* (Skrifter utgit av Videnskapsselskapet i Kristiania, 1915, II Hist.-Filos. Kl., no. 5), pp. 128–35; H. Shetelig, *VA*, i. 56–7; J. Petersen, *VA*, v. 7–12; F. T. Wainwright, 'The Scandinavian Settlement', *The Northern Isles*, ed. F. T. Wainwright (London, 1962), pp. 117–62.
5. See pp. 29–30.
6. See p. 211.
7. See pp. 169–70.
8. Lucien Musset emphasised this in *Cahiers de Civilisation Médiévale*, i (1958), p. 67; see also p. 210.
9. The most important recent discussion is by Fritz Askeberg, *Norden och kontinenten i gammal tid* (Uppsala, 1944), pp. 114–83.
10. For example by J. Brøndsted, *The Vikings* (1960), p. 299.
11. Marc Bloch, *La Société Féodale: La Formation des Liens de Dépendance* (Paris, 1939), p. 30.
12. See p. 35.
13. For Adam see pp. 32–4. It has been claimed that Adam refers to Gotland in iv. 16 as *Holmus*, but it neither fits the description 'a safe anchorage' (see p. 191) nor was it a port of Denmark. The reference may be to Bornholm.
14. See pp. 199–200.

15. A. R. Lewis, *The Northern Seas, Shipping and Commerce in Northern Europe A.D. 300–1100* (Princeton, 1958), pp. 149–50. On this point see the review by P. Grierson, *English Historical Review*, lxxvi (1961), pp. 311–15.
16. See pp. 123–31.
17. See pp. 99–100.
18. See p. 171.
19. See pp. 118, 181.
20. See pp. 143–5.
21. J. M. Wallace-Hadrill, *The Barbarian West 400–1000*, 3rd ed. (London, 1967), p. 151.

2. THE WRITTEN SOURCES: pp. 12–47

1. *Two of the Saxon Chronicles Parallel*, ii (Oxford, 1899), p. xxi.
2. The most convenient introductions to the extensive literature on the Anglo-Saxon Chronicle are by Professor Dorothy Whitelock, *EHD*, pp. 109–16, 129–31 and by G. N. Garmonsway, *The Anglo-Saxon Chronicle* (Everyman Library, 1953), pp. xv–xlviii. The translation quoted here is Professor Whitelock's, *EHD*, pp. 136–235 which has also been published separately as *The Anglo-Saxon Chronicle: a revised translation*, ed. Dorothy Whitelock with David C. Douglas and Susie I. Tucker (London, 1961).
3. F. M. Stenton, *Essays in Medieval History presented to T. F. Tout*, ed. A. G. Little and F. M. Powicke (Manchester, 1925), pp. 20–21. Æthelweard's version of the Chronicle has been edited and translated by A. Campbell, *The Chronicle of Æthelweard* (London, 1962).
4. The compiler cannot have completed his work before 892, see p. 19. This date is accepted here for convenience but it should not be forgotten that there is no proof that he worked in that year rather than sometime in the following decade or even later.
5. A. Jean Thorogood, 'The Anglo-Saxon Chronicle in the Reign of Ecgberht', *English Historical Review*, xlviii (1933), pp. 353–63.
6. J. M. Wallace-Hadrill, 'The Franks and the English in the Ninth Century', *History*, xxxv (1950), pp. 202–18.
7. C. Plummer, *op. cit.*, ii, pp. lxv–lxvi; cf. D. Whitelock, *The Peterborough Chronicle* (Early English Manuscripts in Facsimile, iv, Copenhagen, 1954), pp. 26–34.

8. A very useful list of Irish and other sources is in A. O. Anderson, *Early Sources of Scottish History A.D. 400 to 1286*, i (Edinburgh, 1922), pp. xxi–ci. Francis J. Byrne, 'Thirty years' work in Irish history (II): Ireland before the Norman Invasion', *Irish Historical Studies*, xvi (1968), pp. 1–14.

9. T. Ó. Máille, *The Language of the Annals of Ulster* (Manchester, 1910), esp. pp. 18–19, 118–119.

10. P. Walsh, *The Four Masters and their work* (Dublin, 1944).

11. Seán Mac Airt, *The Annals of Inisfallen* (Dublin, 1951).

12. Ed. J. H. Todd (Rolls Series, 48, 1867). On its date see A. O. Anderson, *op. cit.*, pp. xxxiv–vi, xcix, and A. J. Goedheer, *Irish and Norse Traditions about the Battle of Clontarf* (Haarlem, 1938), pp. 1–12.

13. Ed. J. H. Todd, pp. 50–51.

14. A. J. Goedheer, *op. cit.*, chapters I and III.

15. P. Walsh, 'The Dating of the Irish Annals', *Irish Historical Studies*, ii (1941), pp. 355–75.

16. For these see A. Molinier, *Les Sources de l'Histoire de France*, i and ii (Paris, 1902); A. Potthast, *Bibliotheca historica medii aevi*, 2. Auflage (Berlin, 1895–6). There is much valuable bibliographical material on these sources and on the period in Dahlmann-Waitz, *Quellenkunde der Deutschen Geschichte*, 9. Auflage (Leipzig, 1931), and for the period after 900, W. Wattenbach, *Deutschlands Geschichtsquellen im Mittelalter, Deutsche Kaiserzeit*, ed. Robert Holtzmann, I, i and ii (Berlin, 1942–3).

17. Loup de Ferrières, *Correspondance*, ed. L. Levillain, 2 vols. (Les Classiques de l'Histoire de France au Moyen Age, 1927–35).

18. *Annales de Saint-Bertin*, edd. F. Grat, J. Viellard and S. Clémencet, with introduction and notes by L. Levillain (Société de l'Histoire de France; Paris, 1964).

19. Alexander V. Riasanovsky, 'The Embassy of 838 Revisited: Some Comments in connection with a "Normanist" Source on Early Russian History', *Jahrbücher für Geschichte Osteuropas*, neue folge, 10 (1962), pp. 1–12, argues against the identification of the *Rhos* in this annal as Swedes and suggests that the Swedes were used as ambassadors by the Khaqan of the (Slav) *Rus*. He does accept the annal as evidence that Swedes had reached southern Russia.

20. H. Prentout, *Étude critique sur Dudon de Saint-Quentin* (Paris, 1916).

21. Ph. Lauer, *Les Annales de Flodoard* (Paris, 1905).

22. Richer, *Histoire de France* (888–995), ed. R. Latouche, 2 vols.

(Les Classiques de l'Histoire de France au Moyen Age, 1930–37.)

23. *Vita Anskarii auctore Rimberto*, ed. G. Waitz (SS.R.G., 1884). Cf. W. Levison, 'Die Echte und die Verfälschte Gestalt von Rimberts Vita Anskarii', *Zeitschrift des Vereins für Hamburgische Geschichte*, xxiii (1919), pp. 89–146; *id.*, 'Zur würdigung von Rimberts Vita Anskarii', *Schriften des Vereins für Schleswig-Holsteinische Kirchengeschichte*, 2. Reihe (Beiträge und Mitteilungen) VIII, 2. Heft (Kiel, 1926), pp. 163–85. These two important papers have been reprinted in W. Levison, *Aus Rheinischer und Fränkischer Frühzeit* (Düsseldorf, 1948), pp. 567–630. There is an English translation of the *Vita Anskarii* by Charles H. Robinson, *Anskar, The Apostle of the North* (London, 1921).

24. Ed. B. Schmeidler (SS.R.G., 1917). There is a convenient summary of the work done since 1917 together with a good bibliography by Sture Bolin in *KHL*, v, cols. 283–9. For an English translation see F. J. Tschan, *History of the Archbishops of Hamburg-Bremen* (Columbia, 1959), quoted here.

25. Scholion 142; ed. Schmeidler, p. 262; Tschan, *op. cit.*, p. 210.

26. I, lxi; ed. Schmeidler, p. 59; Tschan, *op. cit.*, pp. 52–3.

27. III, liv; ed. Schmeidler, pp. 198–9; Tschan, *op. cit.*, pp. 160–61.

28. IV, viii; ed. Schmeidler, pp. 235–6; Tschan, *op. cit.*, pp. 191–2.

29. *King Alfred's Orosius*, ed. H. Sweet (Early English Text Society, 79, 1883), pp. 17–21.

30. Sture Bolin 'Danmark och Tyskland under Harald Gormson. Grundlinjer i dansk historia under 900-talet', *Scandia*, iv (1931), pp. 184–209.

31. Adam of Bremen, II, xxx; ed. Schmeidler, pp. 91–2; cf. L. Weibull, *Kritiska undersökningar i Nordens historia omkring år 1000* (København, 1911), pp. 91–101.

32. Theodricus Monachus, *Historia de antiquitate regum Norwagiensium*, ed. G. Storm, *Monumenta historica Norvegiæ* (1880), pp. 1–68; Saxo Grammaticus, *Gesta Danorum*, ed. A. Holder (Strassburg, 1886). On Saxo see A. Campbell, 'Saxo Grammaticus and Scandinavian Historical Tradition', *Saga-Book of the Viking Society*, xiii, 1 (1946), pp. 1–22. For the earliest Scandinavian historical writing see Sture Bolin, *Om Nordens äldsta historieforskning* (Lunds Universitets Årsskrift, 1st Avd., band 27, no. 3, 1931). See also *KHL*, vi, cols. 587–602.

33. G. Turville-Petre, *Origins of Icelandic Literature* (Oxford, 1953).

34. *Ibid.*, p. 89.

35. *Njal's Saga*, translated by Magnus Magnusson and Hermann Pálsson (Penguin Books, 1960).

36. The most convenient introduction to Heimskringla is by Peter Foote, in the revised Everyman Edition (1961), pp. vii–xxxi.

37. G. Turville-Petre, *op. cit.*, pp. 26–47.

38. *Ibid.*, pp. 30–31.

39. Lee M. Hollander, *The Skalds* (Princeton, 1947), p. 151.

40. M. Ashdown, *English and Norse Documents relating to the reign of Ethelred the Unready* (Cambridge, 1930), p. 159. The quotations from the saga are from the same translation, pp. 155–7.

41. Alistair Campbell, *Encomium Emmae Reginae* (Royal Historical Society, Camden 3rd ser., lxxii, 1949), p. 76. Mr. Campbell discusses this poem and elucidates the Icelandic traditions about Olaf's career on pp. 76–82.

42. Sune Lindqvist, *Gotlands Bildsteine*, 2 vols. (KVHAA, 1941–2).

43. On Runic writing in general see H. Arntz, *Handbuch der Runenkunde*, 2nd ed. (Halle, 1944) and Lucien Musset, *Introduction à la runologie* (Bibliothèque de Philologie Germanique, xx: Paris, 1965). The articles by Aslak Liestøl on 'Runer' and by Sven B. F. Jansson on 'Runinskrifter' in *KHL*, xiv, cols. 471–8, 481–94 are useful summaries with good, short bibliographies.

44. Lis Jacobsen, 'Vikingetidens "historiske" danske Runeindskrifter. Bidrag til Spørgsmaalet om Runestenenes Tidsfæstelse', *Scandia*, v (1932), pp. 103–47; Elias Wessén, *Historiska Runinskrifter* (KVHAA Handlingar, Filol.-Filos. Ser. 6, 1960).

45. L. Jacobsen and E. Moltke, *Danmarks Runeindskrifter*, i (København, 1942), nos. 2 and 4.

46. Sture Bolin, *Scandia*, iv (1931), pp. 189–92.

47. Lis Jacobsen, *Scandia*, v (1932), p. 113; *id.*, 'Runeindskrifternes vidnesbyrd om kampene omkring Hedeby. Fra Harald Gormssøn til Sven Estridsøn', *Scandia*, viii (1935), pp. 64–79.

48. Elias Wessén, *op. cit.*, pp. 30–46.

49. S. H. Cross and O. P. Sherbowitz-Wetzor, *The Russian Primary Chronicle* (The Medieval Academy of America, Publication no. 60); see also the very brief summary of K. R. Schmidt, *XIᵉ Congrès International des Sciences Historiques, 1960, Rapports, III*, pp. 26–8.

50. On these names see V. Thomsen, *The Relations between Ancient Russia and Scandinavia and the Origin of the Russian State* (Oxford, 1877), pp. 71–2, 131–41. A revised version of this important work was published in Thomsen's *Samlede Afhandlinger*, i (København, 1919), pp. 231–414.

51. Cross and Sherbowitz-Wetzer, *op. cit.*, pp. 30–35.
52. A. A. Vasiliev, *The Russian Attack on Constantinople in 860* (The Medieval Academy of America, Publication no. 46, 1946).
53. Constantine Porphyrogenitus, *De Administrando Imperio*, ed. G. Moravcsik and R. J. H. Jenkins (Budapest, 1949), vol. 1 (text) ed. G. Moravcsik and R. J. H. Jenkins (Budapest, 1949), vol. 2 (commentary), ed. R. J. H. Jenkins (London, 1962). The commentary on the relevant chapter, 9, is by D. Obolensky, pp. 16–61.
54. A full bibliography is given by V. Minorsky, *Ḥudūd al-'Ālam* ('E. J. W. Gibb Memorial' Series, New Series, xi, 1937), pp. 425–7. The texts referring to the *Rus* are translated into Norwegian with helpful comments by Harris Birkeland, *Nordens historie i middelalderen etter arabiske kilder* (Det Norske Videnskaps-Akademi Skrifter, II. Hist.-Filos. Klasse, 2. Bind, no. 2, 1954).
55. H. Birkeland, *op. cit.*, pp. 10–11.
56. V. Minorsky, *Ḥudūd al-'Ālam*, pp. 216–17.
57. H. Arbman, *The Vikings* (1960), p. 94; cf. H. Birkeland, *op. cit.*, pp. 10–11, 134.
58. The best and most convenient discussion of this question is by V. Minorksy, 'Rus', *Encyclopedia of Islam*, 1st ed., iii (1936), pp. 1181–3. Cf. the bibliography mentioned in note 54 above.
59. H. Birkeland, *op. cit.*, pp. 19–24.

3. ARCHAEOLOGY: pp. 48–65

1. Thomas F. O'Rahilly, *Early Irish History and Mythology* (Dublin, 1946), p. 440.
2. Joseph Anderson, *Scotland in Pagan Times: The Iron Age* (Edinburgh, 1883), p. 43.
3. Mårten Stenberger and Ole Klindt-Jensen, *Vallhagar* (Copenhagen, 1955), ii. 1161–85.
4. Th. Ramskou, *AA*, xxiv (1953), pp. 186–96; xxvi (1955), pp. 177–85; xxviii (1957), pp. 193–201; *Fra Nationalmuseets Arbejdsmark*, 1957, pp. 97–100; *Lindholm Høje* (Nationalmuseets Blå Bog, 1960).
5. See p. 56.
6. See pp. 132–7.
7. See Chapter 8.
8. Bertil Almgren, *Bronsnycklar och Djurornamentik*, pp. 70–97. The

argument of this work is briefly stated in English by D. M. Wilson, 'Almgren and Chronology' *Medieval Archaeology*, iii (1959), pp. 112–19. See also Bertil Almgren 'Datering (*av vikingatida kulturföremål*)', *KHL*, iii, cols. 22–7.

9. See Chapter 5.
10. *KHL*, i, cols. 183–4.
11. H. Arbman, *Schweden und das karolingische Reich* (KVHAA Handlingar 43, 1937), pp. 240–1.
12. G. Gjessing, *Viking*, vii (1943), pp. 105–11; Thorleif Sjøvold, *The Oseberg Find* (Oslo, 1959), pp. 80–81.
13. *VA*, vi. 103.
14. J. R. C. Hamilton, *Excavations at Jarlshof, Shetland* (Ministry of Works Archaeological Reports no. 1, Edinburgh, 1956), p. 129.
15. *VA*, v. 31–2, 92–3, 169, 207.
16. *Birka I*, graves 495, 524.
17. Following Bertil Almgren, *Bronsnycklar*, p. 73 these statistics are from Peter Paulsen, *Studien zur Wikinger-Kultur* (Neumünster, 1933), pp. 83–4, 86–7, 90–3, 95–100. The uncertainty of some of the reported associations may be balanced by discoveries since 1933.
18. *VA*, vi. 102–3.
19. Haakon Shetelig, *Vestfoldskolen* (Osebergfundet III, Oslo, 1920).
20. Sune Lindqvist, 'Osebergmästarna', *Tor*, 1948, pp. 9–28.
21. Holger Arbman, *The Vikings* (London, 1961), p. 122.
22. *Bronsnycklar och Djurornamentik*, pp. 88–95.
23. Harold Barker, 'Radio Carbon Dating: Its Scope and Limitations', *Antiquity*, xxxii (1958), pp. 253–63. He concludes that 'the carbon-14 dating method is at its best in fixing the broad outlines of a chronology rather than the fine detail'.
24. O. Olsen and O. C. Pedersen, *AA*, xxix (1958), p. 174.
25. Sune Lindqvist, 'Fuskhögar och falska båtgravar', *Tor*, iv (1958), pp. 101–12.
26. T. J. Arne, 'Skandinavische Holzkammergräber aus der Wikingerzeit in der Ukraine', *AA*, ii (1931), pp. 285–302.
27. Holger Arbman, *Svear i Österviking* (Stockholm, 1955), p. 94.
28. For example, Ibn Khurdadhbih, see Harris Birkeland, *Nordens historie i middelalderen etter arabiske kilder*, p. 11. See also the list of Muslim imports from Bulghar in al-Mukaddasi, above pp. 193–4.
29. The older excavations are discussed by T. J. Arne, *La Suède et l'Orient* (Archives d'Études Orientales, 9, Uppsala, 1914),

pp. 37–44. For D. A. Avdusin's excavations see *Kratkie Soob-shcheniya Instituta istorii materialnoi kultury*, 30 (1949), pp. 3–14; 44 (1952), pp. 93–103; 38 (1951), pp. 72–81. Dr. Avdusin has also written a short note in English, 'Smolensk and the Varangians according to the Archaeological Data', *Norwegian Archaeological Review*, 2 (1969), pp. 52–62.

30. *The Vikings*, p. 279.

31. The archaeological evidence for Scandinavian activity in Russia has been helpfully discussed by A. Artsikhovsky, 'Archaeological Data on the Varangian Question' in *VI International Congress of Prehistoric and Protohistoric Sciences: Reports and communications by archaeologists of the U.S.S.R.* (Moscow, 1962).

32. *VA*, ii–iv.

33. *VA*, vi. 77–9; C. Clarke and W. Fraser, 'Excavation of Pagan Burial Mounds: Ingleby, Derbyshire', *Journal of the Derbyshire Archaeological and Natural Hist. Soc.*, no. lxvi (1946), pp. 1–23; no. lxix (1949), pp. 78–81. More recent studies of this material include D. M. Wilson, 'The Vikings' Relationship with Christianity in Northern England', *Journal of the British Archaeological Association*, 3rd series, xxx (1967), pp. 37–46; *id.*, 'Archaeological evidence for the Viking settlements and raids in England', *Frühmittelalterliche Studien*, 2 (1968), pp. 291–304, with a map of grave finds in England on p. 295.

34. *VA*, vi. 86.

35. *Medieval Archaeology*, iv (1960), p. 140. Early examples of similar identifications are noted by Albert D'Haenens, *Les invasions normandes en Belgique au IXᵉ siècle* (Louvain, 1967), pp. 167–8.

36. See pp. 132–7.

37. See p. 190.

38. W. Hübener, 'Zur Ausbreitung einiger fränkischer Keramikgruppen nach Nord- und Mitteleuropa im 9.–12. Jahrhundert', *Archaeologia Geographica*, ii (1951), pp. 105–11.

39. H. Jankuhn, *Haithabu* (1956), pp. 167–9.

40. See Chapter 5.

4. THE SHIPS: pp. 66–85

1. For general discussions see A. W. Brøgger and H. Shetelig, *The Viking Ships, Their Ancestry and Evolution* (Oslo, 1953); Thorleif Sjøvold, *The Viking Ships* (Oslo, c. 1957); Harald Åkerlund,

The Ships 241

'Vikingatidens skepp och sjöväsen', *Svenska Kryssarklubbens årsskrift*, 1959, pp. 23–81.

2. O. Olsen and O. Crumlin-Pedersen, 'The Skuldelev Ships (II)', *AA*, xxxviii (1967), pp. 73–174; *id.*, *Fem Vikingeskibe fra Roskilde Fjord* (Roskilde, 1969).
3. H. Shetelig, 'Das Nydamschiff', *AA*, i (1930), pp. 1–30.
4. Knud Thorvildsen, '*Ladby-skibet*' (Nordiske Fortidsminder, vi, 1, Copenhagen, 1957); *id.*, *Vikingeskibet ved Ladby* (National-museets Blå Bog, København, 1959).
5. Sune Lindqvist, *Gotlands Bildsteine*, 2 vols. (KVHAA, 1941–2); for the ships see *id.*, 'Fartygsbilder från Gotlands forntid', *Föreningen Sveriges Sjöfartmuseum i Stockholm årsbok*, 1941, pp. 9–24.
6. O. von Friesen, *Sparlösastenen* (KVHAA Handlingar 46, 3, 1940).
7. *The Bayeux Tapestry*, ed. Sir Frank Stenton, second ed. (London, 1965).
8. See p. 35.
9. N. Nicolaysen, *Langskibet fra Gokstad ved Sandefjord* (Kristiania, 1882); Thorleif Sjøvold, *The Viking Ships*, pp. 12–19. There is an interesting, and well illustrated, account of the Gokstad ship in *The Viking*, ed. Bertil Almgren (London, 1966), pp. 249–69.
10. M. Andersen, *Vikingfærden* (Kristiania, 1895).
11. Harald Åkerlund, 'Áss och beiti-áss', *Unda Maris*, 1955–6, pp. 30–91; 'Vikingatidens skepp och sjöväsen', *Svenska Kryssarklubbens årsskrift*, 1959, pp. 23–81.
12. A. W. Brøgger and H. Shetelig, *Vikingeskipene* (Oslo, 1950), p. 156.
13. *The Viking*, ed. B. Almgren, p. 266.
14. *Unda Maris*, 1955–6, pp. 73–8.
15. Bertil Almgren, 'Vikingatåg och vikingaskepp', *Tor*, viii (1962), p. 190.
16. Bertil Almgren, 'Vikingatågens höjdpunkt och slut: skepp, hästar och befästningar', *Tor*, ix (1963), pp. 215–50.
17. The drawings in *The Viking*, ed. B. Almgren, pp. 26–7 may be compared with Plate IX.
18. *The Bayeux Tapestry*, ed. Sir Frank Stenton, plates 42–5. Part of this section of the Tapestry is reproduced in Plate VIII.
19. Ph. Humbla and H. Thomasson, 'Äskekärrsbåten', *Göteborgs och Bohusläns Fornminnesförenings Tidskrift*, 1934, pp. 1–34.
20. H. Shetelig and Fr. Johannessen, *Kvalsundfundet og andre norske myrfund av fartøier* (Bergen, 1929).
21. Ph. Humbla and L. von Post, 'Galtabäcksbåten och tidigt

båtbyggeri i Norden ', *Göteborgs Kungl. Vetenskaps- och Vitterhetssamhälles Handlingar*, 1937.

22. Harald Åkerlund, 'Galtabäcksbåtens ålder och härstamning', *Göteborgs och Bohusläns Fornminnesförenings Tidskrift*, 1942, pp. 24–49.

23. See note 5 above.

24. For Oseberg and Tune see Thorleif Sjøvold, *The Oseberg Find* (Oslo, 1959), pp. 19–30, 72–3; for Storhaugen see A. Lorange, 'Storhaugen paa Karmøen. Nyt Skibsfund fra Vikingetiden', *Bergens Museums Aarsberetning* for 1887, no. 4.

25. Bertil Almgren, *Tor*, viii (1962), pp. 196–8.

26. For Äskekärr see note 19 above. For Skuldelev 1 see *AA*, xxxviii (1967), pp. 96–109.

27. See note 22 above.

28. *AA*, xxxviii (1967), pp. 153–60.

29. Harald Åkerlund, 'Skeppsfyndet vid Falsterbo 1932', *Sjöhistorisk Årsbok*, 1952, pp. 92–104.

30. *AA*, xxxviii (1967), p. 167.

31. *EHD*, p. 189.

32. A. W. Brøgger and H. Shetelig, *The Viking Ships*, pp. 201–4.

33. O. Olsen and O. Crumlin-Pedersen, *Fem Vikingeskibe fra Roskilde Fjord*, pp. 113–24; cf. G. J. Marcus, *English Historical Review*, lxxi (1956), pp. 59–60.

34. F. Lot, *Bibliothèque de l'École des Chartes*, lxix (1908), pp. 51–2.

35. *Osebergfundet*, ed. A. W. Brøgger, Hj. Falk and H. Shetelig, i (Kristiania, 1917), pp. 240–2.

36. See p. 132.

5. TREASURE: pp. 86–119

1. *SG*, ii, tabular analysis.

2. *SG*, ii, nos. 83, 293, 427.

3. Skovmand, p. 169.

4. The most convenient and best guide to the Kufic coins of Scandinavia and the literature is by Ulla S. Linder Welin, 'Arabiska mynt', *KHL*, i, cols. 182–91. See also the articles by the same writer on 'Dinar', *KHL*, iii, cols. 78–80 and

'Dirhem', *KHL*, iii, cols. 98–100. For Finland the best summary is by Beatrice Granberg in *KHL*, i, cols. 191–4.

5. *SG*, i. 256, 261.
6. T. J. Arne, *La Suède et l'Orient* (Archives d'Étudesientale, Ors 8, Uppsala, 1914), p. 79.
7. *Ibid.*, pp. 70–71.
8. For a summary of the Viking period gold finds of Scandinavia see Holger Arbman, 'Guldsmide', *KHL*, v, cols. 566–70.
9. Sigurd Grieg, *Vikingetidens skattefund* (Universitetets oldsaksamling skrifter, ii, Oslo, 1929), pp. 182–98. For the coins see Hans Holst, 'On the coins of the Hon-find', *Minor Publications of the Norwegian Numismatic Society*, no. 4 (1931); *id.*, 'Nye bidrag til belysning av Honfunnets mynter', *NNA*, 1951, pp. 17–27; Kolbjørn Skaare, 'Die karolingischen Münzfunde in Skandinavien und der Schatzfund von Hon', *Hamburger Beiträge zur Numismatik*, vi (1966), pp. 393–408.
10. Skovmand, pp. 71–4.
11. Mårten Stenberger and Ole Klindt-Jensen, *Vallhagar* (Copenhagen, 1955), ii. 1161.
12. *KHL*, v, col. 567.
13. Hans Holst, 'Roman and Byzantine Gold and Silver Coins found in Norway', *Symbolæ Osloenses*, xiv (1935), pp. 115–18; *id.*, 'Uten- og innenlandske mynter i norske funn, nedlagt før år 1100', *NNÅ*, 1943, pp. 56–112.
14. *Birka I*, tabular analysis, pp. 490–529.
15. *SG*, ii, no. 126.
16. *SG*, ii, no. 590.
17. *SG*, ii, no. 83.
18. *SG*, i. 24.
19. *SG*, i. 370.
20. Skovmand, p. 9 shows how the number of Danish hoards increased until 1940.
21. G. Hilding Rundquist, *NNÅ*, 1946, pp. 36–7 and note.
22. Hacksilver is silver that has been hacked into pieces presumably to obtain a definite weight of the metal regardless of its form. For a brief discussion and references see Mårten Stenberger's article in *KHL*, vi, cols. 37–9.
23. Ulla S. Linder, 'En uppländsk silverskatt från 800-talet', *NNÅ*, 1938, pp. 109–24.
24. See pp. 108–10.
25. G. Arwidsson, P. Berghaus, M. Dolley, B. Malmer and U. S. Linder Welin, 'En vikingatida silverskatt från Gandarve i Alva på Gotland', *Gotländskt Arkiv*, 1957, pp. 22–57.

26. P. Seaby, 'The Sequence of Anglo-Saxon Coin Types, 1030–50', *British Numismatic Journal*, xxviii (1955), pp. 111–46; R. H. M. Dolley, *Some Reflections on Hildebrand Type A of Æthelræd II* (*Antikvariskt Arkiv* 9, 1958); R. H. M. Dolley and D. M. Metcalf, 'The Reform of the Coinage under Eadgar', *Anglo-Saxon Coins*, ed. R. H. M. Dolley (London, 1961), pp. 136–68; Michael Dolley, *Anglo-Saxon Pennies* (London, British Museum, 1964), pp. 24–30.

26a. Philip Grierson, *The Numismatic Chronicle*, seventh series, ii (1962), pp. x–xii.

27. R. H. M. Dolley, *The Hiberno-Norse Coins in the British Museum* (Sylloge of Coins of the British Isles; London, 1966); *Anglo-Saxon Coins*, ed. R. H. M. Dolley, pp. 157–8.

28. *Ibid.*, p. 125.

29. P. Grierson, 'Sterling', *ibid.*, pp. 266–83.

29a. S. Harvey, 'Royal Revenue and Domesday Terminolgy', *Economic History Review*, 2nd series, xx (1967), pp. 221–8.

30. See p. 94 and note 25

31. F. Liebermann, *Die Gesetze der Angelsachsen* ii, ii (Halle, 1912), pp. 344–5; F. E. Harmer, *Anglo-Saxon Writs* (Manchester, 1952), pp. 439–40, 513–14.

32. *Commentationes de Nummis Saeculorum ix–xi in Suecia Repertis*, i (KVHAA Handlingar, Antikv. Ser. 9, 1961), p. 176 note; There was a renewed export of English coins to Scandinavia for a short period at the end of the eleventh century, possibly as the pay of mercenaries or in the form of subsidies to Scandinavian allies of the Norman kings of England, *Sylloge of Coins of the British Isles; Royal Coin Cabinet Stockholm, the Anglo-Norman Coins*, by Michael Dolley with F. Elmore Jones and C. S. S. Lyon (London and Stockholm, 1969), pp. 45–7. See also p. 218.

33. R. H. M. Dolley, 'The Continental Coins in the Halton Moor Find and other Norman Deniers found in the British Isles'. *Hamburger Beiträge zur Numismatik*, iv (1958–9), pp. 53–7.

34. See pp. 112–15.

35. The best hope of scientifically recognising the provenance of silver used in coins seems to lie in the varying occurrence of the radioactive isotopes of lead. On the whole of this subject see the forthcoming volume of proceedings of the Symposium on the Composition and Analysis of Coins organised by the Royal Numismatic Society in London, 9–11 December 1970.

36. A most valuable survey of the subject is by N. L. Rasmusson, 'An Introduction to the Viking-Age Hoards', *Commentationes*, i (see note 32 above), pp. 3–16.

37. P. Hauberg, *Myntforhold og Udmyntninger i Danmark indtil 1146* (Copenhagen, 1900), pp. 15–16.

38. *EHD*, p. 176.

39. Kolbjørn Skaare, 'Et Myntfunn fra Kaupang', *UOÅ*, 1958–9, pp. 106–19; G. Galster,' Karolingiske mønter fundne i Danmark', *NNÅ*, 1951, pp. 28–40 has been translated in his *Coins and History* (1959), pp. 65–78.

40. See pp. 110–11.

41. The word translated here as 'moneyless' is *feohleas* which could mean 'without stock' or 'without property'.

42. C. S. S. Lyon and B. H. I. H. Stewart, 'The Northumbrian Viking Coins in the Cuerdale Hoard', *Anglo-Saxon Coins*, ed. R. H. M. Dolley, pp. 96–121.

43. Michael Dolley, *Viking Coins of the Danelaw and of Dublin* (London, 1965), p. 19.

44. R. H. M. Dolley and K. F. Morrison, 'Finds of Carolingian Coins from Great Britain and Ireland', *British Numismatic Journal*, xxxii (1963), pp. 75–87.

45. *Ibid.*, pp. 80–81.

46. P. C. J. A. Boeles, 'Les trouvailles de monnaies carolingiennes dans les Pays-Bas, specialement celles des trois provinces septentrionales', *Jaarboek van het Koninklijk Nederlandsch Genootschap voor Munt- en Penningkunde*, ii (1915), pp. 1–98. Karl F. Morrison, 'Numismatics and Carolingian Trade: a critique of the evidence', *Speculum*, xxxviii (1963), pp. 403–32, has accepted hoards as evidence of disorder, *op. cit.*, p. 430, and claims that 'the disturbances of these invasions (i.e. by the Danes) and of the civil wars which followed upon Louis's death, and which frequently ranged into Frisia, adequately explain the presence in that area of many finds consisting of issues of Louis the Pious and his sons before 864. The Danes held Frisia undisputed until 880; the absence of numerous finds dating from *c.* 850 until 880 reflects the tranquillity of their tenure.' It is true that very few hoards were deposited there between the Edict of Pitres in 864 and 880, but a relatively large proportion of the known Carolingian hoards (9 of the 15 from the coastal provinces of Frisia and Groningen) appear to have been deposited between 843 and 864, that is during the Danish occupation of Frisia. The explanation must be either that the area was not so tranquil as Morrison suggests or, more probably, that these hoards were deposited by Danes.

47. The most reliable list of ninth-century British coin hoards is in *Sylloge of Coins of the British Isles; The Hiberno-Norse Coins in the*

British Museum, by R. H. M. Dolley (London, 1966), pp. 48–9. Only 6 English hoards are recorded between 830 and 865 as against 36 for the decade after 865.

48. Kolbjørn Skaare, *UOÅ*, 1958–9, pp. 110–14.
49. Sture Bolin, *Studier över Mynt och Mynt fynd i Östra och Norra Europa under Vikingatiden*, pp. 83–92. Many of the analyses given here are from this important but unpublished work and I am very grateful to Professor Bolin for making a copy available to me and for allowing me to quote from it. Professor Bolin has published some of his conclusions in 'Mohammed, Charlemagne and Ruric', *Scandinavian Economic History Review*, i (1953), pp. 5–39, which is a modified translation of an article that first appeared in *Scandia*, xii (1939), pp. 181–222. See also S. Bolin, 'Gotlands Vikingatids-skatter och Världshandeln', *Boken om Gotland*, i (Visby, 1945), pp. 125–37.
50. S. Bolin, *Mynt och Myntfynd* p. 218, table 50.
51. *SG*, i. 254–5; ii, tabular analysis.
52. *SG*, ii, no. 295.
53. Skovmand, pp. 15, 47–9, 77–9.
54. *Ibid.*, pp. 22–3.
55. Ulla S. Linder, 'Salemsfyndet', *Kulturhistoriska Studier, tillägnade Nils Åberg* (Stockholm, 1938), pp. 166–80.
56. Skovmand, pp. 15–23.
57. A. W. Brøgger, 'Et mynt fund fra Foldøen i Ryfylke, Norge, fra xi Aarhundrede', *ANOH*, 1910, pp. 239–82.
58. Skovmand, pp. 192–6.
59. *Anglo-Saxon Coins*, ed. R. H. M. Dolley, pp. 163–5.
59a. G. Hilding Rundquist, 'Tvås ilverskatter från Vikingatiden i Småländsk jord', *NNÅ*, 1946, pp. 35–74.
60. Hoards are particularly frequent in areas that were both rich and vulnerable, and the hoarded wealth of Gotland is therefore not surprising.
61. This is based on an analysis of the hoards in *SG*, ii. Cf. Professor Stenberger's analysis in *SG*, i. 248–9, 252–3 and the comments of U. S. Linder Welin in *KHL*, i, col. 184; see also N. L. Rasmusson in *Commentationes*, i (see note 32 above), p. 7.
62. N. L. Rasmusson and Hans Holst, *KHL*, i, cols. 428–31.
63. U. S. Linder Welin, *KHL*, i, col. 184.
64. See p. 222.
65. S. Bolin, *Mynt och Myntfynd i Europa*, pp. 218–19; *id.*, *Boken om Gotland*, i. 132.
66. See pp. 93–4.
67. *Mynt och Myntfynd*, pp. 102–5.

68. U. S. Linder, *NNÅ*, 1938, pp. 113–14, 124.
69. U. S. Linder Welin, *KHL*, i, cols. 184–5.
70. Skovmand, p. 41.
71. *Birka I*. This does not, of course, mean that the graves in question were earlier than 890, cf. p. 185.
72. U. S. Linder Welin, *KHL*, i, col. 186.
73. *Ibid.*, cols. 186–7.
74. *AA*, xxvi (1955), p. 171 note and map on p. 172.
75. *SG*, ii, nos. 83, 268, 280, 517, 525, 531.
76. Skovmand, pp. 111–13.
77. Kolbjørn Skaare, *NNÅ*, 1961, pp. 20–21.
78. U. S. Linder Welin, *KHL*, i, cols. 186–7; S. Bolin, *Mynt och Myntfynd i Europa*, pp. 119–23; *id., Boken om Gotland*, i. 132.
79. S. Bolin, *Mynt och Myntfynd i Europa*, pp. 396–7; *id., Studier över statsmakten och penningväsendets grundprinciper i det romerska kejsarriket och den äldre medeltidens tre kultursfärer* (unpublished), pp. 300–314; *id., Scandinavian Economic History Review*, i (1953), pp. 19–22; U. S. Linder Welin, *KHL*, i, cols. 185–6.
80. See p. 224.
81. Silver coins were, of course, smelted to make ornaments in both Russia and Scandinavia throughout the Viking period. The argument here is that a sudden increase of smelting is unlikely to be the explanation for the late ninth-century change in the Russian hoards.
82. See p. 193.
83. Professor Bolin has argued that the export of Muslim silver from Russia continued until *c.* 970, *Mynt och Myntfynd i Europa*, pp. 147–50, 479–80 and in *Boken om Gotland*, i. 133.
84. The eleven hoards shown in the map in *AA*, xxvi (1955), p. 172 were all of the period 900–930. The only other British hoards containing Kufic coins are from Croydon, deposited *c.* 874–5 with one dirhem of Harun al-Rasid and some fragments of Kufic coins, J. D. A. Thompson, *Inventory of British Coin Hoards, A.D. 600–1500* (1956), no. 111; and from Machkrie, Islay, deposited *c.* 960–70 with one Kufic fragment, *Proceedings of the Society of Antiquaries of Scotland*, i (1851–4), pp. 74–81.
85. *Mynt och Myntfynd i Europa*, pp. 247, 360–61, 472–8; *Boken om Gotland*, i. 132–3.
86. *SG*, ii, no. 105; Bolin, *Mynt och Myntfynd i Europa*, p. 240.
87. *Mynt och Myntfynd i Europa*, pp. 478–80; *Boken om Gotland*, i. 133.
88. See pp. 108–10.
89. U. S. Linder Welin, *KHL*, i, col. 189.

R

90. This can be seen very clearly in Professor Bolin's table reproduced here, p. 224.
91. See p. 215.
92. U. S. Linder Welin, *KHL*, i, cols. 189–90.
93. S. Bolin, *Mynt och Myntfynd in Europa*, pp. 493–6; U. S. Linder Welin, *KHL*, i, cols. 189–90.
94. *SG*, i. 248–9; Skovmand, pp. 17–23.
95. P. Hauberg and J. Østrup, 'Terslev-fundets Mønter', *ANOH*, 1914, pp. 63–75; cf. R. H. M. Dolley, *NNÅ*, 1957–8, pp. 32, 37.
96. *EHD*, pp. 234–5.
97. See note 32 above.
98. See pp. 199–200.
99. *KHL*, ii, cols. 428–31.
100. Brita Malmer, *Nordiska Mynt Före År 1000* (Acta Archaeologica Lundensia, series in 8°, no. 4; Lund and Bonn, 1966).
101. For Scandinavian coinages see Svend Aakjær, ed., *Mønt* (Nordisk Kultur, xxix, 1936); Brita Malmer, 'A Contribution to the Numismatic History of Norway during the Eleventh Century', *Commentationes de Nummis*, i (KVHAA Handlingar, Antikv. Ser. 9, 1961), pp. 223–376. For a survey of some recent work see Kolbjørn Skaare, 'Vikingtidsnumismatikk', *Nordisk Numismatisk Unions Medlemsblad*, 1961, pp. 189–97 and articles by various writers in *KHL*.

6. THE RAIDS: pp. 120–47

1. Abbon, *Le Siège de Paris par les Normands*, ed. Henri Waquet (Les Classiques de l'Histoire de France au Moyen Age, 1942), pp. 28–30, lines 177–95.
2. *Annales de Saint-Bertin*, edd. F. Grat, J. Vielliard and S. Clémencet (Paris, 1964), p. 37.
3. *The Making of Europe* (London, 1948), pp. 190–91.
4. *Anglo-Saxon England* (Oxford, 1947), p. 242.
5. H. Shetelig, *VA*, i. 122; H. Waquet, *op. cit.*, p. 24 n. 1.
6. See pp. 166–7.
7. See pp. 99–101.
8. See pp. 143–5.
9. Ine 13, 1; F. Liebermann, *Die Gesetze der Angelsachsen*, i (Halle, 1903), p. 94; F. L. Attenborough, *The Laws of the Earliest English Kings* (Cambridge, 1922), pp. 40–41.

10. F. Lot, *L'Art Militaire et les Armées au Moyen Age*, i (Paris, 1946), pp. 336–7.
11. J. H. Ramsay, 'The Strength of English Armies in the Middle Ages', *English Historical Review*, xxix (1914), pp. 221–7.
12. See pp. 16–17.
13. See p. 17.
14. Ed. Waquet, p. 14, lines 28–30.
15. See pp. 80–82.
16. See p. 71.
17. This battle has been discussed by F. P. Magoun, *Modern Language Review*, xxxvii (1942), pp. 409–14.
18. William of Malmesbury, *Historia Novella*, ed. K. R. Potter (Nelson's Medieval Classics, 1955), pp. 73–4.
19. On the battle of Brissarthe see F. Lot, *op. cit.*, i. 99.
20. Stenton, *op. cit.*, p. 241 n.; Lot, *op. cit.*, i. 98.
21. *Op. cit.*, p. 577.
22. I. C. Gould, 'Ancient Earthworks', *Victoria History of the County of Essex*, i. 286–7.
23. C. Fox, *The Archaeology of the Cambridge Region* (Cambridge, 1923), p. 302.
24 *English Historical Review*, xxvii (1912), pp. 512–13.
25. P. Nørlund *Trelleborg* (1948); C. G. Schultz, 'Aggersborg, vikingelejren ved Limfjorden', *Fra Nationalmuseets Arbejdsmark*, 1949, pp. 91–108; O. Olsen, *Fyrkat* (Nationalmuseets Blå Bog, 1959). For a brief summary see J. Brøndsted, *Danmarks Oldtid*, iii *Jernalderen* (København, 1960), pp. 363–9. Olaf Olsen has discussed these camps in two papers, 'Trelleborg-problemer: De danske vikingeborge og deres historiske baggrund', *Scandia*, 28 (1962), pp. 92–109, with an English summary, pp. 109–12; 'Viking Fortresses in Denmark', *Recent archaeological excavations in Europe*. ed. R. L. S. Bruce-Mitford (forthcoming). For Fyrkat see also Else Roesdahl, 'Livet på Fyrkat', *Skalk*, 1969 no. 2, pp. 3–9.
26. Nørlund, *op. cit.*, p. 113.
27. M. D. Knowles, *The Monastic Order in England* (Cambridge, 1940), pp. 69–70.
28. Anglo-Saxon Chronicle, *s.a.* 1013, *EHD*, p. 223.
29. Anglo-Saxon Chronicle, *s.a.* 1012, *EHD*, p. 222.
30. R. H. M. Dolley, *The Hiberno-Norse Coins in the British Museum* (London, 1966), p. 52.
31. Anglo-Saxon Chronicle, *s.a.* 1011, *EHD*, p. 221.
32. See pp. 141–2.
33. R. Poupardin, *Monuments de l'histoire des abbayes de Saint-Philibert*, (Paris, 1905), pp. xxv–xl.

34. L. Delisle, *Littérature Latine et Histoire du Moyen Age* (Paris, 1890), pp. 17–18.
35. Cf. M. Prou, *Les Monnaies Carolingiennes* (Paris, 1896).
36. F. Vercauteren, *Étude sur les Civitates de la Belgique Seconde* (Bruxelles, 1934). p. 123.
37. *Ibid.*, p. 170.
38. F. Lot, *Bibliothèque de l'École des Chartes*, lxix (1908), pp. 21–2.
39. See Figure 9, based on R. H. M. Dolley, *The Hiberno-Norse Coins in the British Museum*, pp. 24, 48–9.
40. *EHD*, p. 818.
41. *EHD*, pp. 273–4.
42. Rose Graham, 'The History of the Alien Priory of Wenlock', *Journal of the British Archaeological Association*, 3rd ser., iv (1939), p. 119.
43. W. de Gray Birch, *Cartularium Saxonicum*, ii (London, 1887), no. 587.
44. See pp. 19–20.
45. *EHD*, p. 818.
46. *The Latin Charters of the Anglo-Saxon Period* (Oxford, 1955), p. 40.
47. R. R. Darlington, *English Historical Review*, li (1936), pp. 422–3; D. C. Douglas, *Proceedings of the British Academy*, xxxiii (1947), pp. 111–12.
48. *Irish Art in the Early Christian Period*, 2nd ed. (London, 1947), pp. 86, 154. Cf. *id.*, *Irish Art during the Viking Invasions (800–1020 A.D.)* (London, 1967), pp. 4–5.
49. A. T. Lucas, 'The Plundering and Burning of Churches in Ireland, 7th to 11th century', *North Munster Studies: Essays in commemoration of Monsignor Michael Moloney*, ed. Etienne Rynne (Limerick, The Thomond Archaeological Society, 1967), pp. 172–229.
50. *EHD*, pp. 190–91.
51. J. Dhondt, *Études sur la naissance des principautés territoriales en France* (Brugge, 1948), p. 28 n.

7. THE DANISH SETTLEMENTS: pp. 148–76

1. F. T. Wainwright, 'Æthelflaed Lady of the Mercians', *The Anglo-Saxons*, ed. P. Clemoes (London, 1959), pp. 53–69.
2. A. Campbell, 'Two Notes on the Norse Kingdom in Northumbria', *EHR*, lvii (1942), pp. 85–97; D. Whitelock, 'The

The Danish Settlements 251

Dealings of the Kings of England with Northumbria in the Tenth and Eleventh Centuries', *The Anglo-Saxons*, ed. P. Clemoes, pp. 70–88.

3. F. Liebermann, *Die Gesetze der Angelsachsen*, i (1903), p. 216.
4. Liebermann, *op. cit.*, ii. 347–8.
5. VI Atr 37—Liebermann, *op. cit.*, i. 256; A. J. Robertson, *The Laws of the Kings of England from Edmund to Henry I* (1925), p. 102.
6. E Cf. 30—Liebermann, *op. cit.*, i. 652, cf. note *e*.
7. *Anglo-Saxon England*, p. 499.
8. O. S. Anderson, *The English Hundred-Names* (Lunds Universitets Årsskrift, 1934), pp. xxi–iv.
9. III Atr 3, 1—Liebermann, *op. cit.*, i. 228; A. J. Robertson, *op. cit.*, p. 64.
10. *Anglo-Saxon England*, p. 497.
11. A. J. Robertson, *Anglo-Saxon Charters* (1939), no. xl.
12. *Op. cit.*, p. 505.
13. J. M. Kaye, 'The Sacrabar', *English Historical Review*, lxxxiii (1968), pp. 744–58.
14. D. M. Wilson, *Frühmittelalterliche Studien*, 2 (1968), p. 295.
15. See pp. 163–6.
16. The best introduction to the study of place-names and its literature is E. Ekwall, *Concise Oxford Dictionary of English Place-names*, 4th ed. (Oxford, 1960). For the elements used in place-names see A. H. Smith, *English Place-name Elements* (English Place-name Society, xxv–vi, 1956). The forms of the names discussed here are from these two works or from the county surveys published by the English Place-name Society.
17. It may alternatively be a translation of a pre-Scandinavian name meaning, 'the *tun* of the Angles'.
18. K. Cameron, 'The Scandinavians in Derbyshire: The Place-Name Evidence', *Nottingham Medieval Studies*, ii (1958), p. 90.
19. F. M. Stenton, *Documents Illustrative of the Social and Economic History of the Danelaw* (British Academy, 1920), pp. cxiv–xv.
20. O. von Feilitzen, *The Pre-Conquest Personal-Names of Domesday Book* (Nomina Germanica, 3, 1937), pp. 18–26.
21. *Saga-Book of the Viking Society*, xii (1937–45), pp. 22–3.
22. 'Scandinavian Personal Names in the Liber Vitae of Thorney Abbey', *Saga-Book of the Viking Society*, xii (1937–45), pp. 127–53.
23. O. von Feilitzen, *op. cit.*, pp. 18–19.
24. Gillian Fellows Jensen, *Scandinavian Personal Names in Lincolnshire and Yorkshire* (Copenhagen, 1968), pp. lxii–iii.

25. E. Ekwell, *Scandinavians and Celts in the North-West of England* (Lund, 1918).

26. Olof von Feilitzen, *op. cit.*, pp. 32–3.

27. A. H. Smith, *English Place-name Elements*, ii. 208–9.

28. The figures given by F. M. Stenton in *Transactions of the Royal Historical Society*, 4th ser., xxiv (1942), p. 12, have been revised by K. Cameron, *Scandinavian Settlement in the Territory of the Five Boroughs: The Place-name Evidence* (University of Nottinhgam, 1965), cited here as Cameron, *Scandinavian Settlement*, part I, p. 8 and Gillian Fellows Jensen in her forthcoming study of the place-names of Yorkshire.

29. F. T. Wainwright, *Archaeology and Place-names and History* (London, 1962), pp. 78–9; F. M. Stenton, *op. cit.* (in n. 28), pp. 20–21.

30. Gillian Fellows Jensen, *op. cit.*, p. xxxiii note, cf. pp. xxxv–li.

31. K. Cameron, *Scandinavian Settlement*, part I, p. 7.

32. *Ex inf.* Gillian Fellows Jensen.

33. A. H. Smith, *The Place-names of the East Riding of Yorkshire and York* (English Place-name Society, xiv; Cambridge, 1937), p. 312, states that only 33 of the 42 place-names in *by* occur in Domesday Book. This is a misprint for 38. The names are listed by Smith on p. 302.

34. A. H. Smith, *op. cit.*, p. 315.

35. K. Cameron, 'Scandinavian Settlement in the Territory of the Five Boroughs: The Place-name evidence, Part II, Place-names in Thorp'. *Mediaeval Scandinavia*, 3 (1970), cited here as Cameron, *Scandinavian Settlement*, part II.

36. *Ex inf.* Gillian Fellows Jensen.

37. Gillian Fellows Jensen, *op. cit.*, pp. x i–ii.

38. K. Cameron, 'Scandinavian Settlement in the Territory of the Five Boroughs: The Place-name evidence, Part III, The Grimston-Hybrids', *England before the Conquest: Studies in Primary Sources presented to Dorothy Whitelock*, ed. P. Clemoes (forthcoming).

39. Gillian Fellows Jensen, *op. cit.*, pp. xxxiv, xxxix, xliii, xlviii.

39a. Cameron, *Scandinavian Settlement*, part I, pp. 12–18.

40. D. M. Wilson and Ole Klindt-Jensen, *Viking Art* (London, 1966), pp. 100–114; A. L. Binns, 'Tenth Century Carvings from Yorkshire and the Jellinge style', *Universitetet i Bergen Årbok* 1956, historisk-antikvarisk rekke, no. 2.

41. W. G. Collingwood, *Northumbrian Crosses of the Pre-Norman Age* (London, 1927), pp. 50–52, 126; cf. T. D. Kendrick, *Late Saxon and Viking Art* (London, 1949), pp. 90–97.

42. Yorkshire examples include North Frodingham (East Riding); Collingham, Dewsbury, Ilkley, Leeds, Otley and Ripon (West Riding); Croft, Lastingham and Northallerton (North Riding).
43. *EHD*, p. 191; P. H. Reaney, *The Place-names of Cambridgeshire and the Isle of Ely* (English Place-name Society, xix; Cambridge, 1943), pp. xix–xxii, 34–5, 129–39.
44. Cameron, *Scandinavian Settlement*, Part II; for Yorkshire see Gillian Fellows Jensen's forthcoming work.
45. F. M. Stenton, 'The Historical Bearing of Place-name Studies: The Danish Settlement of Eastern England', *Transactions of the Royal Historical Society*, 4th Series, xxiv (1942), pp. 1–24; H. R. Loyn, *Anglo-Saxon England and the Norman Conquest* (London, 1962), pp. 52–61; Cameron, *Scandinavian Settlement*, part I.
46. Loyn, *op. cit.*, p. 54; Cameron, *Scandinavian Settlement*, part I, pp. 10–11.
47. Cameron, *Scandinavian Settlement*, part I, p. 19.
48. F. M. Stenton, 'The Danes in England', *Proceedings of the British Academy*, xiii (1927), pp. 205–6.
49. Anglo-Saxon Chronicle, *s.a.* 959; *EHD*, p. 206.
50. William of Malmesbury, *Gesta Regum*, ed. W. Stubbs, i (Rolls Series, 90; London, 1887), p. 165.
51. *EHD*, pp. 217, 545.
52. Loyn, *op. cit.*, p. 61.
53. *History*, xlviii (1963), p. 351.
54. First published as number 1 in *Publications of the Linguistic Circle of New York* (New York, 1953) and reissued 1963, etc., by Mouton, The Hague.
56. P. Skautrup, *Det Danske Sprogs Historie*, i (København, 1944), pp. 95–106, cf. E. Björkman, *Scandinavian Loan words in Middle English*, i (Halle, 1960), p. 8.
57. Weinreich, *op. cit.*, p. 56.
58. *Ibid.*, pp. 57–8.
59. *Ibid.*, p. 59.
60. *Ibid.*, p. 92. My colleague T. E. Hope, Professor of French Language and Romance Philology, has drawn my attention to the importance of the degree of intermarriage as a factor in linguistic interference. In mixed families high frequency words are readily borrowed. He has also pointed out that several of the words quoted above, p. 169, as examples of Scandinavian linguistic influence, e.g. *anger, scant, ugly, happy, thrive, ill* and *die* belong to well known 'dynamic' semantic categories in which synonymy is common and the rate of neologism high.

61. 'Free Peasantry of the Northern Danelaw', *Bulletin de la Société Royale des Lettres de Lund*, 1925–6, p. 79.

62. 'The Proportion of Scandinavian Settlers in the Danelaw', *Saga-Book of the Viking Society*, xii (1937–45), pp. 26–8.

63. F. W. Maitland was sceptical of the association of Danes and sokemen, *Domesday Book and Beyond* (Cambridge, 1897), p. 139.

64. On pre-Scandinavian characteristics of sokemen see R. H. C. Davis, *The Kalendar of Abbot Samson of Bury St. Edmonds* (Camden Society, 3rd ser., lxxiv, 1954), pp. xliii-vii, P. Vinogradoff, *Growth of the Manor* (London, 1911), p. 303. The Sokes of the Danelaw as they existed in the eleventh century and later could have been the result of the English royal government's attempts to create some system of jurisdiction and personal obligations to replace traditional bonds destroyed in the Danish conquests, cf. II Cn 71, 3—Liebermann, *op. cit.*, i. 358; A. J. Robertson, *Laws of the Kings of England*, p. 210.

65. F. M. Stenton, 'The Danes in England'. *Proceedings of the British Academy*, xiii (1927), pp. 238–4; R. V. Lennard, 'The Origin of the Fiscal Carucate', *Economic History Review*, 1st series, xiv (1944–45), pp. 51–63.

66. Poul Rasmussen, 'Plovskat', *KHL*, xiii, cols. 350–51, cf. articles on 'Bol' and 'Byamål', *KHL*, cols. 55–63, 389–96.

67. F. M. Stenton, *Types of Manorial Structure in the Northern Danelaw* (Oxford Studies in Social and Legal History, ed. P. Vinogradoff, ii; 1910), pp. 87–90; R. V. Lennard, *op. cit.*, pp. 56–8.

68. C. S. Taylor, 'The Origin of the Mercian Shires', *Transactions of the Bristol and Gloucestershire Archaeological Society*, xxi (1898), pp. 32–57, reprinted in *Gloucestershire Studies*, ed. H. P. R. Finberg (Leicester, 1957).

69. J. H. Round, *Feudal England* (London, 1895), p. 71.

70. F. W. Maitland, *Domesday Book and Beyond* (Cambridge, 1897), p. 456.

71. A. Tomkinson, 'The Carucage of 1220 in an Oxfordshire Hundred', *Bulletin of the Institute of Historical Research*, xli (1968), pp. 212–16.

72. Henri Navel, *Recherches sur les Institutions féodales en Normandie* (*Région de Caen*) (Caen, 1951), pp. 101–2.

73. D. M. Wilson, 'The Vikings' Relationship with Christianity in Northern England', *Journal of the British Archaeological Association*, 3rd series, xxx (1967), pp. 37–46; D. Whitelock, 'The Conversion of the Eastern Danelaw', *Saga-Book of the Viking Society*, xii, part iii (1941), pp. 160–76.

74. See p. 101.

75. See p. 208.
76. Georges Duby, *L'Economie Rurale et la Vie des Campagnes dans l'Occident Médiéval* (Paris, 1962), i, pp. 133–69.
77. P. H. Sawyer, 'The wealth of England in the eleventh century', *Transactions of the Royal Historical Society*, 5th series, 15 (1965), pp. 145–64, esp. pp. 162–3.
78. The figures in Maitland, *op. cit.*, pp. 400–401, are incomplete and need revision. Unfortunately *The Domesday Geography of England*, ed. H. C. Darby *et al.*, 5 vols. (Cambridge, 1952–67) omits the values, cf. *Economic History Review*, 2nd series, xvi (1963–64), pp. 155–7. R. Welldon Finn, *The Norman Conquest and its effects on the economy 1066–86* (London, 1971) contains a lot of detailed discussion of Domesday values and includes maps showing changes of value recorded in Domesday Book.
79. Northamptonshire was an area of late growth like its neighbour Warwickshire, on which see J. B. Harley, 'Population Trends and Agricultural Developments from the Warwickshire Hundred Rolls of 1279', *Economic History Review*, 2nd series, xi (1958–9), pp. 8–18. For the Scandinavian influence in Northamptonshire see J. E. B. Gover, A. Mawer and F. M. Stenton, *The Place-names of Northamptonshire* (English Place-name Society, x; Cambridge, 1933), pp. xx–xxix.
80. D. C. Douglas, 'The Rise of Normandy', *Proceedings of the British Academy*, xxxiii (1947), pp. 101–30.
81. J. Adigard des Gautries, *Les Noms de Personnes Scandinaves en Normandie de 911 à 1066* (Nomina Germanica, 11, 1954), pp. 265–70; Lucien Musset, 'Pour l'étude des relations entre les colonies scandinaves d'Angleterre et de Normandie', *Mélanges de Linguistique et de Philologie Fernand Mossé In Memoriam* (1959), pp. 330–39; Fr. de Beaurepaire, 'Les Noms d'Anglo-Saxons contenus dans la toponymie Normande', *Annales de Normandie*, x (1960), pp. 307–16; L. Musset in *Mediaeval Scandinavia*, 2 (1969), pp. 187–91.
82. F. M. Stenton, 'The Scandinavian Colonies in England and Normandy', *Transactions of the Royal Historical Society*, 4th ser. xxvii (1945), pp. 1–12, argues that the colonisation of Normandy was essentially aristocratic in contrast to the peasant colonisation in England. D. C. Douglas has questioned this, *op. cit.*, p. 103. See also L. Musset, 'Naissance de la Normandie (V^e–XIe Siècles)', *Historie de la Normandie*, ed. M. de Bouard (Toulouse, 1970), pp. 75–130, esp. pp. 102–6.
83. The study of blood groups sometimes yields valuable clues to migrations and the history of settlement. On their general

value see A. E. Mourant, *The Distribution of the Human Blood Groups* (Oxford, 1954), and for more recent and detailed distribution maps for one series, A. E. Mourant, A. C. Kopeč and K. Domaniewska-Sobczak, *The ABO Blood Groups* (Oxford, 1958). Iceland is remarkable in showing ABO gene-frequencies that are very much like those of the north and west of Britain and quite unlike the average in Norway, see J. A. Donegani, N. Dungal, E. W. Ikin and A. E. Mourant, 'The blood groups of the Icelanders', *Annals of Eugenics*, 15 (1950), pp. 47–52. This would be consistent with a large Celtic element among the settlers of Iceland, many of whom went to Iceland from the British Isles, cf. G. Turville-Petre, *The Origins of Icelandic Literature* (Oxford, 1953), pp. 3–5. The contrast between Iceland and some areas of Norway will probably be less extreme when more detailed figures are available. It is likely that there are areas in Norway with O gene-frequencies that are quite as high as in Iceland, cf. Lars Beckman, *A Contribution to the Physical Anthropology and Population Genetics of Sweden* (Hereditas, xlv, Lund, 1959), pp. 18, 126–40. The areas of Danish settlement in England show strikingly similar ABO characteristics to those of modern Denmark, Ada C. Kopeč, 'Blood groups in Great Britain', *The Advancement Science*, 1956, pp. 200–203, although Mrs. Kopeč has been kind enough to tell me by letter that a more comprehensive survey of over 500,000 cases, shows that the boundary of the high A gene-frequency region (X), will probably have to exclude most of Yorkshire and the north-west part of Lincolnshire. An area of Pembrokeshire shows an even higher A gene-frequency and it has been suggested that this is the result of Scandinavian settlement, I. Morgan Watkin, 'A Viking Settlement in Little England beyond Wales: ABO Blood-group evidence', *Man*, lx (1960), pp. 148–53.

8. TOWNS AND TRADE: pp. 177–201

1. For these sources see pp. 32, 35–6.
2. A. H. Smith, *English Place-name Elements*, i (English Place-name Society, xxvi, Cambridge, 1956), pp. 70–71.
3. This account of Birka is based upon *Birka I*; Holger Arbman, *Schweden und das karolingische Reich* (KVHAA Handlingar, 43, 1937); id., *Birka, Sveriges äldsta handelsstad* (Stockholm, 1939). The importance of the workshops of Birka has recently been emphasised by Birgit Arrhenius, 'Ett tråddragninsinstrument från

Birka', *Fornvännen* 1968, pp. 288–93, English summary, p. 293; *id.*, 'Knivar från Helgö och Birka', *Fornvännen* 1970, pp. 40–50, German summary, pp. 50–1.

4. *Vita Anskarii*, cap. xix, ed. G. Waitz (SS.R.G., 1884), p. 41.
5. *Ibid.*, caps. xx, xxvii, pp. 45, 58.
6. Arbman, *Schweden und das karolingische Reich*, chapters iii and iv.
7. *Ibid.*, p. 240.
8. See p. 118.
9. Agnes Geijer, *Birka Untersuchungen und Studien III, Die Textilfunde aus den Gräbern* (KVHAA, 1938), pp. 58–67.
10. For a map showing former entrances to the lake see *Svenska Turistföreningens Årsskrift*, 1949, pp. 66–7.
11. See pp. 184–5.
12. *KHL*, iii, cols. 112–15.
13. Bertil Almgren, *Tor*, viii (1962), p. 195.
14. Sune Lindqvist, 'Vattenståndet vid Birka på 900-talet', *Fornvännen*, xxiii (1928), pp. 118–20.
15. Nils G. Hörner, 'Fyrisåmynningen och Landhöjningen', *Upplands Fornminnesförenings Tidskrift*, 43: 3 (1943), pp. 207–77 especially p. 250.
16. Bertil Almgren, *Bronsnycklar och djurornamentik*, pp. 96–7; *id.*, *KHL*, iii, cols. 23–4.
17. Holger Arbman, *Schweden und das karolingische Reich*, pp. 240–41.
18. Björn Ambrosiani, 'Birka-Sigtuna-Stockholm. Ett diskussionsinlägg', *Tor*, iii (1957), pp. 148–58.
19. E. Floderus, *Sigtuna, Sveriges äldsta medeltidsstad* (Stockholm, 1941).
20. See p. 116.
21. Holger Arbman, *Svear i österviking* (Stockholm, 1955), p. 135.
22. Wilhelm Holmqvist, *Excavations at Helgö I, Report for 1954–56* (KVHAA, 1961), pp. 124–60, 229–32 for iron, pp. 160–63, 164–82 for glass; cf. pp. 72, 96–7. See also Wilhelm Holmqvist and Birgit Arrhenius, *Excavations at Helgö II, Report for 1957–1959* (KVHAA, 1964).
23. See pp. 194, 198.
24. The best introduction to this site and its literature is H. Jankuhn, *Haithabu. Ein Handelsplatz der Wikingerzeit*, 3rd ed. (Neumünster, 1956). See also *Berichte über die Ausgrabungen in Haithabu*, ed. K. Schietzel of which three have so far appeared (Neumünster, 1969). *Bericht 1* includes K. Schietzel, 'Die archäologischen Befunde (1963–1964)'. Helmuth Schledermann has provided a most valuable survey in two articles entitled 'Slesvig/Hedebys tilblivelse' in *Sønderjyske Årbøger* 1966, pp. 1–65 and 1967, pp. 1–

73. The first part is on 'Stednavne og fund' and the second on 'Historiske meddelelser om kongemagten og byen'.
25. Bertil Almgren, *Tor*, viii (1962), pp. 194–5.
26. H. Jankuhn, *Die Ausgrabungen in Haithabu, 1937–39* (Berlin-Dahlem, 1943), pp. 53–88 especially 87–8; *id.*, 'Sechs Karten zum Handel des 10. Jahrhunderts im westlichen Ostseebecken', *Archaeologia Geographica*, i (1950), pp. 8–16.
27. See p. 43.
28. See the map in *Archaeologia Geographica*, i (1950), p. 13 and in H. Jankuhn, *Haithabu* (1956), p. 195.
29. Charlotte Blindheim, 'The Market Place at Skiringssal', *AA*, xxi (1960), pp. 83–100. *Viking*, xxxiii (1969) contains several important articles on the Kaupang excavations, Charlotte Blindheim, 'Kaupangundersøkelsen avsluttet', pp. 5–39, English summary, pp. 32–9; R. L. Tollnes, 'Bygningsrester fra Kaupang', pp. 41–77, English summary, pp. 77–96; Ellen K. Hougen, 'Leirkar—materialet fra Kaupang', pp. 97–118, English summary, pp. 117–18; *id.*, 'Glassmaterialet fra Kaupang', pp. 119–37, English summary, pp. 132–6.
30. Kolbjørn Skaare, 'Vikingtidsmynter fra Kaupang—en Handelsplass ved Oslofjorden', *Nordisk Numismatisk Unions Medlemsblad*, 1960, pp. 195–7.
31. See the map in *AA*, xxxi (1960), p. 85.
32. Charlotte Blindheim, *AA*, xxxi (1960), p. 100.
33. E. Floderus, 'Västergarn', *Fornvännen*, xxix (1934), pp. 65–83. See also Per Lundström, 'Paviken I, ett vikingatida varv på Gotland', *Gotländskt Arkiv*, xl (1968), pp. 99–114.
34. Adam of Bremen II, xxii; ed. Schmeidler, p. 79.
35. For Novgorod and other Russian towns see M. Tikhomirov, *The Towns of Ancient Rus* (Moscow, 1959). The Novgorod excavations are described by A. V. Artsikhovsky and B. A. Kolchin, *Work of the Novgorod Archaeological Expedition*, I and II (Materials and Researches on the Archaeology of the USSR, nos. 55 and 65, Moscow, 1956, 1959).
36. P. Grierson, 'Commerce in the Dark Ages', *Transactions of the Royal Historical Society*, 5th ser., ix (1959), pp. 123–40.
37. *Vita Anskarii*, cap. xxvii, ed. Waitz (SS.R.G.), p. 58.
38. E.g. IV, vi and xviii; ed. Schmeidler, pp. 233, 245.
39. See pp. 106–7.
40. See pp. 103–4.
41. *Ibid.*
42. Constantine Porphyrogenitus, *De Administrando Imperio*, ed. G. Moravcsik and R. J. H. Jenkins (Budapest, 1949), pp. 56–63.

43. See pp. 107–16, 181.
44. Quoted by I. Hrbek, *Encyclopedia of Islam*, new ed., i (1960), p. 1306.
45. Harris Birkeland, *Nordens historie i middelalderen etter arabiske kilder*, pp. 14–17.
46. *Ibid.*, pp. 17–24.
47. V. Minorsky, *Encyclopedia of Islam*, 1st ed., iii (1936), p. 1182.
48. See pp. 108–10.
49. See p. 118.
50. S. Bolin, 'Mohammed, Charlemagne and Ruric', *Scandinavian Economic History Review*, i (1953), pp. 5–29.
51. See the map showing the mints represented at Dorestad in H. Jankuhn, *Haithabu* (1956), p. 45.
52. Knut Stjerna, 'Lund och Birka', *Historisk Tidskrift för Skåneland*, iii (1909), pp. 171 ff.; E. Wadstein, 'On the relations between Scandinavians and Frisians in early times', *Saga-Book of the Viking Society*, xi (1928–36), pp. 5–25; cf. H. Jankuhn, 'Der fränkisch-friesische Handel zur Ostsee im frühen Mittelalter', *Vierteljahrschrift für Sozial- und Wirtschaftsgeschichte*, 40 (1953), pp. 193–243.
53. See p. 110.
54. See p. 114.
55. See pp. 188–9.
56. See pp. 114, 189.
57. *VA*, v.
58. D. M. Waterman, 'Late Saxon, Viking and early Medieval finds from York', *Archaeologia*, xcvii (1959), pp. 59–105.
59. E. Curtis, *A History of Medieval Ireland* (London, 1938), pp. 6–8. See also Michael Dolley, *The Hiberno-Norse Coins in the British Museum* (1966), pp. 119–45.
60. See p. 116.
61. See p. 95.
62. IV Æthelred, 2– Liebermann, *Gesetze*, pp. 232–4; A. J. Robertson, *The Laws of the Kings of England from Edmund to Henry I* (Cambridge, 1925), pp. 70–73.
63. IV, xviii, ed. Schmeidler (SS.R.G., 1917), pp. 245–6.
64. C. A. Nordman, 'Karelska Järnåldersstudier, *Finska Fornminnesföreningens Tidskrift*, xxxiv, 3 (1924).
65. See p. 67.
66. Bertil Almgren, *Tor*, viii (1962), p. 196.
67. This point is emphasised by J. P. Bjernum, 'Vikingetidens handel og dens betydning for Nordens Folk', *ANOH*, 1948, pp. 294–303.

68. *Transactions of the Royal Historical Society*, 5th ser., ix (1959), p. 128.
69. Elias Wessén, 'Bjärköarätt', *KHL*, i, cols. 655–8.

9. CAUSES AND CONSEQUENCES: pp. 202–18

1. T. D. Kendrick, *A History of the Vikings* (London, 1930), p. 22. Cf. H. Shetelig, *VA*, i. 10, 'It must be confessed at once that a definite cause, suddenly effective at that precise period, has never been discovered, and, indeed, can hardly ever be discovered.'
2. Kendrick, *loc. cit.*
3. *EHD*, p. 740.
4. Tacitus, *Germania*, cap. xiv, trans. H. Mattingly (Penguin Books, 1948), p. 112.
5. *EHD*, p. 165.
6. See p. 147. Another Carolingian who was believed to have treated the Vikings as allies was Lothar, Charlemagne's grandson, see Nithard, *Histoire des fils de Louis de Pieux*, ed. Ph. Lauer (Les Classiques de l'Histoire de France au Moyen Age, 1926), pp. 122–3, cf. W. Vogel, *Die Normannen und das fränkische Reich* (Heidelberg, 1906), pp. 76–7, 85–6.
7. F. Lot, *Bibliothèque de l'École des Chartes*, lxix (1908), pp. 24–8.
8. For this colonisation see F. T. Wainwright, 'The Scandinavain Settlement', *The Northern Isles*, ed. F. T. Wainwright (London, 1962), pp. 117–62 and W. F. H. Nicolaisen, 'Norse Settlement in the Northern and Western Isles: Some place-name evidence', *The Scottish Historical Review*, xviii (1969), pp. 6–17.
9. For a general survey of the period see the Introduction by Kathleen Hughes in A. J. Otway-Ruthven, *A History of Medieval Ireland* (London, 1968), pp. 1–33. There are several valuable papers in *Proceedings of the International Congress of Celtic Studies held in Dublin 6–10 July 1959*. (Dublin Institute for Advanced Studies, 1962).
10. A. T. Lucas, 'The Plundering and Burning of Churches in Ireland, 7th to 16th Century', *North Munster Studies: Essays in commemoration of Monsignor Michael Moloney*, ed. Etienne Rynne (Limerick: The Thomond Archaeological Society, 1967), pp. 172–229.
11. The description is used in *Cogadh Gaedhel re Gallaibh*, ed. James II. Todd (Rolls Series 48, 1867), p. 26. The frequency of raids

can conveniently be studied in the *Annals of Ulster*, i, ed. W. M. Hennessy (Dublin, 1887), The annals for 'the forty years' rest' are on pp. 386–426.

12. *Annals of Ulster*, i, p. 386.

13. G. Turville-Petre, *Origins of Icelandic Literature* (Oxford 1953), pp. 3–4.

14. Gwyn Jones, *The Norse Atlantic Saga* (Oxford, 1964), pp. 19–20.

15. Knut Gjerset, *History of Iceland* (1924), pp. 29–48.

16. For a recent general account see Andreas Holmsen, *Norges Historie fra de eldste tider til 1660*, 3rd ed. (1961), pp. 101–10. Magnus Olsen, *Farms and Fanes of Ancient Norway* (Oslo: Institut-tet for Sammenligende Kulturforskning, 1928), is still a very useful guide to the place place-name evidence.

17. T. Dannevig Hauge, *Blesterbruk og Myrjern: Studier i den gamle jernvinna i det ostenfjelske Norge* (Oslo: Universitets Oldsaksamlings Skrifter, iii, 1946) is the most comprehensive discussion on the subject but it is supplemented by Charlotte Blindheim, 'Smed-graven fra Bygland i Morgedal', *Viking* xxvi (1963), pp. 25–81.

18. See pp. 68–79.

19. Aksel E. Christensen, *Vikingetidens Danmark* (Copenhagen, 1969), pp. 203–6; John Kousgård Sørensen, *Svenborg Amts Bebyggelsesnavne* (Danmarks Stednavne, no. 13, 1958) p. x; *id., Odense Amts Bebyggelsesnavne* (Danmarks Stednavne, no. 14, 1969), p. x.

20. See p. 192.

21. Ernst Dümmler, *Geschichte des ostfränkischen Reiches*, i, 2nd ed. (Leipzig, 1887), pp. 278–9, 343–4.

22. See p. 101.

22a. See p. 176.

23. See pp. 107–16.

24. R. H. M. Dolley, *The Hiberno-Norse Coins in the British Museum*, p. 18.

25. F. T. Wainwright, 'The Battles at Corbridge', *Saga-Book of the Viking Society*, xiii (1946–53), pp. 156–73.

26. *Proceedings of the International Congress of Celtic Studies held in Dublin 6–10 July 1959*, pp. 18–19.

27. Dolley, *op. cit.*, pp. 18–19; cf. *Mediaeval Scandinavia*, 2 (1969). pp. 182–3.

28. The main, apparently contemporary, evidence for close links is the third of the *Three Fragments copied from Ancient Sources by Dubhaltalch Mac Firbisigh*, ed. John O'Donovan (Dublin: Irish Archaeological and Celtic Society, 1866), pp. 114–247. On this see Peter Hunter Blair, 'Olaf the White and the Three Fragments

of Irish Annals', *Viking*, iii (1939), pp. 1–27. The reports
of Harald Fairhair's expedition to the British Isles are all late
and need critical examination, see Alan O. Anderson, *Early
Sources of Scottish History A.D. 500 to 1286* (Edinburgh, 1922),
pp. 388–96.
28a. A. A. M. Duncan and A. L. Brown, 'Argyll and the Isles in the
earlier Middle Ages', *Proceedings of the Society of Antiquaries of
Scotland*, xc (1956–7), pp. 192–220.
29. See pp. 163–6.
30. See most recently Ad. Stender-Petersen, 'Der älteste russische
Staat', *Historische Zeitschrift*, 191 (1960), pp. 1–17. See also his
survey 'Das Problem der ältesten byzantinisch-russisch-nordi-
schen Beziehungen', *X Congresso Internationale di Scienze Storiche,
1955, Relazioni*, iii, pp. 165–88. Stender-Petersen believes that
there were extensive Scandinavian settlements in North
Russia and that a 'State' was established there by Scandinavians in the ninth century. He has treated the discovery of a
runic inscription at Starya Ladoga as the 'missing link' that
proves his hypothesis correct. His views have been criticised by
two Soviet scholars, V. V. Pokhljobkin and V. B. Vilinbakhov
in *Kuml*, 1960, pp. 135–7 and Stender-Petersen replied, *ibid.*,
pp. 137–44. One runic inscription seems insufficient to prove
this hypothesis in the face of the evidence that leads to the
conclusion stated here in the text.
31. See p. 46.
32. M. Vasmer, 'Wikingerspuren in Russland', *Sitzungsberichte der
Preussischen Akademie der Wissenschaften*, Phil.-Hist. Klasse,
1931, pp. 649–74.
33. W. J. Ravdonikas, *Die Norrmannen der Wikingerzeit und das Lado-
gagebeit* (KVHAA Handlingar, 40, 3, 1930).
34. See pp. 62–3.
35. See pp. 118, 181.
36. See pp. 111–12.
37. V. Minorsky, *Encyclopedia of Islam*, 1st ed. iii (1936), p. 1182.
38. *Ibid.*
39. Alistair Campbell, *Encomium Emmae Reginae* (Royal Historical
Society, Camden 3rd ser, lxxii, 1949), pp. 66–91; Arndt
Ruprecht, *Die Ausgehende Wikingerzeit im Lichte der Runenin-
schriften* (Palaestra, 224, 1958), pp. 125–65.
40. See pp. 131–7.
41. L. Musset, 'La pénétration chrétienne dans l'Europe du nord et
son influence sur la civilisation Scandinave', *Settimane studio del
centro Italiano di studi sull'alto medioevo, xiv, La conversione al*

Cristianesimo nell'Europa dell'alto mediocvo (Spoleto, 1967), pp. 263–325.

42. Sven B. F. Jansson, *Swedish Vikings in England: The Evidence of the Rune Stones* (Dorothea Coke Memorial Lecture, University College London, 1966).

43. Florence E. Harmer, 'The English Contribution to the Epistolary Usages of Early Scandinavian Kings' *Saga-Book of the Viking Society*, xiii, 3 (1950), pp. 115–55.

44. Cf. A. J. Goedheer, *Irish and Norse Traditions about the Battle of Clontarf* (Haarlem, 1938), p. 120.

S

Bibliography

This list of books and articles is intended to serve as a guide for further reading. On many topics additional references are given in the notes to the text. The abbreviations are explained on p. 232.

GENERAL

The most recent general account in English is Gwyn Jones, *A History of the Vikings* (Oxford, 1968), but T. D. Kendrick, *A History of the Vikings* (London, 1930), is still useful and for western Europe there is also H. Shetelig, *An Introduction to the Viking History of Western Europe*, *VA*, i (Oslo, 1940). The classic work of Johannes C. H. R. Steenstrup, *Normannerne*, 4 vols. (Copenhagen, 1876–82), remains a valuable guide. Johannes Brøndsted, *The Vikings* (Harmondsworth, 1965), H. Arbman, *The Vikings* (London, 1961), and David Wilson, *The Vikings and their origins: Scandinavia in the First Millennium* (London, 1970), are short, illustrated accounts by archaeologists. The most lavishly illustrated book is *The Viking*, ed. Bertil Almgren (London, 1966). Lucien Musset, *Les Invasions: Le second assaut contre l'Europe Chrétienne (VIIe–XIe siècles)* (Nouvelle Clio, 12 *bis;* Paris 1965), is an excellent guide to recent literature and to current discussions. Many aspects of the subject are treated in *I Normanni e la loro espansione in Europa nell'alto medioevo* (Settimane di studio del centro Italiano di studi sull'alto medioevo, xvi; Spoleto, 1969).

THE BRITISH ISLES

General: W. G. Collingwood, *Scandinavian Britain* (London, 1906).

P. H. Sawyer *et al.*, 'The Two Viking Ages of Britain: a discussion', *Mediaeval Scandinavia*, 2 (1969), pp. 163–207.

England: H. R. Loyn, *Anglo-Saxon England and the Norman Conquest* (London, 1962).

F. M. Stenton, 'The Danes in England', *Proceedings of the British Academy*, xiii (1927), pp. 203–46.

F. M. Stenton, *Anglo-Saxon England*, 3rd edn (Oxford, 1971).

Wales: B. G. Charles, *Old Norse Relations with Wales* (Cardiff, 1934).

J. E. Lloyd, *A History of Wales*, i (London, 1911), pp. 320–52.

Ireland: Charles Haliday, *The Scandinavian Kingdom of Dublin*, 2nd edn (Dublin, 1884).

Kathleen Hughes, *The Church in Early Irish Society* (Cambridge, 1966).

Kathleen Hughes, 'Introduction' in A. J. Otway-Ruthven, *A History of Medieval Ireland* (London, 1968), pp. 1–33.

A. T. Lucas, 'Irish Norse Relations: Time for Reappraisal?', *Journal of the Cork Historical and Archaeological Society*, lxxi (1966), pp. 62–75.

Proceedings of the International Congress of Celtic Studies held in Dublin 6–10 July, 1959 (Dublin, Institute for Advanced Studies, 1962).

A. Walsh, *Scandinavian Relations with Ireland during the Viking Period* (Dublin, 1922).

J. Young, 'A Note on the Norse Occupation of Ireland', *History*, new ser., xxxv (1950), pp. 11–33.

Scotland: A. O. Anderson, *Early Sources of Scottish History, A.D. 400 to 1286*, i (Edinburgh, 1922).

W. F. H. Nicolaisen, 'Norse Settlement in the Northern and Western Isles: Some place-name evidence', *The Scottish Historical Review*, xviii (1969), pp. 6–17.

F. T. Wainwright, 'The Scandinavian Settlement', *The Northern Isles*, ed. F. T. Wainwright (London, 1962), pp. 117–62.

Isle of Man: B. R. S. and Eleanor Megaw, 'The Norse Heritage in the Isle of Man', *The Early Cultures of North-West Europe* (H. M. Chadwick Memorial Studies), edd. Sir Cyril Fox and Bruce Dickins (Cambridge, 1950), pp. 141–70.

THE NORTH ATLANTIC

General: Gwyn Jones, *The Norse Atlantic Saga* (Oxford, 1964)

Iceland: Kristjan Eldjarn, *Kuml og haugfé ur heiðnum sið á Íslandi* (Akureyri, 1956).

K. Gjerset, *History of Iceland* (London, 1923).

F. Jonsson, *Island fra Sagatid til Nutid* (Copenhagen, 1930).

Jon Steffensen, 'Aspects of Life in Iceland in the Heathen Period', *Saga-Book of the Viking Society*, xvii, 2–3 (1967–8), pp. 177–205.

The Faroes: G. J. Marcus, 'The Norse Emigration to the Faroe Islands', *English Historical Review*, lxxi (1956), pp. 56–61.

Alan Small, 'The distribution of settlement in Shetland and Faroe in Viking Times', *Saga-Book of the Viking Society*, xvii, 2–3 pp. 145–55.

Greenland: K. J. Krogh, *Viking Greenland* (Copenhagen, 1967).

P. Nørlund, *Viking Settlers in Greenland and their Descendants During Five Hundred Years* (Cambridge, 1936).

America: Magnus Magnusson and Hermann Pálsson, *The Vinland Sagas; The Norse Discovery of America* (Harmondsworth, 1965).

WESTERN EUROPE

General: H. Arbman, *Schweden und das karolingische Reich*, (KVHAA, Handlingar 43, 1937).

W. Vogel, *Die Normannen und das fränkische Reich bis zur Gründung der Normandie (799–911)* (Heidelberg, 1906).

Low Countries: W. C. Braat, 'Les Vikings au pays de Frise', *Annales de Normandie*, iv (1954), pp. 219–27.

Albert D'Haenens, *Les invasions normandes en Belgique au ixe siècle* (Louvain, 1967).

I. H. Gosses, *Deensche heerschappijen in Friesland gedurende den Noormannentijd* (Amsterdam, 1923).

Normandy: D. C. Douglas, 'The Rise of Normandy', *Proceedings of the British Academy*, xxxiii (1947), pp. 101–31.

L. Musset, 'Naissance de la Normandie', *Histoire de la Normandie*, ed. M. de Bouard (Toulouse, 1970), pp. 75–130.

H. Prentout, *Essai sur les origines et la fondation du duché de Normandie* (Caen, 1911).

J. C. H. R. Steenstrup, *Normandiets Historie under de syv første Hertuger* (Copenhagen, 1925).

Spain: Claudio Sánchez-Albornoz, 'Invasions normandas a la España cristiana durante el siglo IX', *I Normanni e la loro espansione in Europa nell'alto medioevo* (Spoleto, 1969), pp. 367–408.

EASTERN EUROPE

H. Arbman, *Svear i Österviking* (Stockholm, 1955).

T. J. Arne, *La Suède et L'Orient* (Archives d'Etudes Orientales, 9; Uppsala, 1914).

H. Paskiewicz, *Origins of Russia* (New York, 1954).

H. Paskiewicz, *The Making of the Russian Nation* (London, 1963).

Ad. Stender-Petersen, *Varangica* (Aarhus, 1953).

See also pp. 239–40, notes 29, 31, p. 262, note 30.

SCANDINAVIA

Aksel E. Christensen, *Vikingetidens Danmark* (Copenhagen, 1969).

P. G. Foote and D. M. Wilson, *The Viking Achievement* (London, 1970).

Andreas Holmsen, *Norges Historie fra de eldste tider til 1660*, 3rd edn (Oslo, 1961).

L. Musset, *Les peuples Scandinaves au Moyen Age* (Paris, 1951). *Nordisk Kultur*, 30 vols. (Stockholm, 1931–56) and KHL contain many very helpful articles with good bibliographies. The literature on towns has been surveyed by Birgitta Fritz, 'Stadtshistoria och arkeologi', *Historisk tidskrift* (Stockholm, 1965), pp. 472–98. See also *Die Zeit der Stadtgründung im Ostseeraum*, ed. Mårten Stenberger (Acta Visbyensia I; Visby, 1965). Per Sveaas Andersen has surveyed the literature on the Norwegian *Vikingtid og riksamling* in the first part of *Nytt fra Norsk Middelalder* (Oslo, 1969).

BIBLIOGRAPHIES

The best current bibliographies, which between them list almost all publications on the subject, are *Bibliography of Old Norse–Icelandic Studies* (Copenhagen) *Cahiers de Civilisation Médiévale* (Poitiers) and *International Medieval Bibliography* (Leeds).

Index